The Dancing Peacock

Indian Insights into Religion and Development

The Dancing Peacock

Indian Insights into Religion and Development

Editors
Kuruvilla Pandikattu SJ
James Ponniah

SERIALS PUBLICATIONS
NEW DELHI (INDIA)

First Published - 2010

ISBN: 978-81-8387-341-3

Published by

SERIALS PUBLICATIONS
4830/24, Prahlad Street, Ansari Road
Darya Ganj, New Delhi-110002 (India)
Phone: 23245225 Fax : 91-11-23272135
E-mail: serials@satyam.net.in

Dedicated Gratefully to

Rev Prof. Kurien Kunnumpuram SJ (Emeritus)

The founder-publisher-editor of Jnanadeepa: Pune Journal for Religious Studies since 1996

"It is already becoming clear that a chapter which had a Western beginning will have to have an Indian ending if it is not to end in self-destruction of the human race. At this supremely dangerous moment in human history, the only way of salvation is the ancient Hindu way. Here we have the attitude and spirit that can make it possible for the human race to grow together in to a single family." Arnold Toynbee (1889-1975)

Contents

Preface

"Economic development of a country is not judged by the number of billionaires, but from the condition of poor, backwards and dalits (SCs/STs)", L. K. Advani said after unveiling Dr. B. R. Ambedkar's statue on his 117th birthday (*The Hindu*, April 14, 2008).

The articles in this volume focus on development with special reference to India. Its scope is not limited to economic or material prosperity alone, though that forms its core concern.

The authors in this volume share the common vision of setting the tone in providing a discourse on development that is multifaceted and multidisciplinary. They have come together to reflect on a development suitable for India, which does justice to individual well-being, economic prosperity and religious profundity. It also draws insights from philosophical thoughts and environmental issues.

Fortunately India has been a land abundantly endowed with multiplicity of traditions, plurality of cultures and richness of life-styles. Keeping this in mind the authors suggest some ways of continuing and cultivating development in India, thinking specially of the poor and the marginalised in India.

So in this volume, criteria for development are suggested, critiques are made, questions posed, visions are developed and symbols studied, with a view to articulating a development which is creative and constructive both to India as a nation and Indians as persons.

In keeping with the Indian tradition a few foreign scholars, along with their Indian counterparts, who are familiar to India, have been invited to share their experiences and insights on development with special emphasis on the marginalised and the poor.

We are delighted to dedicate this volume to Prof Kurien Kunnumpuram who has tirelessly committed himself to creating a culture of life and fostering a climate of development and well-being, inspired by the Indian wisdom. By his dedicated work in bringing out *Jnanadeepa: Pune Journal of Religious Studies,* for more than a decade, he has contributed substantially to the development of Indian thought. For that the editors are grateful to him and so dedicate this volume with love and affection.

It is our fond hope that the readers will be inspired by the insights offered in this book to articulate a vision of human and societal development that is liberative, integrated and people-centred.

Kuruvilla Pandikattu SJ
James Ponniah

Acknowledgements

This volume on *The Dancing Peacock: Indian Insights into Religion and Development* is the product of a great deal to the generous support and active collaboration of many organizations and persons. We are indebted to Prof. Dr. Job Kozhamthadam, the President of Jnana-Deepa Vidyapeeth, and Albert Menezes, its Registrar, Pradeep Sequeira, the Rector of Papal Seminary and Jacob Kulangara its Administrator, for their active support and encouragement. Prof Kurien Kunnumpuram, the editor of *Jnanadeepa: Pune Journal of Religious Studies* is specially thanked for his permission to republish or revise some of the articles from the same journal. Rev Lionel Macarenhas went over the manuscript several times and gave many valuable comments and suggestions. We are indeed grateful to them and to the many young scholars of both Jnana-Deepa Vidyapeeth and Papal Seminary, who have encouraged us in our studies.

Kuruvilla Pandikattu SJ
James Ponniah

Our Contributors

Binoy Pichalakkatt SJ, based in New Delhi, has specialized in Mathematics and is involved in interfacing creatively science and religion.

Christian Bauer, has finished his doctorate on Chenu and is currently teaching systematic theology at the university of Wurzburg, Germany.

Cyril Desbruslais, is Playwright and Professor of Philosophy at Jnana-Deepa Vidyapeeth, Pune.

Gnana Patrick, is a Professor at the University of Madras, Chennai, is a prolific writer.

Indunil Janaka Kodithuwakku, is a Sri Lankan missiologist teaching Pontifical Urban university Rome.

James Ponniah, is the Head of the Dept of Indian Studies at Jnana-Deepa Vidyapeeth, Pune and is currently doing his post-doctoral research at Berkeley, USA.

Jose Thayil SJ, is the Head of the Dept of Moral Theology at Jnana-Deepa Vidyapeeth and has been involved in inter-religious dialogue, specially with Buddhists.

Keith D'Souza SJ, is an eminent writer and Professor of Philosophy at St Pius College, Mumbai.

Kuruvilla Pandikattu SJ, is the Coordinator of Master's Programme in Philosophy at Jnana-Deepa Vidyapeeth, Pune.

Roger Burggraeve SVD, from the Catholic Univeristy of Leuvein, Beligum is the world-renowned Levinas scholar.

Sharon D'Cruz, is a creative historian teaching at the University of Goa. She has numerous articles to her credit.

Subhash Anand, the Professor of Indian Philosophy at Jnana-Deepa Vidyapeeth, Pune, is an eminent scholar and prolific writer.

Walter Fernandes SJ, is a social scientist and activist and is a well known writer taking up the cause of the marginalised. Currently he is based in Shillong.

Introduction

There once was a time, in the not so distant past, when penguins ruled many lands in the Sea of Organisations, promoting progress and development. These penguins were not always wise, they were not always popular, but they were always in command.

The top management wore the same outlook in their distinctive black and white suits. They believed that uniformity is the way to do things; Uniformity is Unity.

On the other hand, worker birds wore colours and outfits that reflected their work and lifestyles. Birds who aspired to move up the corporate ladder were encouraged to adopt the penguins' code of conduct and wear the penguin suits. They learn the penguin stride and follow the example of their leaders towards efficiency and progress.

One day, Perry the peacock joined the Land of Penguins. He was loud, colourful and full of new ideas. Although he was different, the penguins were impressed by his new ideas. They felt that he has real Penguin Potential.

Initially, everyone was happy. The penguins were pleased with their new recruit. Perry was creative and he brought in good results. However, as time went by, the penguins began to murmur against Perry. His colourful ideas invaded the penguins' comfort zone.

Perry was also unhappy. The penguins tried to turn him into a penguin. He was told to "try to be like the rest of us, wear a penguin suit". Both parties were unhappy. Creativity and innovation are seen to be "a breath of fresh air" in every developmental efforts.

Many "Perrys" are recruited for their creativity. Yet, along the way, their creativity is stifled by the need to conform to the norm. Peacocks bring in varieties and new ideas, But, the stability provided by the penguins must not be ignored.

Penguins, being the backbone of the organisation, need to recognise that diversity can exist in an organisation if there is acceptance and trust. When we learn to appreciate one another's differences, we become more willing to listen, more open to new ideas and more eager to grow. Birds of different feathers can progress together in harmony and bring healthy development.[1]

Not long ago the astute British historian and critique of civilisations Arnold Toynee (1889-1975) asserted: "It is already becoming clear that a chapter which had a Western beginning will have to have an Indian ending if it is not to end in self-destruction of the human race." Inspired by this insight, the editors are convinced that an Indian approach to the issues of human development can contribute significantly to a sustainable world order, preventing the assured self-destruction caused by unlimited progress and unguarded greed. Indian with its deep spiritual resources and human resilience offers a sign of hope in the troubled times of today.

In recent years there has been a renewed interest in the role of religion, a forte of Indian heritage, in the course of development and its ethics within the context of globalization and the emerging world order. The latest concepts in developmental theories such as self-cultivation, the face of the other, etc., bring the agenda of development close to the question of religion. Some authors think of development itself as quasi-religious. It is against this background that this volume seeks to bring both religion and development together for a meaningful dialogue between the two in the global world of today.In recent years there has been a renewed interest in the role of religion in the course of development and its ethics within the context of globalization and the emerging world order. The latest concepts in developmental theories such as self-cultivation, the face of the other, etc., bring the agenda of development close to the question of religion. Some authors think of development itself as quasi-religious. It is against this background that this issue of *Jnanadeepa* seeks to bring both religion and development together for a meaningful dialogue between the two in the global world of today.

There are three articles in this issue which deal with Indian perspectives on religion and development. The first seeks to put forward some Gandhian criteria for authentic development. The author feels that well-being is an experience of integration. He believes that Satya should be the goal of development; that Ahimsa should be its ethos; that Svadeshi offers the resources for development; and that Swaraj creates the right environment for development. The second discusses the relationship between Hinduism and development. After pointing out some of the problems involved in the discussion of this issue, the author tries to clarify the concept of development. To his mind development is the dynamic process of the actualization of a dream, a journey from one situation to another, a transformation of something into something. Development is concerned about transforming the lives of the people, not just transforming economies. Hinduism has made a remarkable contribution to the development of a great civilization. But at a particular point in time a certain degree of closure of mind and its exploration intervened which has adversely affected the growth of human persons and the development of society. The third deals with folk/subaltern religion and development. Folk religions can help to clarify the concept of development and release forces that can promote holistic development. Such religions can function as a subaltern agency to defy the oppressive social order, to negotiate a new egalitarian social identity and restore the human dignity of the oppressed. They can also promote a type of development which is eco-friendly and people centred.

Included in this issue are three articles which discuss the ethical dimension of development. The first deals with development in the social teaching of the Christian Church. The author points out that the Church's understanding of development has undergone change. While the promotion of development in underdeveloped nations is primarily the responsibility of each such nation, the more advanced countries should come to their aid. The Church also calls attention to the need for moral development along with economic and social development. The second deals with the need to cultivate a global mentality in the contemporary world. This is an essay in ethics applied to the phenomenon of globalization and social development, guided by the role and influence of religion. Dialogical pluralism, creative visualization, collaborative solidarity, transnational responsibility and proactive optimism are some of the virtues the article advocates. The third seeks to broaden and deepen development ethics with the thought of Emmanuel Levinas. Responsibility is the basic concept of development ethics. While we should feel responsible for the poor and the marginalized we should see to it that our altruism does not promote egocentrism in the poor. We are responsible for the poor and the marginalized for others.

There is an article in this issue which discusses some of the features of development which make it quasi-religious. It points out that new approaches to development that are emerging today need to be supported by new forms of religious intervention. Liberation theology is an example of the critical intervention of religion in societal transformation. Another article deals with the role of the Christian Church in the development of Goa. There has been a progressive abandonment of the Portuguese legacy. The post-colonial Church in Goa has made a renewed commitment to the promotion of the development of the State and expressed its readiness to be an active partner in the collaborative effort for regeneration. The Church believes that it is her sacred duty towards humanity to help in the integral development of the human person and the human society. This is certainly a progressive step.

The title of this volume, it must be mentioned, is inspired by the insight from Arnold Toynbee mentioned earlier. It is our fervent wish that the unique Indian contribution to human and social development will promote a progress that is dynamically humane, creative and peaceful. The best symbol for such a scenario is the Peacock, India's national bird, that brings with it harmony, creativity, play, joy and spontaneity into the process of holistic and integrated development. So the title: The Dancing Peacock.

In a truly inclusive vein, it may be mentioned that not all the scholars are Indian. There are a few foreign scholars who vibrate with the Indian ethos and mentality and so can honestly suggest new vistas for development for both India and the world.

It is our fond hope that this volume will promote a serious reflection on religion and development which will lead to new approaches to the process of personal and societal development. May we draw from the rich Indian spiritual resources so that our progress–economic, technological and religious–does not lead to our own annihilation. May we grow into a single family, *vasudheva kudumbham*, where diversity is cherished, plurality is affirmed and prosperity offered for all.

Editors
James Ponniah
Kuruvilla Pandikattu

Notes

1. Adapted from BJ Gallagher Hateley & Warren H. Schmidt, A Peacock in the Land of Penguins: A Fable about Creativity and Courage Berrett-Koehler Publishers, Inc., 2001.

1

Authentic Development Some Gandhian Criteria

SUBHASH ANAND

Of late one hears a lot about "India's emergence as a fast-growing economic power."[1] India's "growth rate is now approaching that of Asia's other economic juggernaut, China."[2] This, however, is not the full truth.

> Prosperity and progress haven't touched the 550,000 villages where two-thirds of India's population live... Millions of women are not getting the education they need. Transportation networks and electrical grids, which are crucial to industrial development and job creation, are so dilapidated [that] it will take many years to modernize them.[3]

Writing in 1908, Gandhi made a statement that today comes across to us as prophetic: "The generally accepted principles of economics are invalid. If acted upon, they will make individuals and nations unhappy. The poor will become poorer and the rich richer..." (*CW* 8.371).[4]

The success of a recent movie "Lage Raho Munnabhai", portraying Gandhian ideals, is an indication that Gandhi continues to have an appeal to people even today. Even though all of us may not always follow his advice, he can still challenge us. He may impart to us some wisdom that may guide us in our struggle to become a developed nation. Gandhi was no economist: "I know very little of economics" (*EW* 93). He was even advised that, given his ignorance, he ought to stop "experimenting in matters of economics at the expense of the public" (*EW* 93). Yet a deep inner voice tells him: "You are on the right track, move neither to your left nor right, but keep to the straight and narrow way" (*EW* 93). I believe that our inner wisdom can sometimes give us a deeper understanding of human growth and development than formal studies can do.

Satya: The Goal of Development

Gandhi makes clear his purpose in writing his autobiography, *The Story of My Experiment with Truth*: to share with others the insights of his many years of spiritual striving, i.e., "to see God face to face, to attain Moksha" (*Au* x). For him 'God is Truth' is not merely a theoretical statement, but the driving force of his life, giving it a direction and unity: "I live and have my being in pursuit of this goal. All I do by way of speaking and writing and all my ventures in the political field are directed to this same end" (*Au* x). The integration he experienced was not merely imposed from outside by the one purpose of his life—satya, but also experienced from within because "truth is the sovereign principle, which includes numerous other principles" (*Au* xi). "The word *satya* is derived from *sat*, which means that which is. *Satya* means a state of being" (*EW* 231). Thus truth (satya) is above all a mode of being: being what we should be, an experience of wellbeing.[5] Hence satya must be the goal of development. Only then will development be authentic.

Advaita: Well-being as an Experience of Integration

To understand Gandhi's approach to development we need to appreciate the basic presupposition of his thought. Though not an Advaitin in the traditional sense, Gandhi believes in some kind of *advaita*, "in the essential unity of man and for that matter of all that lives," and as a consequence, "if one man gains spiritually, the whole world gains with him and, if one man falls, the whole world falls to that extent" (*CW* 25.390).

A contemporary writer puts it more tersely: "Poverty anywhere is a threat to prosperity everywhere."[6] Gandhi suggests some kind of symbiotic relation binding the whole of creation, a creation held together by "the universal and all-pervading Spirit of Truth" (*Au* 420). Thus, there is a certain oneness, a certain non-duality in all reality, because all reality comes from, is sustained by, and finds it fulfilment in the Real, in Truth. The whole of creation mediates the presence of "the one and the same Creator" (*Au* 230).

Humans do not have independent goals. "One's respective *dharma* towards one's self, family, nation and the world cannot be divided into watertight compartments" (*EW* 183). Like Gandhi, we to are called to see God face to face, and all our undertakings are to be directed to this goal. What is actually happening is just the opposite. "The predominant character of modern civilization is to dethrone God and enthrone Materialism" (*CW* 28.127). The deepest dimension of being human—our openness to transcendence—is put aside. "The flesh has taken precedence over the spirit" (*CW* 48.442). Carried away by the more popular understanding of development we "make bodily welfare the object of life" (*HS* 23). For Gandhi *advaita*, being an ontological principle, becomes an existential ideal: human life must be an experience of integration. "There must be a return to simplicity and proper proportions" (*HS* 23).

When we put aside our quest for the supreme Truth, as the ultimate and, therefore, the normative goal of human life, we become victims of materialism,

> all the while conveniently forgetting that its greatest achievements are the invention of the most terrible weapons of destruction, the awful growth of anarchism, the frightful disputes between capital and labour and the wanton and diabolical cruelty inflicted on innocent, dumb, living animals in the name of science, 'falsely so called'" (*EW* 83).

Development is authentic only when it promotes the total well-being of persons, who constitute a just society and maintain the integrity of creation.

The Well-being of Persons

To be wholesome persons we need to have health of body, peace of mind, and joy in our health. Good health is the greatest wealth. "We must search for wealth not in the bowels of the earth, but in the hearts of men. If this is correct, the true law of economics is that men must be maintained in the best possible health, both of body and mind, and in the highest state of honour" (*CW* 8.325). Hence "economics that ruins one's health is false, because money without health has no value. Only that economy is true which enables one to conserve one's health" (*CW* 60.268). To be healthy we need to take care of the basics of life. "Every human being has a right to live and therefore to find the wherewithal to feed himself and where necessary [if need be] to clothe and house himself" (*EW* 94).

Peace of mind is essential for good health. A disturbed mind leads to many psychosomatic diseases. "Ignoring the emotion is to forget that man has feelings" (*CW* 61.250). Inner joy and peace is much more important than all the forms of pleasure the consumer market promises us. The family is the primary source of our emotional well-being. It provides us with our first experience of belonging, of being wanted and cared for. Yet, sad to say:

> more than any other institution, it has been affected by the profound and rapid changes witnessed by the world today. Many families are struggling to live in fidelity to authentically human values, while some others have become totally bewildered. Some even doubt if the institution has any purpose at all.[7]

The life-styles that emerge from being part of a developed society tend to minimize our human interactions.

> We've forgotten the magic of sharing a meal with our family members... it is also important to remember that sharing a meal is not just about eating, but also about strengthening family bonds and making pleasant memories... The more often families eat together, the less likely that kids are going to smoke, drink, do drugs or get depressed.[8]

Any development that tends to undermine the family in unhealthy.

Many "economists do not take men's conduct into account but estimate prosperity from the amount of wealth accumulated and so conclude that the happiness of nations depends upon their wealth alone" (*CW* 8.371). But humans have an ethical dimension. Therefore "True economics must follow ethics. Even if we fail in this we shall have succeeded" (*CW* 62.241).[9] As long as we continue to be ethical we have not failed. An ethical collapse would mean the end of our humanity. Any development that makes money the primary concern is detrimental to our well-being. "Rome suffered a moral fall when it attained high material affluence. So did Egypt [suffer a moral fall] and so perhaps most countries of which we have any historic record" (*EW* 95). Moral decadence is suicidal. Yet, this is happening even today "Western nations today are groaning under the heel of the monster-god of materialism. Their moral growth has become stunted" (*EW* 97). On the other hand moral discipline gives us power. "When we can be certain that once the spirit of discipline comes to pervade our lives, we shall be able to get anything we may want" (*EW* 103).

If we are not ethical in our personal life, then we cannot claim to have integrity in other areas of life.

> I am firmly of the view, and it is my experience too, that, if a person has violated a moral principle in any one sphere of his life, his action will certainly have an effect in other spheres. In other words, the belief generally held that an immoral man may do no harm in the political sphere is quite wrong. And so is the other belief that a person who violates moral principles in his business may be moral in his private life or in his conduct in family affairs" (*EW* 181-82).

Without morality, development can only be distorted. Morality is not merely avoiding evil. We need to cultivate positive attitudes.

> Love is a rare herb... and this herb grows out of non-violence... We should act only through love; thus alone

> shall we succeed. So long as we do not have unshakable faith in truth, love and non-violence, we can make no progress. If we give up these... we shall be doomed (*CW* 14.299-300).

The Well-being of the Society

The development of persons cannot be confined to the well-being of individuals. "Not the good of the few, not even the good of the many, but it is the good of all that we are made [by God] to promote, if we are `made in His own image'" (*CW* 61.250). The vast majority of the people of India live in "about half a million villages."[10] Only when the village economy prospers will India prosper. We need to encourage the villagers "to revive their lost industries and arts by assuring them a ready market... If we neglect our duty to our villagers, we shall be courting our own ruin" (*CW* 60.256).

Wealth has a social function. Gandhi tries to explain this by giving two examples: "The circulation of wealth among a people resembles the circulation of blood in the body... the concentration of blood at one spot is harmful to the body and, similarly, concentration of wealth at one place proves to be a nation's undoing" (*CW* 8.303). The more the wealth is distributed the better it serves society. On the other hand accumulation of wealth in the hands of a few can be counterproductive:

> Most of the rivers run out their course unregulated, their marshy banks poisoning the wind... Similarly the uncontrolled use of wealth will multiply vices among men and cause starvation; in brief, such wealth will act like poison. But the selfsame wealth, if its circulation is regulated and its use controlled, can, like a river whose stream has been properly harnessed, promote prosperity" (*CW* 8.337).

The rich are the trustees of the wealth they have (*EW* 389). It is not easy to be a trustee. I need to discipline myself:

> My requirements also should be like [that] of the millions. My requirements cannot be greater because I happen to be the son of a rich man. I cannot spend the money [I get

> from my father] on my pleasures. The man who takes for himself only enough to satisfy the needs customary in his society and spends the rest for social service becomes a trustee (*EW* 403).

The real test of social development is the deepening of the bonds of fellowship among people, going beyond traditional boundaries of caste, creed, etc.

> Brotherhood is just now only a distant aspiration. To me it is a test of true spirituality. All our prayers, fasting and observances are empty nothings so long as we do not feel a live kinship with all life. But we have not even arrived at that intellectual belief, let alone a heart realization. We are still selective. A selective brotherhood is a selfish partnership. Brotherhood requires no consideration or response (*EW* 244).

Hence economic disparities that keep people apart cannot be part of authentic development.

The Well-being of the Environment

As the greater part of India is found in her many villages, Gandhi gave great importance to the development of our villages. He believes that "if the village perishes India will perish too. It will be no more India. Her own mission in the world will get lost (*CW* 63.241). It is not merely a concern for economy. For Gandhi a village has a great potential for human development.

> Those whose minds are fresh will find new things to see and to learn in villages. It is not true that your mental development becomes stunned when you go to the villages. My reply to those who say this would be that they must have gone there with closed minds. Actually the village, and not the city, is the place for the development of the mind (*Ibid.* 420).

This explains why both in South Africa and in India, Gandhi located his ashram in a rural setting. "The key to swaraj is not in the cities but in the villages" (*Ibid.* 417). I am inclined to believe that Gandhi's fondness for life in a village is not merely a concern for the vast majority of Indians who live there. It is also an expression of his desire to be with nature.

Our experience of being human is intimately related to our experience of nature around us. For the vast majority of Indians this is what the villages offer:

> Villages are normally recognized as significant social units, which are defined and constituted by relationships among villagers themselves, their local deities, and the land on which they live. There should always be harmony between the deities and the population and territory that they protect and rule over, as well as compatibility between the people and their land, whose qualities are ingested by eating food grown in village fields and drinking water drawn from village wells.[11]

This is true of all primal communities, communities that have not been fundamentally disfigured by the impact of modernisation. My experience convinces me that, by and large, the rural folks are much more integrated persons than urban people, even though the former may claim to be more modern, more cultured, more educated. Gandhi too seems to have had a similar impression. "Forest-dwellers everywhere are less often overcome by evil desires than city-dwellers" (*CW* 33.435).

The symbiotic relation with nature around us is vital for our total health. "A human being is made of earth. His body springs from the earth and derives its sustenance from the various forms which earth takes" (*CW* 28.206). We instinctively see life as a continuum: the individual is nurtured by the family constituted by blood relations. This is itself a member of a larger family, the world of life around us, and this is turn is sustained by the complex network of non-living realities that surround us. The evolution of the universe and of life upon planet earth tells us that we are born not merely from the womb of our mother, but also from the womb of the earth, from the womb of the cosmos. Just as people around us affect us emotionally, so too life around us shapes our emotions. Nay, even the non-living creatures that constitute our environment—the soil that nourishes our plants and trees, the hills and the valleys, the winds and the clouds, etc., have a significant role in the formation of our emotional make-up, in the discovery of the symbols we need to communicate more intimately, in the genesis of art forms that embody our deeper experiences. Hence we need to be in touch with nature as much as possible, and hence authentic development will not only avoid distancing us from mother earth, but will also safeguard the integrity of creation and promote a more beautiful environment.

Forests are part of our natural resources. Their presence ensures rain and adds to the fertility of the soil, on the other hand "the rainfall is low wherever there is no vegetation (*CW* 28.469). We need to protect our forests and engage in the work of afforestation. Hence in some parts of our country "tree plantation would be... a religious necessity" (*CW* 28.457).

Ahimsa: The Ethos of Development

Gandhi concludes his autobiography with the words: "I can say with assurance, as a result of all my experiments, that a perfect vision of Truth can only follow a complete realization of Ahimsa" ((*Au* 420). Ahimsa "translated `love', is the supreme law for human beings. It knows no exception" (*EW* 353). For the same reason ahimsa provides the ethos that should guide human development. If ahimsa is understood as love, then it denotes not merely a negative attitude—not hurting others, but a positive task—actively wanting the good of others.

Non-violence Towards Oneself

According to popular understanding, industrialization is one essential aspect of development. In an agricultural setup, the farmers need not live together. Their houses can be located on their own land. Even when they do live together, it is in small villages. On the other hand, industrialization means greater concentration of workers. Hence

> rapid urbanization is the process that usually accompanies industrialization in the developing countries. There is a mass exodus of peasants, the landless, the destitute and the youth from the villages to the cities... This exodus has

> created innumerable slums and squatter colonies, which present a pathetic sight of misery and squalor.[12]

What is still more tragic is that "some workplaces are so substandard that people are depersonalized, if not almost dehumanized."[13] When the worker returns home after a day of hard labour he is less human than when he left his home for work. Thus the villager who leaves his village in search of job in some way inflicts violence to himself.

We put in more hours of work to earn the money we need to be effective in the consumer market—the other side of development. The pace of life in an urban setup is characterized by acceleration. For instance, our mode of travel is much faster, and "this is considered the height of civilization" (*HS* 23). All this makes the lives of millions very stressful. This causes bodily and mental sickness. To get some idea of the stress people go through, we just need to travel by the Mumbai local trains during the peak hours, when commuters are either rushing to their work-sites or are returning home. They seem to lose all sense of humanity. Gandhi anticipates this when he speaks of modern cities whose

> roadways are traversed by rushing engines dragging numerous cars crowded with men mostly who know not what they are after, who are often absent-minded, and whose tempers do not improve by being uncomfortably packed like sardines in boxes and finding themselves in the midst of utter strangers who would oust them if they could and whom they would in their turn oust similarly (*EW* 97-98).

We are victims of the consumer market because we do not have the inner strength needed to swim against the current. Ahimsa comes to our aid:

> Non-violence in its dynamic condition means conscious suffering. It does not mean meek submission to the will of the evil-doer, but it makes the putting of one's whole soul against the will of the tyrant. Working under this law of our being, it is possible for a single individual to defy the

> whole might of an unjust empire to save his honour, his religion, his soul and lay the foundation for that empire's fall or its regeneration (*EW* 238).

Resisting the pressures of our times is an act of true love for oneself. It is also a loving service of others: others can be empowered by what we do.

Non-violence Towards Others

Contemporary development promotes competition in all spheres of life. We are once again in the sub-human level of life, where survival of the fittest is the law. "Not killing competition, but life-giving co-operation, is the law of the human beings" (*CW* 61.250). Gandhi rejects the idea that "the Indian population requires to be roused by `the lash of competition' and the other material and sensuous, as well as intellectual, stimuli..." (*EW* 89). Nay, competition leads to unethical tactics: whatever leads to success is allowed. This leads to the "lowering of standards and regulations governing the interests of labour, consumers and the environment."[14]

The emphasis on capital generation brings about many forms of injustice, that violate human dignity. Let me give just two examples. Many TNCs are either shifting their factories from the First World to the Third World, or are opening new factories in poorer nations—where labour and raw materials are comparatively cheap, and where labour laws are not so stringent—and then exporting the products to richer countries. "The retail price of goods produced in the Third World is often up to 10 times higher than the prices at which the commodity was imported."[15] The people who work to produce these items and the country whose raw material is used to produce them get very little. This means "the bulk of the earnings of primary producers is appropriated by merchants, intermediaries, wholesalers, and retailers.[16] Second, if we can replace humans by machines we can save more money. "Between 1972 and 1992 the 500 largest TNCs... laid off 4.4 million workers."[17] In poorer countries, "workers are forced to endure inhuman working conditions because their governments want to attract elusive foreign investment."[18]

International cooperation involves compromises, and the weaker nations have to accept laws that are not quite fair. Gandhi rejects this way of going about. "It happens these days that many things which are legal are not just. The only right way, therefore, to acquire wealth is to do so rightly. And if that is true, we must know what is just" (*CW* 8.337). What happens between nations, happens within a nation, when poor people have to find jobs. There are so many wanting to work that they are willing to accept the terms of the employer. This too is a form of violence. "It is not enough to live by the laws of demand and supply. God has endowed man with understanding, and with a sense of justice. He must follow these and not think of growing rich by devouring others—by cheating others and reducing them to beggary (*CW* 8.337).

Our inter-connectedness means that we cannot think of development just for our nation. "Love has no boundary. My nationalism includes the love of all the nations of the earth irrespective of creed" (*EW* 245). Richer nations must not only avoid benefiting from the helplessness of poorer nations, but also positively help them in their struggle for development. This is in their own interests. When peoples experience injustice and have no peaceful way of righting the wrong, then they take to violence. This is one explanation of the growing menace of terrorism and conflicts between the nations. "Present-day capitalists are responsible for widespread and unjust wars. Most of the wars of our times spring from greed for money" (*CW* 8.371). Unfair developmental approaches are forms of violence, and violence always begets violence.

Non-violence Towards the Environment

Unbalanced development has lead to a lot of environmental damage. According to the U.S. Worldwatch Institute, "between 1975 and 2000 20 percent of all living species will have disappeared."[19] In the last fifty years "we have lost a fifth of the cultivable surface and of the tropical rain forests.[20] Among other problems resulting from our modes of development are acid rains, air and water pollution, destruction of the ozone layer, deforestation and desertification. All these adversely affect human well-being. "Doctors say that 99 per cent of all the diseases are caused by insanitation, by eating things not fit to eat and by lack of proper nutrition. Today pure water, pure earth, and pure air are not available" (*CW* 85.213). If we wish to be healthy we need to respect the basic laws of life. "Disease springs from a wilful or ignorant breach of the laws of nature" (*CW* 85.264).

Svadeshi: The Resources for Development

In his struggle for India's independence, Gandhi gave great importance to swadeshi. For many this denotes the use of things—especially cloth—produced in India. For Gandhi, however, this is another way of explaining the unity of human life and the inter-connectedness of all creation. "I would like to apply it [swadeshi] in our religious, political and economic life" (*CW* 13.251). Swadeshi calls us to bring about harmony in the whole universe, "Swadeshi then means the creation of a most perfect organization in which every part works in perfect harmony with every other" (*CW* 17.331). This will be possible if we look at the whole of creation as our home. It is an invitation to go beyond narrow boundaries. "In its ultimate and spiritual sense swadeshi stands for the final emancipation of the human soul from its earthly bondage... [which] stands in the way of its realizing its oneness with other lives. A votary of swadeshi seeks to be emancipated from the bondage of the physical body" (*CW* 46.254).

Initially swadeshi invites us to take our immediate neighbourhood seriously, to believe that we have within ourselves and within our God-given surroundings the resources we need for development:

> *Swadeshi* carries a greater and profound meaning. It does not mean merely the use of what is produced in one's own country. That meaning is certainly there in swadeshi. But there is another meaning implied in it which is far greater and much more important. Swadeshi means reliance on our own strength. We should also know what we mean by 'reliance on our own strength'. 'Our strength' means the strength of our body, our mind and our soul (*EW* 362).

Development reaches its height only when we actualise all our potential. "Human development is about much more than the rise or fall of national incomes. It is about creating an environment in which people can develop their full potential and lead productive, creative lives in accordance with their needs and interests."[21]

Resources from within Persons

For centuries we Indians have been ruled by outsiders. We have developed some kind of national inferiority complex. We think that what comes from the west is always the best. Also, it is not easy to practise swadeshi, because foreign goods appear to be seductively attractive. Hence swadeshi calls for inner discipline. "Those who are not attached to pleasure and personal adornment, I venture to say, can give a great impetus to *swadeshi*" (*EW* 364). Real development will give us a sense of confidence, and without it development would only further enslave us.

Swadeshi also calls for the promotion of cottage industries, the spinning wheel being one example. "It supplements agriculture and therefore automatically assists materially to solve the problem of growing poverty. Thus swadeshi is our veritable *Kamadhenu* supplying all our wants and solving many of our difficult problems" (*CW* 17.331). Our farmers have a lot of free time while they wait for their crops to be ready for harvesting. They can make a more fruitful use of this time. Remaining idle can also lead to moral problems. Swadeshi will prevent a lot of Indian money from going out of the country (*CW* 17.470). More positively, "it is capable of limitless expansion and of producing, without any capital outlay, new wealth in the country and providing honourable employment to those who are starving for want of it" (*CW* 58.445).

Resources from the Society

Swadeshi calls us to be concerned about the people who live in our neighbourhood. "If this interpretation of swadeshi [as oneness with other lives] be correct, then it follows that its votary will as a first duty dedicate himself to the service of his immediate neighbours" (*CW* 46.254). In doing this he is also reaching out to others. "Pure service of one's neighbours can never, from its very nature, result in disservice to those who are remotely situated, rather the contrary" (*CW* 46.354).The resources of a given locality must be used first and foremost to meet the needs of the people of that place. Development enables us to transport our products to places where we can get more money. "Railways have also increased the frequency of famines, because, owing to facility of means of locomotion, people sell out their grain, and it is sent to the dearest markets" (*HS* 36).[22]

We have a large work force. Any form of mechanisation that will leave these people unemployed will be counter-productive.

> How can a country with crores of living machines afford to have a machine which will displace the labour of crores of living machines. It would spell their unemployment and their ruin. We have to employ all these crores of living machines... and unless cities decide to depend for the necessities of life and for most of their other needs on the villages, this can never happen (*CW* 60.256).

The workers will be encouraged if their products find a good market. Hence we need to patronize them.

> A votary of swadeshi will carefully study his environment and try to help his neighbours wherever possible by giving preference to local manufactures even if they are of an inferior grade or dearer in price than things manufactured elsewhere. He will try to remedy their defects but will not give them up because of their defects and take to foreign manufactures" (*CW* 46.256).

This patronizing of local products is in the long run for the good of all. When our neighbours have a productive job, they have a sense of dignity, and then peace has a better chance.

It would however be a mistake to think that swadeshi is a rejection of machine made items or of machinery. "Pure *swadeshi* is not at all opposed to machinery" (*EW* 366). Machines would be out of place were they to displace the local resources:

> Opposition to mills or machinery is not the point. What suits our country most is the point. I am not opposed to the movement of manufacturing machines in the country, nor to making improvements in machinery. I am only concerned with what these machines are meant for. I may ask, in the words of Ruskin, whether these machines will be such as would blow off a million men in a minute or they will be such as would turn waste lands into arable and fertile land (*EW* 367).

So too, Gandhi is open to the constructive use of modern forms of power. "If we could have electricity in every village home, I should not mind villagers plying their implements and tools with the help of electricity" (*EW* 401).

Our mother-tongue is one the resources of our society. Hence it "should be given proper importance and its development encouraged" (*CW* 88.403). This is also true of our culture taken as a whole. So too our ability to rule ourselves. Sad to say, the forces of development are "homogenizing diverse cultural and social sectors and marginalizing the political process."[23]

Resources from the Environment

The more the process of development uses local resources, the greater will be the well-being of the locals. Among different ways to utilize local resources to the maximum, Gandhi suggests the use of organic manure,

> made from human and animal excreta. We will then be able to save golden manure worth crores of rupees, which is being wasted because of our ignorance. The soil will become fertile and we will get better crops than what we are getting. As a result we will be rid of famines, crores of people will get enough to eat and the surplus can be exported (*CW* 90.270).

This manure does not "require expenditure but a little labour" (*CW* 90.306).

Gandhi was not totally opposed to things of foreign origin. "Boycott of all foreign things is neither possible nor proper" (*CW* 40.374). The emphasis is on the maximum use of local products. Imported goods should not displace local products. This is the reason why Gandhi insists on khadi: "it is our dharma to use those things which can be or are easily made in our country and on which depends the livelihood of poor people; the boycott of such things and deliberate preference of foreign things is adharma" (*CW* 40.374). For the same reason we need to use home-made dyes (*CW* 40.23).

Swaraj: The Environment for Development

Gandhi gives us a very simple rule for evaluating developmental activity:

> Whenever you are in doubt, or when the self becomes too much with you, apply the following test. Recall the face of the poorest and the weakest man whom you have seen, and ask yourself if the step you contemplate is going to be of any use to him. Will he gain anything by it? Will it restore him to a control over his own life and destiny? In other words, will it lead to swaraj for the hungry and spiritually starving millions? Then you will find your doubts and yourself melting away (*EW* 418).

Amartya Sen, who received the Nobel Prize for his work on economics, agrees with Gandhi.

> Expansion of freedom is viewed... both as the primary end and as the principal means of development. Development consists of the removal of various types of unfreedoms that leave people with little choice and little opportunity of exercising their reasoned agency. The removal of substantial unfreedoms... is *constitutive* of development.[24]

Freedom for Persons

Modern development is very much market-related. If the market does not flourish many multinational corporations will collapse. Hence they invest a lot of capital in promoting the sale of their goods, and for this they employ highly sophisticated advertisements that convince many uncritical moderns that they need many more consumer items to be happy. They are brainwashed by the market mafia. They are not really free. "Formerly, men were made slaves under physical compulsion, now they are enslaved by temptation of money and of the luxuries that money can buy" (*HS* 24). Gandhi, on the hand, rejects this craze for more, for the latest. "Civilization, in the real sense of the term, consists not in the multiplication, but in the deliberate and voluntary reduction of wants. This alone promotes real happiness and contentment, and increases the capacity for service" (*EW* 378). He does not "subscribe to the belief that everything old is bad. Truth is old and difficult" (*EW* 399).

To be able to resist the lure of the consumer market, we need to cultivate a critical approach to life, and nurture inner strength that will enable us to resist the superficial glamour of our times. Then we will be free to fulfil our obligations towards others. "Real swarajya consists in restraint. He alone is capable of this who leads a moral life, does not cheat anyone, does not forsake truth and does his duty to his parents, his wife, his children, his servant and his neighbour (*CW* 8.373). Today so many aged parents feel abandoned by their children, who are doing very well in life. They regularly send money to their parents, but have no time for them. We are so taken up by consumer items that we "have hardly leisure for anything else" (*HS* 25), not even for our loved ones. We lose the aesthetic and creative dimensions of being human.

Freedom for Society

According to Gandhi, the development of our villages is the development of our nation. "Independence must begin at the bottom. Thus, every village will be a republic or panchayat having full powers" (*EW* 347). For this the village must be

> (I)ndependent of its neighbours for its own vital wants, and yet interdependent for many others in which dependence is a necessity. Thus every village's first concern will be to grow its own food crops and cotton for its cloth. It should have a reserve for its cattle, recreation and playground for adults and children. The village will maintain a village theatre, school and public hall. It will have its own waterworks, ensuring clean water supply. (*EW* 358-59).

Our villages will be autonomous to the extent our nation is truly independent. With globalisation, weaker nations are forced to compromise on their autonomy. When powerful nations bully the weaker ones, then the latter may retaliate in the way they can. This is one explanation for the growth of international terrorism.

This [permanent peace on earth] is clearly impossible without the great Powers of the earth renouncing their imperialistic design. This again seems impossible without great nations ceasing to believe in soul-destroying competition and to desire to multiply wants and therefore increase their material possessions (*EW* 175).

Years ago I heard a professor of economics, who gave us a lecture on Gandhian economics. He concluded by saying: "Gandhi does not teach us a particular brand of economics. He gives us a comprehensive vision for human growth and development. Only within this framework can we understand and appreciate what he says about economics." I fully agree with this insight. If we disregard the overall Gandhian vision, then what he has to say about economic development sounds non-sensical. But any approach to economic development, that ignores the totality of human well-being, will in the long run be detrimental to human happiness. On the other hand if we follow what Gandhi has to offer then we as a nation will blossom and fulfil our mission.

> Ours will then be a truly spiritual nation when we shall show more truth than gold, greater fearlessness than pomp of power and wealth, greater charity than love of self. If we will but clean our houses, our palaces and temples of the attributes of wealth, and show in them the attributes of morality, we can offer battle to any combinations of hostile forces without having to carry the burden of a heavy militia. Let us seek first the kingdom of God and His righteousness and the irrevocable promise is that everything will be added with us. These are real economics. May you and I treasure them and enforce them in our daily life" (*EW* 99).

What we need is a different way of looking at life. Gandhi believes India can help the world to acquire this vision. "Many of us believe, and I am one of them, that through our civilization we have a message to deliver to the world" (*CW* 13.262). I agree with Gandhi.

Notes

1. Pradeep Pillai, "India spins its charm", *The Week*, April 23, 2005, p. 18.
2. Jim Erikson, "A Place in the Sun", *Time*, June 19, 2006, p. 26.
3. *Ibidem*.
4. I shall indicate references to Gandhi's own writings in the text itself, using an abbreviation, followed by the page number. For *CW*, the volume number will be followed by a point (.) and then the page number. I am basing my study on the following sources:

   Au An Autobiography: *The Story of My Experiments with Truth*, Ahmedabad: Navajivan Publishing House, 14th rep., n.d.

   CW The Collected Works of Mahatma Gandhi, 90 viols., New Delhi: Publication Division, Ministry of Information and Broadcasting, Government of India, 1958-84.

   EW: The Essential Writings of Mahatma Gandhi, ed. Raghavan IYER, New Delhi: Oxford University Press, 1993, 11th rep. 2004.

   HS: Indian Home Rule or Hind Swaraj, Madras: G. A. Natesan, 6th rep., 1947.

   When quoting from these books, I have kept the spelling of non-English words as it is in the text. There is also no consistency with regard to the italicising of these words. Hence they will not be italicised when these texts are quoted.

   Certain words – *satya, ahi×sâ, svadeœa, svarâj*, etc. – very frequently used by Gandhi, have become part of the English language. Hence when I use these words, I shall spell them as they are commonly spelt in Gandhi's writings and not italicise them.

   Sometimes the text as it stands appears to have some grammatical error. This could be either because Gandhi himself wrote in a hurry or because the persons who transcribed his talks and speeches did not notice their errors. Whenever possible, I have tried to clarify what Gandhi is saying by supplying some words within square brackets [...].
5. See "Satyagraha: A Theological Model for India", in Subhash ANAND, *Hindu Inspiration for Christian Reflection: Towards a*

Hindu-Christian Theology, Anand (Gujarat): Gujarat Sahitya Prakash, 2004, pp. 171-201, here, pp. 179-80.

6. Victor L. Anthuvan, *The Dynamics and the Impact of Globalisation: A Subaltern Perspective*, Madurai: Amirtham Pb., 2006, p. 276.
7. Catherine B. Haliburn, "The Family and the Child: The Asian Family's Struggle for Life", *FABC Papers*, 72f, Hongkong: FABC, 1995, p. 5.
8. Nona Walia, "A family that eats together..", *Ibid.*, November 5, 2006, p. 2.
9. This sentence is a bit prolematic. I suggest the following reading: "Even if we fail [in terms of economics] in this we shall have succeeded [by maintaining our humanness."
10. Christopher John Fuller, *The Camphor Flame: Popular Hinduism and Society in India*, New Jersey: Princeton University Press, 1992, p. 128.
11. *Ibidem.*
12. Haliburn, "The Family and the Child", p. 13.
13. *Ibid.*, p. 7.
14. Anthuvan, *The Dynamics and the Impact of Globalisation*, p. 94.
15. *Ibid.*, p. 77.
16. *Ibidem.*
17. *Ibid.*, p. 83.
18. *Ibid.*, p. 84.
19. Leonardo Boff, *Ecology and Liberation: A New Paradigm*, Maryknoll (NY): Orbis Books, 1995, p. 15.
20. *Ibidem.*
21. Anthuvan, *The Dynamics and the Impact of Globalisation*, p. 285.
22. Gandhi wrote this in 1908. Amartya Sen cites an instance of famine in Wollo (Ethiopia), when food was taken away from Wollo to be sold elsewhere, "where people had more income to buy food." Amartya Sen, *Development as Freedom*, New Delhi: Oxford University Press, 1999, p. 167.
23. Anthuvan, *The Dynamics and the Impact of Globalisation*, p. 48.
24. Sen: *Development as Freedom*, p. xii. Emphasis in the original.

2

Hinduism and Development

TK JOHN SJ

Introduction

Four considerations have to be brought in while treating *Hinduism and Development*. First that India is a country of many religions and so the religious ethos largely determines the socio-economic mores of the people. Second, that there is a cause-effect relationship between the social formation and the economic dynamics and status of the country: both are marked by sharp contrast and distance. The lowest placed in the social structure are also the lowest possessors of economic goods, for centuries. Third, the not yet-properly scrutinized caste system has largely compounded and contributed to this anomaly. Fourth, the system that is operative seems to be marked by certain irreversibility. A bad mix of anthropology and psychology seem to be at work, apart from the callousness of collectivity.

A most distinctive feature of India is that India is proud of and enjoys a unique title and claim to being a land of religions. The recent plunge of this land into the global merge of economic streams now baptized as globalization with visions and values devoid of the ethical and the moral has generated much debate. Faster development is the proclaimed objective.

The assumption behind this drive which is not yet scrutinized boldly and ruthlessly is that the western corporate capitalism will remove poverty and distribute well-being evenly and sufficiently for all. On to an already distraught social and economic system the elites of India have attached the economic policy and mode of operation of globalization stamped with inequality. We all have to be in the bandwagon and reach wherever the impersonal dynamics take us. Our collective memory is too short to recall that colonialism was the child of capitalism, and that western capitalistic model of development cannot but behave in the manner in which India was treated by the colonizers. The only difference is that this time it is the internal colonizers and capitalists that are the masters and holders of the keys, in close collaboration and network with the global contenders. We have a western capitalistic culture joined to the Indian caste hierarchical culture, a hard mix that is almost irrefragable. Both are devoid of what some world economists describe as economics with a human face. It may be useful to be forewarned that dive down into the pool by someone with insufficient skill in swimming from the dive-board can bring either disaster or invite temerity. Will the *Hindu ethos* examine the dynamics of development at work in the country so that the Indian people will critically operate in order to evolve a thrust that will help everyone and help to keep our country on the right track– is the question. The following pages are devoted to a brief investigation of Hinduism's resourcefulness to face the challenges of 'development', on the one hand, and how the Hindu ethos is capable of taking a critical stand *vis-à-vis* the march of development that is a global phenomenon.

Here are some pace-setting questions. Does India know the roots and dynamics of development in the West that virtually destroyed religiosity in Europe and America and made many nations there disoriented and created "Iraq' as Nazi Germany gifted Spandau and Auschwitz to the world and to history? Will the land of religions survive 'development', if the phenomenon in the West is a lesson for all. One moot question too: is religion capable of contributing to development?

or will it be an obstacle to it? Derived from the same: What role can Hinduism play in the realization of the dream India entertains of becoming a developed nation? If India has been developing is it because of religion/HINDUISM? or is it in spite of religion/Hinduism?

Some Christian authors (Christopher Dawson, Arnold Toynbee and others) have claimed that Europe is the creation of Christianity and Hellenism. The assumption is that there is a case of religion contributing to the making of nations. There seems to be much truth in the claim. The first phase of the making of Europe was by monks that fostered and nurtured centres of learning like Bologna, Sorbonne, Florence. But with the birth of the empirical sciences and modern philosophy religion was left behind. Why? Is it because religion could not keep pace with the development brought in by science, technology industry and related developments. Although there is not much evidence of Christianity being practised in the West, yet, it is asserted, that the essence of the Gospel has been the very progenitor of western humanism. Can Hinduism play a role in helping a nation to develop integrally?

Japan is a 'developed' nation. But there is a Japanese stamp, so to speak, about Japanese development. China's partial withdrawal from the world culture was to preserve and to promote what is the Chinese version of development. Their understanding of 'development' is not a mere copying of the Western patterns. What about India? An intimate link between a sound religious-cultural ethos and development seems to be the answer. India should decide what kind of development we need. Not an uncritical copying of what happens elsewhere but a choice that befits our national ethos and the needs of the people.

Indian religions, with the numerically larger Hinduism, are now faced with a major challenge: to run with the hare pulling the gold-plated cart of globalization and its progeny development. Will Hindu ethos, known the world over for what it is, promote the kind of development that befits humankind and eradicate problems like poverty, equally known the world over? Great Indians like Ashoka, Akbar, and the mythical Janaka of the puranas and the epics, are held out as examples of evolving state policy inspired by ethics and a spiritual vision. The essential core of the Indian religious ethos they tried to inject into political, social and other sectors of the state. Gandhi and Nehru of our times too are credited with such farsightedness and comprehensive vision. Nehru and Gandhi in own times tried to combine the essentials of the Indian ethos with the western and introduced and integrated what the two had drawn from both these streams. They were 'modern' yet Indians.

Conceptualizing 'Development'

(a) *Development was about transforming the lives of people, not just transforming economies'* stated Nobel laureate Joseph Striglitz during his lecture in Chennai as reported by the Special Correspondent of *The Hindu* covering the session (*The Hindu*, Friday, January 5, 2007). The report further added that "Professor Stiglitz underlined the importance of India continuing to maintain its programmes for the weaker sections and the poor, for health and education projects and rural development measures and said that the state should not withdraw from these sectors". This warning from this informed economist is actually also the voice of the majority of the Indian people. That was demonstrated by movements and trends in the country. Mumbai's World Social Forum and New Delhi's Asian Social Forum are crystallizations that illustrate.

Battling vigorously against this trend is a powerful minority that thinks differently and acts accordingly. It is involved in directing the nation in the opposite direction. Thus India is virtually at the crossroads. India is in a state of parting of ways. It is like the mythical scene of Kurukshtra: Duryodhana and his small but powerful holders of ill-gotten power and accumulation of wealth on one side ranged against the larger in their millions who are the losers in an unequal all-out war.

(b) Uppsala based Dag Hammarskjold Foundation in its journal *Development Dialogue* ("Another Development," 1981: 1) argues that our understanding of development has to be widened and made comprehensive. The research document demands that authentic development should aim at the greatest improvement in the *quality of life of the people.* This takes place when all the possibilities people have to adequately satisfy their fundamental human needs are met. These refer to areas of a person's being having doing and interacting. Subsistence, protection, affection, understanding, participation, leisure, creativity, identity, and freedom are a person's fundamental needs and these have to be adequately fulfilled. Development then should address these comprehensive needs of the human person. Religions would add one more to this list: transcendence. Obviously the State's understanding of development falls short of this overarching description of what ought to be the real components of development.

Hence the pertinent question: What then is *development?* And what is the role of Hinduism in the common task of development of India? The following nuances need to be taken into account when we use the term development.

(c) Strictly speaking development refers to a dynamic process of actualization of a dream or a project or a potentiality, a journey from one situation to another, a transformation of something into something, an attainment of a stage envisioned, inbuilt and pursued. The best examples are available in abundance from a close observation of development in nature around us: the seed's development into the full grown plant that blooms blossoms and become laden with fruits brimming with sweet juice and health-promoting nutritives. The journey of the power-charged white powder in the seed that sprouts, passes through the various stages like entry into the wet soil, growth and development of the sapling, maturing unto a plant or a tree, leading to the birth of the bud that blossoms into flowers, then the birth of the fruit with its many seeds within until the maturing and ripening—is a vital organic process of development. Here we observe the *vital/organic* process in developing and blossoming and blooming.

Close analysis of this daily event in all vital organic activities reveals the following elements:

First of all, it is the very nature or essence of the species that is being transmitted, is present in all stages, and manifests as the fruit. The fidelity to the nature or essence of the apple tree is preserved and operative at all stages. Hence continuity of the essence of the journeying subject is the first component in the process. The fruit that is the apple contains 'appleness', so to speak, all through the stages of the life-force dynamism at work. This is important for our understanding and critiquing of development and Hinduism.

Secondly, there is a goal or destiny towards which the journey is undertaken by the vital dynamism or impulses imparted to the organic process. The destiny inherent in the seed and which activates the dynamics of the journey is the fully grown tree, and full growth takes place when flowers appear and they blossom and produce fruit. Here is a genuine case of development.

Thirdly, there is the necessary sine-qua non role of the agents and ingredients in the forward and upward journey of the vital process. The moisture from water, the energy from the sun, the chlorophyll responsible for light absorption for generating the energy required for the vital process in the plants, are essential ingredients that contribute to the 'development' of the plant. The energy from the sun is also a catalytic agent that facilitates full development.

(d) We take next another use of 'development'. For this we enter the field of education. Those well-versed in the field of education trace the meaning to its Latin root, 'educere', i.e. 'bring forth' the various potentialities imbedded in the child in order to promote or 'develop' them and facilitate the full becoming or 'development' of the child as a healthy member of the society. Reference here is to the development of the physical, the mental, the affective, the kinetic, the artistic, the aesthetic, the transcendent and other potentialities and capabilities of every child.

(e) The Christian understanding of the development of the human person will underscore all these, and more, because the origin nature and destiny of the human person are all traced to the creative act of God that creates the human being in the image and likeness of God. It is consequently evident that the term development can be applied to the human person, and collectively to the society, when the essential potentialities that constitute human nature is imparted the required stimulus so that actualization of these potentials take place.

First of all central to the concept of the human person is *reason.* When rationality is recognized with all its demands and human behviour and social relationships are guided by the sine qua non of rationality we can say development is taking place.

Second, *freedom* is a non-negotiable second component of the human person. If the individual and the society of which one is a member honour freedom, foster freedom, and sufficient space is available for the legitimate exercise of freedom, development of the human person is taking place. Compulsion, regimentation, homogenization etc. are hostile forces.

Third, the *dignity* of the human person flows from the very nature of the person. If values like equality, fellowship, are enjoyed by everyone in a given society, it will be considered a developed society. The much honoured phrase, being and not having,' needs to be recalled again and again.

(f) The expectation of this line of thinking is that the target of 'development' by the State *ought to be* the all round well being of all the citizens of a country, leaving none behind unattended. Availability of resources to fulfil satisfactorily the basic needs of all citizens and every citizen ought to be the set objective of planned development. Growth, advancement, prosperity and well-being are concerns of the State when it aims at development. Availability of food, health care, housing, literacy, transport, employment, security, is part of the schemes aimed at development. Economics, industry, agriculture, technology, energy, natural mineral resources, labour, management, financial institutions, and other agencies are closely associated with development of the country. Rate of production, gross national product, growth in income, sufficiency of resources for meeting the basic needs of the citizens like food, health care, education, entertainment and relaxation and other items are considered as indicators of development. Space and freedom for the exercise of one's rights and live a lie worthy of the nature and dignity of the human person are the crowning of such state policy on development.

Development as Conceived by the State

However the thrust and dynamics of development pursued by the State have merits and demerits. They are influenced primarily by the laws of economics where growth, production, and profit are the guiding principles and values. From the era of competition among mega corporations to that of merger in order to have greater control and greater profit, the trend is set. This powerful merger movements in industries and in trade climaxed in the much-debated globalization. It is a cultural mutation that has taken place. It is the global financial institutions that control and direct these trends. With the collapse of the Soviet Union and the imposition on the world of the unipolar imperialist capitalism of the United States, development is under the dictates of market economy, the child of globalized and globalizing economy. The human rights of peoples, the chief concern of the U. N. Charter, democratic culture and structures are subordinated to the demands of the market culture. Corporates have grown stronger over sovereign States.

What is the Criterion of the State and the Planners?

Growth is the central criterion. Growth in economy dictates other policies. High rate of growth, booming stock exchange, increase in benefits of free trade are enjoyed by people because a variety of goods non-available hitherto when control was strict, are available now. Indian mega corporates like Mittal and Tata are entering the international market and buying. Our information technology competes effectively with other known and powerful companies the world over. We have a booming economy!

There is Absolute Reliance on the Laws of Economy and the Favours and Benefits of the Market

The laws and dynamics of the market are allowed to have their sway which will eventually percolate and fill the plates and cups of those below, eventually even of the deprived of India, neglected for millennia, we are told. Free enterprise encourages and stimulates private initiative which is key to economic growth. Rise in GDP is a reliable index of the health of the nation, it is held. India is credited with a booming economy. The Stock exchange and the bahaviour of the shares market are the index.

These developments are commendable in themselves. But then how do the people on the other side fare?

Ground Realities that Need to be Attended to

But signals sent from a wide spectrum of the Indian peoples carry messages that need to be taken seriously in order to balance the picture. The nation has a soft belly and is vulnerable.

First, the already bleeding farmers' serial suicide, over 9000 in the last six years, according to official statistics, in at least four States in the South, seem not to disturb the planners and their pursuers. This is appalling since the phenomenon exposes the Indian rural sector, the mainstay of India's economy, as undeveloped or under-developed. Indian farmers for centuries lived in contentment though struggling hard against the vagaries of nature and other forces. But today desperation has overtaken them and the industry-enticed State seems slow to take note of.

Besides, conversion of prime agricultural land for mega factories, malls, IT colonies, has become part of the process. Industry that swallows agriculture in a country like India where the farmlands feed the people has fatal consequences for the future.

The farmers are suddenly waking up to meet the invading forces symbolized by the new child of globalization, namely, Special Economic Zones. Political parties with different ideologies fall in line as in the game of ninepins. The suppression of peasants meets with democratic resistance. But brutal force is used by the State. Brutal police violence on the workers of Honda factory in Gudgaon Haryana, firing and killing of tribals in Kalinga, similar acts of state violence in

Singur and Nandigram are among the latest indicators of the direction of development of which the State is only an obedient servant. Elected representatives toe the line easily forgetting the truth that they are to represent the voice and the needs of the people.

What has recently been called 'development terrorism' by the State, inspired by a fundamentalism in economics, a new and deadly kind of land grab has been planned unilaterally by the elites without the consensus of the electorate and pursued ruthlessly by people's representatives and by the bureaucracy. Livelihood is destroyed, land is forcedly taken away by the State at low price and sold to the Corporates at ten times or more higher level. In this process the till-recently observed laws pertaining to the tribal lands sale has been violated by the State.

Where does the land go? It goes to the over 250 special economic zones set up by the peoples elected representative at the hem of the State without consulting the people. More than 250 such Special Economic Zones have been sold out. Kalinga, Nandigram, Singur testify to the killing by the Indian State to satisfy the demands of corporates. People are expendable and disposable for the purposes of what the State decides. This is immoral and anti-democratic, and damages the current mode of ownership and livelihood.

Second, the tragedy among the farmers needs to be linked with the fast growing concern for ecology. The message that human interference with the laws of nature is fraught with very serious consequences is being sent repeatedly by nature but listening to that is yet to become effective The experiment with seeds (cotton, rice, and others) seem to have brought us to a T-point. In order to secure fast and copious yields, disproportionately higher than the normal, chemically treated varieties of seeds have been supplied to the farmers almost under compulsion. The disappearance of hundreds of varieties of plants, cereals like rice etc are signals we can ill-afford to ignore.

Third, the cruel phenomenon of the Indian State evicting millions of Indian citizens from Indian cities on the plea that they are illegal occupants of space in the city is unpardonable. The State cannot consider such migrants as a law and order problem. The effort to develop Indian cities and make them be on a par with 'world-class cities' should be with due consideration for the rights of the Indian people. The rural poor have to give way to the demands of the new set of holders of power. The nation is haunted by this spectrum. Both the suicide by the farmers and those taking refuge in the cities show our planning and development vision and dynamics as flawed. Indeed it is a blot on our culture known to be humane. Who are these evictees? They are not outsiders, but Indians, all of them, people whose knowledge of their rights is limited. The evictees are those who migrated to the cities for their living, since rural situation failed them. The voluntary migrants are turned back, thrown out of Indian cities, to become forced migrants. Law, and not humaneness, is the criterion since the evictees are on illegal land in the cities.

Fourth, large scale sale of rivers to Corporates is also part of that scheme. Corporates will make money and deprive thousands of farmers of their use of water, agricultural labourers will suffer loss of work, fishermen, the boatmen and others related to the process of traditional fishing and living will be deprived of their occupation for living..

Fifth, displacement of population without proper rehabilitation in order to facilitate the growth of such corporations is taking place on a colossal scale the world over. From Hattia in Ranchi in Bihar to Narmada in Madhya Pradesh the record of the State as regards settlement is dismal because shabby.

Sixth, the growing Naxalite movement tells the nation loudly that the governance of the nation since independence was faulty. According to the figures available from Ministry of Home at least 150 out of a total of 607 districts are already affected by naxalite movement. The non-fulfilment of aspirations raised during the freedom struggle days and promises made after Independence landed them in this situation. Land distribution has not taken place adequately. The functioning of the many Sate apparatuses in the rural areas leaves the villagers only in despair. The Naxalites intervene to correct and to improve. Where the State failed Naxalites won. The unchanged status of the millions who are still landless strengthens the movement.

Seventh, the percentage of the illiterate Indians remains still forbidding. And without literacy opportunity for employment is very limited. Present economic and industrial development has added to the already swollen number of the unemployed. The number of the men and women who lack employment to live is staggering.

Eighth, large-scale borrowing from IMF and the World Bank and Asian Development Bank for the purposes of development is comparable to drinking sea water to quench thirst. Ramifications are such. It is the multinational corporations that are employed by the government at their terms for giant projects. Such steps further contribute to the already existing debt traps. To respond, other projects are launched in order to feed them. Drinking salt water is no remedy for thirst, wise fish workers know, but not the planners.

Ninth, welfare policies of early days have been abandoned in favour of the laws of economy. Financing welfare schemes are unproductive investment, managers of financial institutions tell the State.

Finally, a combination of illiteracy, unemployment and poverty has gripped those still lower than the middle class and those below with apathy and hopelessness. The benefits of development have not yet reached them. Drinking water, health care, electricity, transport, are among the urgent needs the far-flung villages are badly in need of. Their patience is exhausted.

In other words, commoditization of nature and of social relations has subjected everything to the demands of rude consumerism and the faceless laws of the market that attend only to growth. Bulldozing of the weak in the name of the demands of new economy and a devaluing of the people without resources (social, political, economic) is a major fall out.

From the strict understanding of the term development, the above black sports in human history are signs of undeveloped human thinking, being and relating. We can say that an 'undeveloped' 'development' is at work. We need to correct and move towards 'real development.'

Some Factors Responsible for the Distorted Vision and Action

Elitism and Absence of Peoples' Influence in Development

We need to take note of an important perhaps less noticed factor about post independent planning. The first Prime Minister, Jawaharlal Nehru, during his days of the freedom struggle had travelled through the country side, and engaged with the rural population. He was deeply moved by their situation. In his autobiography he describes the shock that this Eaton educated humanist lawyer and visionary had registered when confronted with the lives of the nearly famished ill-clad village folks living in their simple dwellings with little amenities. India is largely rural, he was convinced, and the rural population shows a picture different from the affluent elitist urban population. This experience of rural India, the greater India, had influenced much of his planning and decisions once he became the Prime Minister. In other words it was the voice of the people still ringing loud in his ears and their picture vivid and moving that was a major clinching factor for policy deliberations and decisions while he worked in the present day Teen Murty Bhavan in New Delhi. He introduced planned development with the people and for the people based on his perception and experience of the Indian people..

Gandhi, on his return to India, travelled through rural India and acquired first hand experience and knowledge of the Indian people. He listened to India. The planners and the industrial-trade magnates should listen to India and feel the pulses of the people and plan.

Are the Indian peoples' voices heard and listened to by our present day planners and performers, is the moot question before us today. The shrill voices from Narmada, Kalinga, Nandigram, Sangru, Kalahandi, Netrahat, Koel Karo, 'Noida' Kheirlangi, are treated with apathy and contempt by the destiny-makers of the nation at all levels since they are considered blocks to the 'development' which the neo-foreign colonies known as 'SEZ' will bring about for all the people of India!? Dictates from outside and from above and not the voices of helplessness from below rule development. How far do people's voice and needs influence those who design and execute the plans for the nation?

This takes us to further questions. What could be the experience and knowledge of the planners and economists about the actual situation of the majority of the Indian people? Minds shaped by the World Bank-generated economy and culture can be immune to shocks when confronted, if at all, with the life of the great majority of the Indian people. Ambedkar had the fire within. That fire was born of his bitter experiences of humiliation as a dalit. This fire, combined with profound scholarship, gave him the drive to battle ceaselessly for the socially transforming steps he envisaged for India. But are the majority of administrators, bureaucrats, and planners that come from the affluent classes able to register the anxiety and anguish of villagers of the caste-affected rural India? For instance, the Musahars of Bihar live on gathering the fallen rice from fields, rat-holes and the precincts of FCI go downs! Recently some States that under-utilized the fund allotted for the rehabilitation of the tsunami affected people returned the balance to the Centre. The news shocked the sensitive citizens across the country. Bureaucrats and administers at the helm seem not to be fired by the wretchedness of our people. Another Nobel laureate Professor Amartya Sen had experienced the famine of Bengal in his early days, and that coloured his economics and helped evolve an economics with a human face..

The development of the human person and society takes place in the first place when all substantially inhibiting and enslaving constraints are removed and a correct vision is evolved. In India it is the Brahmins and those associated with them in sharing power in a graded manner that are planning for the country, governing the country, and making judicial pronouncements. *There is an inherent flaw in the very make-up of that governance.* How can the tainted clean the indigent! A major factor is the hardened and valueless institution of caste in India.

Caste taints the enforcer of caste. India needs to be free of this major block to development. This needs further elaboration.

In India the major flaw in the development of the very concept of the human person intervened with the introduction of caste since its very essence is grading of the human nature and grading of the exclusion of those below. As a category this determines the mindsets of the upper castes and vitiates them, and afflicts those below. The malady affects the dominating and the dominated, suppressed and the suppressor, the excluded and those excluding, equally and adversely.

Since it is this dominant group or class that is governing the country, planning for the people, allotting resources for the maintenance of the various departments of administration, it is inconceivable that the caste prejudices will be left behind when planning and decision making take place. For example in the reports submitted to the nation after riots and orgies in Gujarat, it was made clear that community caste or class or gender prejudices vitiated the enforcement of law. The fact that what is now known as dalits as a body, all over India, are largely still kept outside the society and regarded as polluting and hence to be avoided, is a clear indication that 'development' in the full sense is not yet ready to be applied to the human situation in India. Economically, proliferation of goods is taking place and flooding the house kitchen parlour or even the bedrooms of the affluent. But human development and consequent social transformation is slow to take place.

Significance of Peoples' Movements

A distinguishing feature of governance in India is the space given to protest and to activism in order to attend to grievances the State is unwilling to listen to and address. It is to make up for that deficiency in democracy that various civil society initiatives in the form of peoples' movements, protest groups, and voluntary organizations are in the field utilizing the space available to them in the Constitution.

However, the future of this corrective presence and contribution to the democratic cultures and structures will diminish since the power in governance of the nation is still largely in the hands of the upper strata that are impervious, increasingly, to the voices of dissent. The best case in point is the campaign against tribals' displacement in the Naramda valley. In spite of over twenty years of protests by the tribals, the upper class/caste combine has been consistently unyielding. The voice of dalits, tribals and other weaker sections have no impact upon the hardened minds of the ruling block. The power-holders in the society are unwilling to listen to them, honour their protest and consider their stand.

Below we need to trace the roots of this cultural malaise that intervenes in the process of development. We need to detect the perceptions, values and modes of deciding that shape the mindset. Religion has much to do with it since bureaucrats, legislators, judges, ministers, members of planning institutions all shape perceptions and organise actions

Hinduism and 'Development'

In this land of many religions Hinduism is the largest numerically. Therefore its potentiality to shape the behaviour of the people is greater than that of the other religions. Hence Hinduism is called upon, as are the others, to play a role.

The expectation of the people is that religions, as the meaning dimension of a culture, are expected to wake up and redeem the situation in favour of the concept of development that will enable healthy and full growth of the human person, and of all persons in this large country of contrasts..

Hindu Humanism and Development

There seems to exist a close connection between the development thrust of a nation and the humanism of the culture. For the assessment of the situation of the people, planning, execution and evaluation are all conditioned by class/caste/gender and value bias and mindset. Humanism to a large extent is influenced by the world-view of a culture. Religion as the meaning dimension of a culture is a necessary, even major, component. Hence it is necessary that we consider the role of Hinduism for development linking it with the kind of humanism Hinduism has generated. A religion can influence the birth of humanism although other factors are also there to influence its shaping. For instance, elements of Christianity are present in what could be called western humanism. But the western model of development is generated by humanism and also capitalism.

What could be the components of a humanism facilitated by Hinduism.

The following may be considered as components of Hindu humanism. It is not an exhaustive or researched data, but elements that seem decisive and significant are listed.

First of all, set against the Vedic cosmogonism and running through subsequent developments, is an evolutionary vision of all reality (*parinama/vivarta vada)* . Accordingly there is a graded manifestation of different realities, inclusive of humankind, from one primal source. When we come to the human level in that scale there is the inception of the humans (in India) *caste-wise: brahmans* on top and *shudras* at the bottom. This original classification was later on modified to create another group, called the *panchamas* (dalits), outside the recognized the fourfold division. The origin of caste, however, is a much disputed topic in Indian anthropology/mythology combine.

Already, exclusion of one section of the human community has taken place, namely, that of the *panchamas,* the present-day *dalits.* The economic social and political powers and privileges begin to move away from them and move upwards towards the upper castes. Development benefits are only for the upper castes: land, resources, powers, privileges, rights. The lower we descend the duties increase and powers and privileges decrease. Dalits are assigned only abhorrent and despicable duties with neither power nor privilege, neither rights nor freedom. The era when this ideology was generated and matured could be now considered the most unfortunate. For, this is seen today as playing a major role in the development programmes and performances of the Indian nation.

Second, conceptually there is a mode of participation of all, especially of humans, in the nature of that one primal source, Brahman: (*tat tvam asi,* Aruni is told in Chand.Up.). Yet occupation for each caste is specified and there is no crossing of the fixed order. Rigidity and fixation as character traits are born and begin to mature and fossilize.

Life by prescription is introduced and walls are being created between profession and profession and between human agents.

Third, the axis of all thinking and doing in the early phase of Hinduism, known as the Vedic times, was *sacrifice.* And sacrifice was the key to the world of the gods on whom depended entirely the life of the Vedic Indian. *Yajet swarga kama* was the injunction ('Let the one desirous of heaven perform sacrifice) (*Artha Samgraha, by Laugakshi Bhaskara*). Sacrifice was endowed with power even over the gods. This power came from the *mantra,* the sacred formula uttered by the designated priest at the appropriate time. The performer of the *yajna* and the reciter of the *mantra* also share that power.

Performer of the sacrifice rises higher in the social hierarchy and hierarchy formation deepens and becomes rigid.

Fourth, *mantra* has *power, even over the gods,* because it is rooted in the Vedas that are of non-human origin (*apaurusheyam vakyam veda*). Vedas are eternal and have an existence of their own. The recipients of the Vedas, the *rishis,* and the dealers of the *mantra,* the priests, the brahmans, gradually began to be 'powerful' in society because they handle the Veda and the *mantra.* This religio-cultural phenomenon added to their social standing. Those without that power were kept at a distance.

Since the Vedas are sacred and liberating knowledge received from a realm beyond the human mind, they are received *obediently* and *submitted* to unquestioningly. This submission is extended to the recipient of the Veda, to the samhitas and injunctions, to the mores that were derived later on in the Sutra literature, and further down, to thousands of details worked out in course of time. This has resulted in the shaping of a mindset marked by fixation, rigidity in customs, beliefs and traditions. This uncritical acceptance has its unintended effect on the recipient, as well as on the community that receives them. What happened in this process was that the critical in the human faculty had to give way, and submission became part of that acceptance. At the popular level this led to a closure of the critical in humans.

However, critique of such a stand had been taking place periodically. The Upanishadic times, for instance. The Buddhist revolt, for instance. The long history of Hinduism is seen as being punctuated by protest and stagnation, renaissance and relapse into traditionalism and blind veneration of the Past.

Manussmrti dealt with the Indian mind as those small men of Liliput did with Don Quixote as we have in Gulliver's Travels: tied it down with prohibitions and prescriptions. Promotion of exploration of further avenues and of alternatives, exploration and discovery of the mystery and power in nature are yet to take birth. To tear asunder the binding ropes, and to break open the closed and frozen minds and to respond to the new challenges, powerful stimuli are needed. The demands of development need to be felt and met by our culture marked by this twofold features.

Fifth, the law of *karma* determines practically everything: your future, your present social economic and other status and fortunes. Ills of empirical life in society like poverty, misfortune, ailments etc are traceable to this law of determinism. And determinism ruled the roost for a long time. It did ravage many minds in all castes. Human science tools are needed to unravel and heal and restore.

There have been sprouts of insights demanding service and welfare of all like *lokasamgrha (welfare of the established* order: Gita 3,25)) and pauranic concepts like *ramrajya* (welfare of all subjects – Ayodhya kanda). Yet the fatal consequence of the law of *karma* reduced the impulse to serve others to minimum. To repair the damage it is not *karuna* that is needed but *nyaya Swadharma* dominated. We recall here its crude economic form as in Adam Smith's economic theory and how it has come to today's economic global policy.

Six, as a result of a dualism that intervened (*sreyas-preyas* (Kath.Up.); *purusha-prakrti* (Yoga Sutra of Patanjali) and the growth of the institution of *samnyas* (life of the renouncer) an exaggerated spiritualism and other-worldliness grew and a downgrading of the empirical historical life, in spite of the later summing of Hindu view of life as guided by four-fold objectives namely *dharma, artha, kama and moksha* took place.

However, two counter developments kept challenging constantly this view, namely the *charvaka* view of life and the intermittent rise and disappearance of dissent and protest against the institution of caste ritualism and polytheism etc. The former, with the entry of the affirmation of the sex-gift via *Kamasutra* of Vatsyayana, re-affirmed the value and legitimacy of earthly pursuit. Both these much-repressed and devalued systems have vigorously re-surfaced with vengeance in our times.

What had been the IMPACT of some of these features upon the human community need to be reflected upon. In the light of what has happened, predictability of what could happen may be possible. It is possible then to reflect upon this ethos vis-à-vis development.

The fact that the land and much of the resources of the rich land were in the hands of a very limited few was known to the patrons of religion. That means production and accumulation, though according to the rate and kind of the different ages, before the Moghal era, during the colonial period, were controlled and motivated by the interest of a few. Profit and accumulation of the profit guided further investment. The thought that others also should benefit, that others also have the right to the resources of the land, that others also have a share in the production of knowledge that was behind the systems of the times, was not part of the economists and resource-holders of pre-Moghul, Moghul, and British times. Still less was such thinking among the protagonists of religions. Is not this trend still continued?

We monitor diligently the Indian social structures. There is no mitigation of the rigour of the social hierarchy in India. The lower we go in the social hierarchy there is less space for the lower, and least for the lowest. The excluding culture has been operative at all levels in the new Indian governance culture. Maintaining this excluding mindset undiluted acts only against the incentives for social transformation, a major component of development.

Inter-dining, inter-marriage and other dynamic of levelling social barriers are only minimally practised. A sound humanism will advocate the rejection of social customs that are inhibitive of the development of the human person, and consequently of the community. B. R. Ambedkar was correct in holding that without social transformation freedom is in chains.

It is *religion that was a silent bystander and approver when caste was shaped.* It is so even today. Religion created the caste system. The same religion is unwilling to recast that religion in the light of the insights from the human sciences which reject these institutions as irrational and anti-human.

Caste system was and still is a social system which has led to the concentration of all powers in the hands of the upper castes and which deprives the dalits of these powers. Caste is also an economic system in so far as land and all resources are in the hands of the upper castes.

Caste also is a political structure. The upper castes largely constitute the upper class which even today, rule the country. They design the development plans for the people. They supervise their execution, although some from the lower rungs have succeeded in climbing the ladder – the so-called *creamy layer.* Three or four times anti-reservation fumes and flames warmed and burned Indian social landscape. The resistance to and protest against affirmative action for the low castes continue. That shows that the inherited social system and structure with its economic benefits and support system refuses to relent.

Development at the economic level without development of the social system, Ambedkar had warned, will give us only mutilated freedom and punctured dignity of the human person with all rights eroded. Ambedkar rebelled against Hinduism since he considered it a block to social transformation. Without social transformation economic development alone will benefit only the already beneficiaries of the inherited systems.

Under the inspiring and committed leadership of the first Prime Minister India embarked on a major national venture towards 'development'. And drawing inspiration from the Soviet and Chinese experiments planning became a major strategy for the development of the country. And the Planning Commission was created as the supreme body in order to design the development of the Indian nation. Similar approaches were made by other countries belonging to the so-called 'under developed' nations. Development became a global concern. International institutions like the United Nations created under its aegis departments like the UNESCO to address the educational scientific and cultural and other aspects of the international community. World Health Organization was created to address in a focused manner the problem of health in the world at large. Because of the phenomenal growth and ramification of industrialization and to meet with the mounting labour problems the International Labour Organization was also created. Development became a major concern at the national and international level. It continues to be so even today even as the phrase 'under-developed' nations began to be replaced by 'developing' nations. But Nehru, the visionary, died a broken man because of the failure in execution. The reasons are clear:

First, the upper caste people have scarce experience of the degraded situation of the dalits.

Secondly, untouchability and pollution-purity fear keeps them away from the dalits not only physically but mentally, intellectually and emotionally. The officers keep them at a distance, as has been abundantly testified by the dalits.

Thirdly, the waves of anti-reservation campaigns have demonstrated to the Indian people their conviction that the dalits have no way to regain their lost space in the society and to enjoy the rights granted by the Indian Constitution. These are major factors impeding the social transformation which is a necessary component of development

Closure, Stagnation, and Regimentation

Moderns like Subhayu Dasgupta (1990) calls this mindset as the ossification and stagnation of the Hindu mind. Sociologist

G.S. Ghurye (1932) locates much of the consequences of such walled-in mindset in the caste system which according to him gave the Hindu society the look of a hive with its "snug living by surrendering the inbuilt fluidity and flexibility of the human groups. Human freedom and the colourful adventures and hazards that it might lead to were sacrificed to gain security, stability and the stagnancy of a hive" (Dasgupta 1990: 162).

The unhindered journey of the human mind in India began to get signals from promoters of the conservation of what has been achieved. Freezing of the mind and drawing of lines and building of walls began to emerge. Prohibition of the free wandering of the mind, and dominance of convention led to imposition of ban on innovative thinking and acting. With the advancement of thought fixation of the mind too caught up with the process.

One aspect of development is to promote and draw benefits for life from industrialization. True benefits from industrialization depend on the cultural ethos. Commitment to work and to duty is a major requirement. Religion and ideologies that promote consciousness of and application to duty are required. One unintended consequence of karma is minimizing this personal aspect and attributing behaviour or result or even temperament to an untraceable vague past action in a previous birth. This evasiveness and disclaiming would adversely affect commitment and production.

Red tapism, corruption, and non-performance are held out as factors associated with Indian bureaucracy. Failure of the implementation of national or State programmes for the people are traced to these negative traits in individual and collective behaviour. Religious and cultural ethos determine these traits in individuals. Religions promote purificatory rites to free individuals from guilt and culpability without linking rectitude and truthfulness, as well as personal responsibility. This caution needs to be carried into the offices, the laboratory, the mines and the factories. It is here that such beliefs and rituals block development. A ritual bath draws lakhs of devotees to the holy waters. On return to their place of duty does the devotee carry a purified ethics of work, duty and responsibility? If yes, our country will benefit immensely.

Concluding Observations

The human process of planning, deliberation and making decisions need to be guided by a prioritization of values. The supreme value and concern is all that pertains to the origin nature dignity and destiny of the human person. Full and all round development of the human person is non-negotiable priority, and there is almost universal consensus on this. The human person is body-spirit integral reality. Close on the heels of human development is the need for all that pertains to other needs of the person in society, the person in community, the person in the 'modern city'. A major concern of the State is on this issue of development.

Hinduism had made a remarkable contribution to the development of a great civilization. At the same time at a particular point in time certain degree of closure of mind and its exploration intervened that began to affect adversely the human person. Caste system was one major consequence. It impeded the pace of human development. The current society, along with the State, is engaged in pursuing development. The light of the fast growing human sciences could be focused on socio-cultural mores to help them become creative tools for the development of the country.

References

Dasgupta, Subhayu (1990), *The Hindu Ethos,* Cosmo Publications.

Dawson, Christopher (1967), *Formation of Christendom,* Sheed and Ward, New York.

Ghurye, G. S. (1969), *Caste and Race in India,* 5th Ed. Populal Prakashan, Bombay.

Toynbee, Arnold J. (1949-57), *A Study of History,* abridgment by D.C. Somervell, London Oxford University Press.

3

Folk/Subaltern Religion and Development[1]

James Ponniah

This article endeavours to investigate the question of the relationship between folk or subaltern religion and development, bringing into dialogue two seemingly contradictory historical human initiatives: the phenomenon of folk religion which is often regarded as pre-modern, and the idea of development which is conceptually intertwined with the process of modernisation. While the latter is taken to mean primarily the economic dimension, the article takes into account other models of development evolved in the last few decades, in which the concept has undergone change and the horizons of its understanding have expanded to include the overall well-being of humans, as many authors have pointed out. Subsequently, the article has two parts: *part one* which focuses on the nature and dynamics of relationship between the economic terrain of development and the phenomenon of folk/subaltern religion, and *part two* which dwells on the new meanings of development, and the mediating role that the folk religions can play both at the conceptual and the concrete levels of such development schemes.

Part–I

Folk Religion and Economic Development

Though today's understanding of development means more than the economic aspect, yet we need to take up the relationship of folk religion and development not only because Weber's theory of religion, which remains very influential till today, focuses on the relationship between religion and economic development, but also because most of the social scientists following Weber have found Hinduism as obstructing development. For instance K.W Kapp[2] held that the general beliefs and values of Hinduism like the law of karma and astrology denied history its transformative role in social and economic development. Another writer, Mishra, attempts to establish that the other-worldliness of Hinduism stresses the release from the cycle of rebirth, and this, he believes, has adversely affected economic growth. While we cannot take up this issue in detail, the questions that need to be asked are "Are these observations true? Are they applicable to the whole of Hinduism? Or to part of it? What brand of Hinduism if any is anti-development?" Is the kind of Hinduism that we are interested in, namely, folk religion against development? or does it promote development?

While scrutinising the relationship between Hinduism and economic development, most of the authors following the hypothetico-deductive method have derived their conclusions from the abstract ideas of higher Hinduism's values which are either favourable or unfavourable to economic development. Such conclusions deduced from beliefs and values of the conceptual domain remain alienated from concrete social and cultural contexts. Instead, one has to shift the focus from text-bound Hinduism to practice-oriented Hinduism. The latter includes not only the practices of the elite Brahminic order, but also the rituals of the ordinary common folk. "In considering Hinduism in relation to economic growth, the character of the former as it is practiced by the common people is more important than its metaphysical aspects."[3]

The common people's folk ritual observances and practices such as vows and votive offerings and a consideration of these in relation to economic activities present a different perspective on the relationship between religion and economic action. Rao notes that people keep the *vratas* to various folk deities not only in the rural areas but also in the urban habitats, in order to seek benefits which are often mundane and material.

In the folk religious practices, a worshipper is promised success and prosperity in this world, and often such mundane prosperities are regarded to be the result of accumulated ritual merit. The folk gods and goddesses are perceived to have enormous powers over the prosperity of the village and the fertility of the village lands. These deities who represent the powers of nature offer not only promises and assurances to people to improve their economic lot in the agrarian settings, but also hope to those who have failed in business or who seek employment. "The ritual practices seeking the divine assistance in achieving a specific objective belong to the realm of religion and they seek to establish a bridge between the mundane activity on the one hand and supernatural beings on the other."[4] This integrating function of folk rituals enables the common folk to harmoniously reconcile the needs and demands of modern life with their day-to-day living through their belief in the powers of gods and goddesses.

Thus, contrary to popular belief, the folk ritual observances and practices emphasise the this-worldly aspect of Hinduism, which has been ignored by those who have written on Hinduism and economic development. Ritual practice, often enacted through the folk religious realm, "emphasising the worldly character of Hinduism acts as a corrective to the hypothetico-deductive view of the other-worldliness of Hinduism. But this worldliness of Hinduism does not by itself guarantee a positive orientation to economic action"[5] As Rao rightly observes whether ritual promotes an outlook for the positive pursuit of economic activities is a question which requires empirical investigation.[6]

Folk/Subaltern Religion and the Process of Modernity

In the sociological studies of religions in India, folk religions are generally treated as pre-modern or mere remnant of the old feudal system, and as static or stagnant with the mechanical routinisation of their rituals. The latest studies on the folk and subaltern religions conducted in their socio-economic-historical milieus take issue with such understandings.

My own research done on the folk religious phenomenon of Sudalaimadan Cult in Tirunelveli district of Tamilnadu has contested such a view. The study has shown that in the origin and growth of a folk religious phenomenon such as Sudalaimadan cult changes can occur in the symbolic meaning schemes as a result of the *advent of modernity*. It has indicated how old religio-cultural forms can obtain new schemes of socio-economic meanings in course of history.

The changes in the district occurred following the initial phase of modernization inaugurated by the British in the nineteenth century in this region. The policy decisions regarding land-holdings, new revenue systems (such as *ryotwari*), education, employment, market, etc., made by the colonial state brought about transformation not only in the socio-economic systems, but subsequently, it became a collateral factor for the emergence of different folk religious forms. It was not a mere change that took place in the past and was pertinent only to a particular point of time in history. It was not experienced as a residual phenomenon that passed away along with the death of the colonial state. The changes brought about by the colonial state were carried out by the independent Indian state which has carried over the impact of modernity to the present. Modernization has undoubtedly acquired new accents and varied emphases through different economic systems such as capitalism, liberalisation and globalisation, but has also yielded different benefits to different sections within the caste hierarchy. The different agents of change have provided impetus to different actors by bringing in alternative economic systems and schemes at different times, and, through them, new opportunities for the liberation of the subalterns from the old economic system of caste hierarchy.

Thus, it has effected a change in society over a period of time. All these phenomena have brought about not only fluidity within the socio-economic systems but also transformations in the religious systems such as folk religions.

The study shows that by making use of temple honours and the nuances of ritual power, social actors can articulate the newly acquired symbolic power. It has been appropriated by different social actors across the spectrum of the caste hierarchy at different times in different intensities. The changes experienced by the people by their appropriation of new systems have shown up in the symbolic universe. New cohorts of castes and families have appropriated the subaltern religious terrain and generated new forms of socio-symbolic discourse in the district of Tirunelveli. They have not drastically altered the folk forms of worship, but have infused new social meanings into the old symbolic systems. Thus they have altered the old cultural conceptual schemes and meaning systems in the ever-growing new contexts, be it the colonial state, independent India, or the global world. Here, modernity, through various agents such as the colonial state, the independent state and the global world order, has provided new socio-economic constructs to social actors within the caste hierarchy. They, in turn, have apprehended and appropriated the benefits and the privileges of such contexts on the one hand, and, in the process of social transformations, have constructed, constituted, adduced, disseminated and explored new systems of meanings to old religious forms, and have created new socio-symbolic cultural discourses, on the other.

The study has thus unfolded the interplay between culture and modernity in the domain of folk religious cults, in the process of demonstrating 'how the symbolic can mirror–and can be mirrored by – the subtle transformations in culture and society.' It shows that, through the medium of a subaltern religious universe, folk culture can provide new cultural schemes to the subalterns to display new forms of power acquired by the appropriation of the benefits of modernity and industrialisation. Thus modernity has its insidious effects on the delicate balance of power relations within the caste hierarchy, and can become a partner with religion and culture to generate new texts of discourse of symbolic power. It is to be noted that, as modernity can add colours to religion, so, too, culture and religion can add new shades of meaning to the thesis of modernity.

Saurabh Dube, in his seminal study on the history of a subaltern religious sect of the Chamars known as Satnamis, has nuanced the relationship between folk/subaltern religion and modernity further. He has held that through religion arena, the subaltern communities can also engage in construction of creative cartographies defining spaces in time and places in history.[7]

In the above mentioned work, Dube shows that the subaltern Satnamis, while challenging the terms of ritual power and caste hierarchy, colonial authority and nationalist imperatives, can carve out their own visions, designs and practices surrounding sect and caste, myth and history, highlighting the interplay and interpenetration between symbols of modern state and forms of communities in India. Thus, as he claims, he has tapped the potentiality of subaltern religious domain to suggest the importance of linkages between the pre-colonial, colonial and the post-colonial. To achieve this, he has followed the method of conducting fieldwork in an engagement with the historical imagination which addresses the key analytical relationships between sect and caste, myth and history, religion and power, gender and order, community and hegemony, resistance and domination.[8]

Thus, Dube would claim that the entangled endeavours of ethnographic histories and untouchable pasts is capable of unravelling process "involving myths and the making of modernities, orality and the construction of histories, writing and the fashioning of traditions to interrogate the place and persistence of binary categories—of modernity and tradition, state and community, rationality and ritual, reason and emotion—within influential strands of social and political theory."[9] His work calls into question the taken-for-granted overarching opposition between tradition and modernity, "which is often accompanied and animated—at the very least implicitly—by equally grand divisions between myth and history, ritual and reason, magic and the modern."[10] These binary schemes and categories are actually rooted in reified representation of a singular modernity. The study of subaltern religions in India has unfolded the power of the subaltern religious initiatives to question such conceptions of singular modernity. Thus the historical phenomena of subaltern religions is perceived to have the potentialities to expose the falsity of a representation of modernity, to put it in the words of Saurabh Dube himself, "as a self-realising project of progress, a self-evident embodiment of development and a self-contained incarnation of history."[11]

Public Sphere, Folk Religion and Modernity

The concept of public sphere as proposed by Habermas meant "a domain of social life in which such a thing as public opinion can be formed .... A portion of the public opinion is constituted in every conversation in which private persons come together to form a public. Citizens act as a public when they deal with matters of general interest without being subject to coercion.... The coercive power of the state is the counterpart, as it were, of the political public sphere, but not part of it."[12] In his opinion, public sphere is a mediating category between the civil society and the state. To our Indian context, we have to broaden the outreach of this concept so as to include public spheres other than those envisaged by Habermas, and focus upon the multiplicity and plurality of spheres as well as groups that create them. There is no single monolithic public sphere as there is not single monolithic notion of civil society. Different socio-historical conditions generate multiple spheres and public groups that are engaged in the continuous process of defining and redefining the state and the individual, the caste-hierarchy and the marginal castes. With the production of new and altered symbolic cultural schemes, the subalterns raise voice that transcends hierarchical boundaries of gender and caste through the medium of folk religion and folklore. Folklore and folk ritual performances serve as a medium for contesting dominant world-views. Through them public opinions are generated, discussed and debated. They could be used for articulating heterogeneity rather than stressing homogeneity.[13] Study of folklore and folk religious forms can reveal how communities can break hierarchies, articulate aspirations and constitute new identities. As identities are constantly created and recreated, what we encounter through the generation of such folk forms is a complex cultural phenomenon "not necessarily rational but in alignment with the logic of cultures concerned. Such process do create and influence public opinion."[14] As Muthukumar notes, what we see here is a 'performing society' that generates public opinion not necessarily through rational verbal arguments and dialogues but *also through gestures, genres, versions, performances, stories, narratives and codes.*[15]

Besides, public sphere plays a vital role in the process of modernisation. The changes that modernity brings in its wake become more socially acceptable and the conflicts that are created find a medium in public sphere through which they can be resolved. The various folk forms, including folk religious performances, provide and create public sphere in India, and they help in bringing into focus ideas, values and contentions into public discourse, a kind of unshackling of inhibitions in a stress-free manner.[16] Here folk religion functions as a notable instance in which the creation and sustenance of public sphere becomes significant to achieve the multi-level interests of different performers and patrons.[17]

Thus, in some cases, the folk religious arena is perceived to have undergone a shift from the usually 'private sacred space' to a site of construction of what can be called "public sphere." As Bhaduri notes in the case of the origin of community Durga[18] Pooja in 18th and 19th century Bengal, such public spheres arose in the process of the modernisation process initiated by the British. As the author observers, it evolved "in response to the colonial state machinery and often included subversive strategies."[19] The fact that Raja Nabo Kissen Deb in 18th cent. celebrated Robert Clive over the Muslim ruler, Shiraz-ud-dowla with Durga Puja indicates that the Hindu upper class took the opportunity of British control over Bengal to demonstrate its negative reaction to its erstwhile repression under Muslim domination. Keeping in line with their general policy that the British would not meddle much in the religious affairs of the natives, they abolished the festival tax introduced by the Muslim rulers. However, the British also introduced a more rigid system of taxation, which means the Zamindars had to pay more to the new masters. But, making use of the privileges and freedom given by the British in religious matters, "an annual extravagant event like the Durga Puja became an easy route for Zamindars to get major tax reliefs and even manage extra allowances from the British."[20] Thus folk or popular religious practices have the potential of becoming an interface between the modern state and civil society, "in this case between the emergent British colonial state and the Hindu Bengali religio-cultural space."[21]

Folk Religion as a Counter-Public and Identity Politics

One of the social consequences of development and modernisation in India today is the identity politics of religion and caste which is often displayed in the religious realm, more so in the case of folk religious realm. Kaushal, who made a study on the Gaddi community in the western Himalayas, notes that "another very important sub-text of public ritual performances is construction and presentation of a group's identity to oneself and to others."[22] Blackburn, who made a study on the folk religious performances of South India, also arrives at a similar conclusion. According to her, folk performances "help to shape a community's self identity" and "they have that special ability to tell a community's own story and thus help to create and maintain that community's self-identity."[23]

Now, folk religion's capacity to construct and uphold the identity of a social group is appropriated by different groups with ingenuity to display their social status and to assert their identity. For instance, the folk cults/ folk rituals like *Kodai* in the southern part of India can become the site of assertion of the newly gained autonomy of the depressed classes in this district, as insightfully shown by Diane P.Mines in a recent study.[24] She has demonstrated that identity politics has not only impacted upon the meta-narrative of Hindutuva but also has transformed the folk religious arena into a site of contestation by the subalterns who dared to defy caste-hierarchy empowered by the newly gained economic status thanks to modernity and its fruits such as education and employment. She explains how the people of Yanaimangalam in Tirunelveli district drew on regional and national socio-politico-religious movements, and contested the social and spatial contours of their local lives and their villages through ritual action.

Making a study on the folk community festivals called *jatar*(s) in the western region of Himalayas, Kaushal holds that while *Bharmour jatar* and *Chchtarari jatar* were the community festivals of the dominant castes in the region, the *Guggal jatar* – celebrated by low caste Halis and Rehars created a space for the articulation of voices of protest against mistreatment and neglect, and can be "generative of multiple public spheres that may use the language of myth and ritual, which seem to overlap, but nonetheless facilitate articulation of counter-hegemonic voices that contest and compete."[25] He concludes that the public sphere created through the medium of folk religious rituals, rather than defusing boundaries may actually become arenas for public display of hostilities and tension that exist in the society.[26]

Thus, in our contemporary times, the public sphere of folk religions is bound to have within itself fissures and spaces for subversive appropriation leading to the possibility of counter-public discourse.

Ambivalent Character of Folk Religion in Urban India

Folk Religions, especially in the urban setting of today's India, can be described to have ambivalent picture. On the one hand, you have folk temples in the urban setting, which seeks to transcend the boundaries of caste, gender and religion. For instance, Kalpagam, having made a study on roadside temples in the urban areas, observes that, the creation of an urban popular culture through roadside temple activities is an expression of working class culture that seeks to synthesise the Hinduism of the "great tradition" and "little tradition," and in its everyday practices transcends caste, class, religious and gender boundaries. "It is also simultaneously the constitution of a social text that allows people to draw meanings of nationhood and their sense of belonging in cultural terms that are rooted in local practices, everyday life and localities, and seeks to evolve new perspectives and ideas of a secular society" This signifies the harmonious side of evolving civil society in the cities and towns.

On the other hand, we can also witness the opposite characteristics of folk religions. Folk religious forms, which assert caste-identity as noted earlier in the article, can also function as a source of subaltern agency. In some urban settings, they can operate as an instrument of negotiating civil space through creation of folk or popular religious sites such as the celebration of 'Kanwad'[27] in cities like Delhi. These religious sites are fundamentally ritual domains wherein, through the rituals, people display their identity, re-member themselves into the cultural habitus they belong to, draw resources to face life, and sometimes even negotiate a new civil space according to their terms.

The above mentioned presence of such contradictory characteristics reveals the ambivalent portrait of folk religions in India. But, in as much as the Indian society that we live in has ambivalent characteristics of equality and discrimination, harmony and conflict, folk religions can be found to depict them in the religious realm. Thus the opposite functions of folk religion can be described to mirror the society which is in conflict itself.

Part–II

In this Part, let me deal with the different meanings that the concept of development has acquired over a period of time and the new areas of interaction such new understandings can create for the folk religious phenomenon to engage in the process of development.

The Development of 'Development'

We are at the cross-road now in our vision and practice of development. Much of our difficulties here relate to our inability to look at and participate in the field of relationship and as a quest of a shared responsibility which brings the self and the other together. The project of development has been subjected to much criticism and rethinking in the recent years in the midst of which agenda of development has been broadened to include human development from mere economic development and rise in per capita income.[28]

The above quotation shows us the shifts that have taken place in the very conception of 'development.' In order to have a better grasp of the problematic of development, let me dwell briefly on the history of development.

The concept of 'development' meant different things to different people at different times. Authors identify three post-World War II phases of development. In the first phase (1947-1949), the liminal phase between the World War and the beginning of the cold war, the world grappled with the future after an extreme crisis. In this period, development was seen as a 'work of hope.'[29] It primarily aimed at alleviating poverty. It did not go beyond economic growth. In the second phase (1949 -), of the cold war, development entered the domain of politics, application and administration. In 1960, development was defined as 'growth with change,' referring to economic and cultural change, influenced by structural functionalism.[30] Development thus meant a simultaneous transformation in all these dimensions. In the mid 1970s, there again occurred a shift of focus of development which aimed at a decent standard of living for all humans, in line with the basic human rights as defined in the UN charter, and measured by 'human development indicators.'[31] In the third phase (1990-), the natural environment and its ecology became integrated into the development discourse, and 'sustainable development' became the watchword. Sustainable development drew attention to formerly ignored marginal regions and people, like the gold miners in the Amazon, the peasants in Africa, the hill tribes in Thailand etc.., who were previously rather ignored.[32] Development had little to do with equity, justice or with people and social relations since the subject matter at that time was growth and not distribution. It was in this context that the UN General Assembly resolution called for the renewal of political will to invest in people and their well-being in what could be the trend setter for the next millennium, and set up a special committee in the year 2000 to review the process of development.[33] Following these, a whole array of new discourses of development, such as Amartya Sen's idea of development as freedom (i.e., development as expansion of substantive freedom to achieve alternative functions), development as human dignity and human rights,[34] development as 'global responsibility,' and development as cultivation of 'self'[35] etc., has acquired significance in the development theories.

Folk/Subaltern Religion as A Process of Development in the Restoration of Equality for All and Human Dignity of the Oppressed

As Aloysius notes, in the subaltern religions, there is a privileging of the ethical over the transcendental and they are often manifestations of voluntary construction of the morally just in place of involuntary acceptance of the 'religiously given' as found in the case of dominant religions. "These transitions need not only be seen as historical, that is, from pre-modernity to modernity, in religion. They are, in fact, dimensions or aspects of religion of all times."[36] No doubt one immediately tends to link development of the ethically religious worldview, embodying a social order that is egalitarian, with the emergence of modernity and its democratic institutions. But there were in the pre-modern times protest religious movements in India proposing an ethical world-view, although they came to be subordinated and often submerged as we see in the example of Buddhism in India.

These types of religious movements strive for collective emancipation rather than individual salvation. It has "the power of motor force moving a collectivity to effect a change in human-social reality, a change that takes the reality nearer to the conceptual ideality"[37] But in the emancipation of the collective, the human and the dignity of the individual human is restored developed and constructed. The historical examples of The Satnami movement, which reformed the lives of the Chamars in Chattisgarh, Ayyavazhi Movement that transformed the status of Nadars in Kannyakumari District in Tamilnadu, the Narayanguru movement which revolted against the oppression of Ezhavas in Kerala reveal the fact that religion can function as a subaltern agency to defy the oppressive social order, to negotiate a new egalitarian social identity and to restore the human dignity of the oppressed

But not all folk religious phenomena such as CM cult in Tamilnadu, Virabhadra cult in Andhra Pradesh etc, could fit into this type. These pre-modern cults have not emerged as a separate and a distinct subaltern religious phenomena. But they are sites of contestation of the dominant religious ideology. In fact, both these types contest the hierarchy and both embody the aspirations of the oppressed for liberation from the clutches of gruesome caste hierarchy.

Folk Religion: An Idiom of Reversal?

Kaulpagam, in his/her study on roadside temples in Chennai, takes note of a case in which the poor auto drivers have employed a Brahmin as a priest wherein the high caste Brahmin is made answerable and accountable to the low caste men. My own PhD research in the district of Trinvelveli on Folk Religion reveals that a good number of most backward castes get the Brahmin priests to perform rituals in their folk temples. Through such folk religious sites, there is a reversal of social dynamics as regards the construction of human dignity in the Indian society. In the traditional agrarian Indian society, the Sanskritic Hinduism had provided a socio-economic structure through its caste-hierarchy wherein the Brahmin-Kshatriya alliance had the power of determining the human dignity of the Sudras and Dalits. The self-worth of a Sudra or a Dalit or his/her self perception was dependent upon the kind of treatment meted out to him/her but within the parameters of caste-hierarchy. The Dalits and Sudras always remained dependent on and accountable to the high castes. In folk religious realm today, on the contrary, as we see in the case of a Brahmin above, the Sudras/Dalit (the auto drivers in Chennai or the most backward castes in Trinelveli district) have a significant role to play in the self-making of a Brahmin priest. The Brahmin priest in Chennai openly acknowledged this. Kaulpagagm writing about him says, "Post-retirement employment as a priest of a roadside temple is really the fulfilment of a long-long yearning as in his youth he was trained in a gurukulam in Mahabalipuram on Agama sastras." While such occurrences point to the new kind of social dynamics that take place in the folk religious realm, they also mirror the subtle social transformations that could occur in the process of development like modernisation or urbanisation and folk religion's potentiality in being instrumental to bring about such transformations.

Folk Religion and Holistic Development

Another major step in the evolution of the concept of 'development' is the realisation that care of the human is intrinsically related to the care of nature. The actualisation of the human cannot take place in isolation or in the abstract. It has to take place in the concrete material world and along with the other creatures and beings in the world. This implies that, during the process of transformation of the humans, the human beings have to work for the promotion of well-being for the whole of the cosmos. While such a task calls for a proactive involvement of the humans in the world, it implies a total rejection of any dichotomy between matter and spirit, sacred and profane. This entails a holistic view of the universe which underscores a fundamental unity between the humans and the cosmos. This basic unity and the symbiotic relationship between the humans and the cosmos is best inscribed, created and established in the embodied human beings through concrete human practices. Such human practices obtain religious overtones in most of the cultures wherein the sacred character of nature is made aware of through folk religious rituals. For instance, Madhu Kanna holds that the folk festival of *navapatrika* worship can be related to the issues of ecological sensibility.[38] Similarly the various folk festivals such as *karam* in the tribal belt of Chotanagpur, *kodai* in South India and various season-transition festivals in different parts of India are at once the expressions of the religious and the ecological concerns of the common folk. Folk religious rituals such as *Bihu* in Assam or *Pongal* in Tamilnadu play a major role in making humans realise the inalienable relationship between nature and humans. More often than not, religious beliefs/practices and the earth's ecology are inextricably linked, and organically related. "Religious beliefs—especially those concerning the nature of powers that create and animate—become an effective part of ecological systems."[39] Rather than the major religious traditions, it is the folk/indigenous religious traditions which ensure the creation and the maintenance of the human being's intrinsic relationship with the natural environment.

Conclusion

This paper which has attempted to discourse on the proactive role of *folk religions* in the evolving concept *'development'* has dwelt on the various possibilities of interaction between the two at different levels and between their different aspects. Since both these realities have been undergoing evolution themselves in human history, the attempt of discourse, like that of this paper, on interaction between the two can never get exhausted, but rather will remain open-ended.

Notes

1. Folk religions stand for the original religious representations and categories of the non-twice born and non-brahminic masses (Sudras and Dalits), found in the agrarian setting. Unlike Sanskritic Hinduism, folk religions are centred on gods who are carnivorous, and served by priests who are non-Brahmins. Folk religions are believed to have their origin in the feudal system. When a folk religious phenomenon becomes for a subordinate group a site of assertion of their identity and of negotiation with the dominant (the powerful) social groups, be it in the rural and in the urban setting, in the past or in the contemporary time, we can name that religion as subaltern religion.

2. Kapp, K.W, *Hindu Culture, Economic Development and Economic Planning in India,* Asia Publishing House, Bombay, 1963.
3. M.S.A. Rao, "Religion and Economic Development" in Rowena Robinson (ed.,) *Sociology of Religion in India,* Sage Publications, New Delhi, 2004, 68-83, p.74.
4. *Ibid*, p. 78.
5. *Ibid.*, p. 79.
6. *Ibid.* p. 79.
7. Dube, *Untouchable Pasts,* State University of New York Press, Albany, 1998, p. xii
8. Cf. Dube "Entangled Endeavours," in PostColonial Passages, edited by Dube, Oxford University Press, New Delhi, 2004, pp. 196-209.
9. *Ibid.*, p. 209.
10. *Ibid.*, p. 206.
11. *Ibid.*
12. Habermas, "The Public Sphere" in Habermas, *Kultur and Kritik,* Trans.S.W. Nicholson in Paul Marris and Sue Thornham, eds. Media Studies: A Reader, Edinburgh University Press, Edinburgh, 1996. p. 55.
13. Muthukumarasamy & Molly, "Introduction" in (eds.), Folklore, *Public Sphere and Civil Society,* IGNCA, New Delhi, 2004, 1-16, p. 3.
14. *Ibid.*, p. 4.
15. *Ibid.* p. 3.
16. Bhattacharya, "Preface,"
16. Muthukumarasamy & Molly (eds.), Folklore, IX-X.
17. *Ibid.*
18. One might wonder if Durga is a folk deity, as it is often associated with Kali. But the characteristics of the folk deity is clearly seen in Durga. Bhaduri observes that Durga has no permanent temple to her credit and can be worshipped only once a year as a temporarily sculpted idol in temporarily erected community pandals under a temporarily festive public gaze, and a Durga puja is an annually generated mass activity and not a solipsistic religious function. Cf. Bhaduri, "Of Public Sphere and Sacred

Space: Origin of Community Durga Puja in Bengal," in Muthukumarasamy & Molly (eds.), Folklore, pp. 77-89, p. 80.

19. *Ibid.* p. 7.
20. *Ibid.*, p.82.
21. *Ibid.*, p. 88.
22. Kaushal,, "From Mythic to Political Identities: Folk Festivals and Cultural Sub-texts," in Muthukumarasamy & Molly (eds.), *Folklore*, pp 186-196, p. 187.
23. Blackburn et al., *Oral Epics in India*, University of California Press, Berkeley, 1989, p. 11.
24. Diane P Mines in "Hindu Nationalism, Untouchable reform, and ritual production of a South Indian Village," *American Ethnologist*, Vol. 29, No. 1, Feb. 2002.
25. Kaushal, *From Mythic.*, p. 194.
26. *Ibid.*
27. Naresh Goswami notes that the celebration of this festival has as much to do with religion as an assertion of identity in urban social dynamics. Cf. "Songs of the Road," in *The Times of India*, August, 17, 2005, 14.
28. Ananta Kumar Giri, *New Horizons of Social Theory*, Jaipur: Rawat Publications, 2006. p. 200.
29. Cf. Wiebe Nauta, "A Moral Critique of Fieldwork," in Ananta Kumar Giri et al.(eds.,)*The Development of Religion and the Religion of Development*, CW Delft: Eburon Delft, 2004, p. 89-100, p. 90.
30. Cf. Rudiger Kroff & Heiko Schrader, "Does the End of Development Revitalise History?" in Ananta Kumar Giri et al. *The Development of Religion and the Religion of Development*, 9-17, p.12.
31. *Ibid.*
32. *Ibid.*, p. 14.
33. Cf. John Mohan Razu, "Introduction," Bangalore Theological Forum, 3&4 (30), 1998, *A Special Issue on Development*. pp 2-6.
34. Cf. Bas de Gaay Forman, "In Search for a New Paradigm" in Ananta Kumar Giri *et al. The Development of Religion and the Religion of Development*, pp. 18-28.
35. Cf. Ananta Kumar Giri, *New Horizons of Social Theory*, pp.199-222.

36. G. Aloysius, *Religion as Emancipatory Identity,* New Age Publishers, New Delhi, 1998. p. 10.
37. *Ibid.*, p. 11.
38. Cf. As noted by Bhaduri, *Of Public Spheres*, p. 88. See also, Madhu Kanna, "The Ritual Capsule of Durga Puja: An Ecological Perspective," in Christopher Key Chapple et al. (eds.,) *Hinduism and Ecology: The Intersection of Earth, Sky, and Water,* Oxford University Press, New Delhi, 2001.
39. Sullivan, "Preface" to John A. Grim ed., *Indigenous Traditions and Ecology, Centre for the Study of World Religions,* Harvard University School, Massachusetts, Cambridge, 2001, p. xi.

4

Cultivating a Global Mentality Virtue Ethics for an Age of Globalisation

Keith D'Souza SJ

This is an essay in *virtue ethics* applied to the phenomenon of globalization and social development, guided by the role and influence of religion. I intend to present the basic virtues or elements of an appropriate practical mentality or disposition necessary in order to both experience personal and social well-being (*eudaimonia*) in the current scenario of globalization and to orient global processes towards integral social development using adequate practical wisdom (*phronesis*).

In order to both experience personal fulfilment within our contemporary world of globalization and to make this world more humane and harmonious, one needs an adequate social and moral education–an education which virtue ethics is better suited to provide as compared to *deontological* and *teleological* ethical schools of thought.[1] There is a considerable amount of literature available with regard to critical perspectives relating to the merits and demerits of globalization from a deontological or teleological position. From a deontological position (which is largely concerned with rules and duties), one can provide a critique of globalization in terms of whether its processes and products are *in principle* suitable or detrimental to human nature and social relations (i.e, whether they are right or wrong). From a teleological position (which is largely concerned with social consequences), one can provide a critique of globalization in terms of whether it is *ultimately or proximately socially beneficial or destructive* (i.e, whether they are good or bad).[2] Compared to these deontological and teleological perspectives, there is comparatively little literature available with regard to the adoption or the cultivation of relevant virtues which would serve to better prepare ourselves to live in an increasingly globalised world. Such an approach is necessary, so as to both enjoy the benefits of globalization and to necessarily guide, to the best of our ability, the shape globalization will take in the future.

The Context of our Discussion

We live in a world of increasing globalization. We also live in a world where religion seems to be playing a more significant role in the public sphere, for better or worse. The challenge before us is to orient both globalization and religious currents–separately and connectedly–into more productive channels in terms of social development.[3] By 'religion' I do not include only the mainstream organized systems of faith, but indeed any organized or relatively unorganized movement which is governed by a set of meanings, values, beliefs and rituals based on a transcendent reality. By 'globalization' I do not just include transnational eco-political processes, but the whole gamut of a transnational exchange of goods, services, capital, knowledge, values and lifestyle. The more specifically eco-political aspect of globalization may be termed 'global capitalism,' which is a movement mainly concerned with the development of a transnational system of liberal, market-driven trade, which is of course influenced and restricted by global political currents.

In *Making Globalisation Good: The Moral Challenges of Global Capitalism*–a seminal work closely related to the theme of this essay[4]–John Dunning, the editor, defines globalization as:

> the *connectivity of individuals and institutions across the globe, or at least, over most of it.* Such connectivity may be shallow or deep; short or long lasting. It may be geared to advancing

> personal or institutional interests; and economic, cultural, or political goals . . . Globalisation is a morally neutral concept. In itself, it is neither good nor bad, but it may be motivated for good or bad reasons, and used to bring about more or less good or bad results. (original italics)[5]

The concept of 'global capitalism,' as has been pointed out, is relatively more restrictive, as it has to do primarily with eco-political manoeuvring. It is thus ideologically more problematic, as it is rooted in traditional economic presuppositions and practices which have given rise to the current eco-political imbalance within and between nations. However, as a contemporary adage goes, "capitalism is the worst economic system on the face of the earth, except for all of the other alternatives!" In contrast to this more narrow concept of 'global capitalism', Dunning proposes a wider and richer concept of 'responsible global capitalism' (RGC), which

> includes the set of non-market institutions within which the market is embedded and which, together, characterize a global society . . . it is the task of these institutions to set the rules and monitor the behaviour of markets; to engage in a variety of market facilitating and/or regulatory activities; and to produce such socially desirable products, which, left unaided, the market is unable or unwilling to produce. RGC then is a system made up of individuals, private commercial corporations, non-governmental organizations (NGOs), governments, and supranational agencies. Each has a unique and critical role to play. (original italics)[6]

A virtue ethics suited for the world of globalization would need to be cultivated within this matrix of personal, social, governmental, non-governmental and corporate responsibility. Joseph Stiglitz too advocates this "more holistic approach to development . . . Such an approach should embrace a social, moral and environmental dimension as well as an economic one."[7]

There is no doubt that we are living today in a situation of increasing globalization (and increasing global capitalism), and it appears that we will continue to do so in the near future.

There are two primary responses to such a situation. One is to fight the processes of globalization, especially those processes which are based on 'neo-liberal' eco-political policies leading to apparently draconian 'structural adjustment policies' which seem to harm weaker nations and peoples. The second is to channelise the social energies which globalization has released along productive and integrally developmental pathways, including that of maximizing the possibilities for transnational fair trade. This essay will adopt the logic of the second alternative, for two main reasons:

Firstly, at a more realistic level, I do not see any viable and widespread alternative to globalization–and its attendant global capitalism–gaining international currency. The past couple of decades have seen the collapse of communism as a viable eco-political alternative. Even China has pragmatically given way (economically, if not politically) to primarily capitalist means of production and distribution. The Communists today in West Bengal are also struggling to come to terms with this reality.

Secondly, I see that globalization, in spite of its many drawbacks, has the potential to raise humanity to a new level of consciousness, so as to shake off the shackles of much of debilitating tradition and replace them with more emancipatory mentalities. Also, responsible globalization has the potentiality to overcome artificial problems such as famine, hunger, epidemics, illiteracy and war, among other human-made problems. Here it is good to recognize that the strengths of globalization may also be considered to be its weaknesses, even though we may attempt to make it a responsible process. For example, even in a situation of fair trade, global capitalism could lead to job insecurity, for jobs can move overnight to locations favouring more lucrative production opportunities (this is certainly adversely affecting citizens of more economically developed nations today). At the cultural level, openness to transnational cultures may lead to the gradual erosion of one's more traditionally salubrious cultural values. One may be more influenced to adopt lifestyles, relationships and commitments which are easy, convenient and gratifying, rather than those which are more substantial, wholesome and longer-lasting. This in turn will play out at the economic level in terms of a focus on the production of needless sophisticated consumer goods instead of more wholesome and cheaper sustainable-oriented goods and services which are relatively of greater benefit for those more socially disadvantaged. For these and other reasons, globalization and (economic, political, and cultural) marginalisation may well go hand in hand for some time to come.[8]

It is debatable, however, whether the contemporary processes of globalization are the *causes* of this marginalization or the potential *solutions* of impoverishment and marginalization. A substantial amount of the literature with regard to the current state of social development is rather polarized, depending largely upon the agency and individuals presenting the material, and the parameters or criteria being considered. As a result, value-laden theories and instruments of investigation give rise to ridiculously different social scenarios, ranging from a frenzied apocalyptic rally call at the one end, to annunciations of the Kingdom of Heaven on earth itself at the other. The former clarion call is usually issued by singularly anti-MNC[9] NGOs, while the latter acclamation is enunciated by a good number of corporate and management gurus who seem to worship unashamedly and uncritically at the shrine of opulence. Such a polarized situation is unhelpful, even though partially unavoidable, for exaggerated rhetoric unfortunately still remains one of the most powerful tools for social mobilization.[10] Keeping these excesses in mind, I will instead attempt to adopt a comparatively conciliatory, practical and realistic approach in this essay.

Globalisation has to do with integral social development, somewhat matching the purpose and direction of the different religions, which are concerned with salvation or personal and communitarian wholeness or integrity (Latin '*salvus,*' Greek '*holos,*' and Sanskrit '*sarvam*'). Today, the influence of religion seems to be on the ascendancy with regard to contemporary social processes. The task before us is to channelize religious interests and forces so that salubrious processes of globalization are fostered and less healthy processes are challenged and overcome. Sustained religious instruction and education could well provide the foundations for an adequate virtue ethics in such a situation. The role of religion is pivotal in the development of these virtues simply because of the power which religious organizations and movements have over the minds and hearts of billions of human beings worldwide.

We will now focus on the specific virtues or dispositions or attitudes governing practical action which need to be cultivated in this world of globalization. These attitudes are necessary not only to help one to survive in such a world, but hopefully more than that, to thrive in such a world, and even more, to act responsibly so as to guide processes of development towards a more integrated pattern of personal and social well-being (*eudaimonia*). I have chosen five prominent virtues, viz., *dialogical pluralism, creative visualization, collaborative solidarity, transnational responsibility and pro-active optimism*. These are by no means an exhaustive list of virtues necessary for our contemporary world, but they seem to be some of the more basic ones, both on a personal as well as on a communitarian level. Also, these are not virtues to be cultivated mainly by the more privileged beneficiaries of globalization, so that they may further benefit from these processes of globalization, but instead by each and every member of the human community, even those who are at present the victims of globalization, so that they may better prepare themselves to be victims no more.[11]

Dialogical Pluralism

Perhaps one of the more helpful insights of 'post-modern' thought is that every metanarrative or worldview is a partial, limited perspective which needs to be complemented by other perspectives. It would be too much for religious believers and even believers in any form of developmental work to go along with Lyotard's more radical suggestion of an adoption, along post-modern lines, of "an incredulity toward metanarratives." For no individual or institution engaged in developmental work could truly be said to be free of the power and influence of some form of 'ideology,' or in terms of a temporal construction, a 'metanarrative. Indeed metanarratives are not only the consequent construction of a community's search for truth, but concomitantly serve as powerful means of motivation towards personal and social development. Thus, instead of a rejection or a forfeiting of these metanarratives (an act which would do violence to the human spirit), what would prove to be more helpful and productive is a concerted strategy of *dialogical pluralism* between the adherents who live by these metanarratives. Negatively, dialogical pluralism entails the readiness to renounce any form of aggressive dogmatism or fundamentalism associated with these grand narratives, be it socio-political, cultural or religious. Positively, dialogical pluralism is an attitude which is aimed at cultivating at the very least a basic tolerance of the 'other' (community), with a more ultimate objective of fostering a deeper respect for the 'other.' J. Orstrom Moller provides us with a helpful and somewhatcomprehensive understanding of tolerance:

> Tolerance does not mean opening the floodgates for everybody to behave as they like. Tolerance means the right to think and act differently from other people but within a mutually agreed framework. . . Thinking in this way opens the door for realizing that what is best for us may not necessarily be best for others. And that gives birth to the crucial observation that the heart of tolerance is that we care for other people's destiny even if we do not agree with them.[12]

Tolerance, then, is not an excuse or condition for relativistic thinking. A globalized world cannot afford such a luxury, especially since we are compelled to interrelate with different peoples in different social circumstances. An educated tolerance rather entails the virtue of humility, viz., a recognition of the limitedness of one's perspective with regard to personal and social development. This in turn entails the necessity of the creation of an adequate hermeneutical (interpretive) and social space for the 'other' to function and relate, while at the same time sharing a common social space ("within a mutually agreed framework," according to Moller).

The full flowering of this virtue of tolerance is thus the virtue of respect for the other, and if this respect is genuine, what will necessarily follow is the desire to borrow from the wellsprings of the other. For even if we do not entirely agree with the perspective of the other, there are surely some aspects of the worldview of the other which may be incorporated into one's own paradigm or way of life. Respect, then, is not just a recognition of the validity of the 'other,' but a conscious desire to interact with the other in order to both learn from and contribute towards each other's development. The foundation of these virtues of tolerance, humility and respect is human relationships - not just the formal relationships constructed at forums of interreligious or intercultural dialogue, but informal relationships with one's neighbour at home and at work, and, in a situation of globalization, this may mean with one's neighbour living halfway around the globe.

Globalisation has the potentiality to raise us all beyond the 'we' versus 'them' discourse. This discourse is based on a narrow understanding of the self as belonging to one primary community. In fact, as Amartya Sen convincingly argues, a sense of multiple-identity is both true to a phenomenological description of our being-in-the-world, as well as is a powerful means of overcoming communally divisive ideological forces.[13] As a matter of fact, we belong to different communities–not just religious, but also national, ethnic, regional, class, caste, occupational, guild, neighbourhood, sportsclub, etc. To identify ourselves with one primary community seems to belie all other identifications. Furthermore, even if this is widespread, and in some sense inevitable, because of primary indoctrination and social pressure, it is unfortunate that these forms of identification sometimes result in inter-communal strife and even violence. Indeed, Sen's interest in pursuing this topic initially arose from a first-hand witness of the bloody interreligious violence in West Bengal during his childhood.

Religious sentiments have played a powerful role in fermenting interreligious strife, often linked with political interests, and based upon fundamentalist religious and inadequate secular education. But religion can also play a powerful role in reversing this trend, and in fostering a spirit of interreligious dialogical pluralism. The virtue of pluralism leading to respect for the other is not an optional luxury but a pressing necessity, especially as interreligious relations will only become more intense with the increase of global trade and exchange at different levels. This means a greater openness to as well as a greater challenge between adherents of the different religions to reinterpret their respective religions in more salubrious terms, not only for themselves, but for the sake of the common good. In the long run, and even in the short, this virtue will help religious practitioners and the human community in general not only to experience peace between the different communities, but more so, to make progress as one borrows from one another's traditions. A reinterpretation of the past is necessary if one has to move towards a peaceful and prosperous future–which brings us to the next of our shortlisted virtues, viz. creative visualization.

Creative Visualization

Perhaps one of the most important virtues to develop in this new age of globalization is that of creative thinking or creative visualization. Those individuals and institutions ready for significant 'paradigm shifts' will survive, while those who refuse to emerge from their comfort zones and modify their traditional ways of thinking and doing will likely have to struggle to survive. For the only thing one can be certain about in the world of globalization is that it is characterized by change.

Perhaps the most significant change that has been brought about in our world over the last two decades is the possibility of instant and widespread communication via the internet. Primarily on account of the power and omnipresence of the internet, each one of us is increasingly capable of raising global levels of creativity. This is already happening in terms of projects undertaken by TNCs which span whole continents and which thus enable an almost uninterrupted '24/7' work schedule. But besides this, creativity in terms of productive solutions for current problems is considerably enhanced, because projects placed on the internet are being increasingly transnationally executed by faceless and even nameless individuals, and often for little or no remuneration.[14]

The communication revolution in general has brought the world much closer, not only at the level of multinational business conferences and sophisticated scientific (medical/engineering) ventures, but even at the very ordinary level of cell-phone conversation which allows very small scale entrepreneurs like the streetside vegetable seller to optimise his or her sales. The days of state-controlled media in most nations is a thing of the past, as it has become well-nigh impossible for totalitarian regimes to successfully employ strategies of media-censoring or to disseminate monopolistic propaganda. Indeed, conventional media sources too stand threatened on account of the power of omnipresent 'bloggers' who are capable of operating more independently with regard to the reporting and analysis of events.

Knowledge and the 'service' industry in general has replaced goods and manufacturing as the key ingredient in any fast-growing economy. Today India has an edge in this sector simply because of the number of skilled workers available. For the moment, at least, we are capitalizing on the English-based educational infrastructure of the past. But this situation could change overnight, unless one is ready not only to be trained adequately to perform specific skills, but to be trained to think creatively as well. What is already perceived is a dearth of competent CEOs for corporations which are currently driving the Indian economy. Soon there may be a vast amount of capital in India, but not enough creative visionaries and competent heads of organizations to sustain and drive economic growth.

Perhaps this virtue of creative visualization is most needed in international relations, for politics and economics are intrinsically related. The new world order, pulled along headlong by the fast pace of global capitalism, cannot travel very far if political relations are sour and unstable. While it is true that the permanent members of the Security Council are paradoxically the world's largest producers and exporters of arms, this situation seems to belong to a logic of the past, when instability in a distant country did not affect these host nations which export war and its accoutrements. Today global terrorism which at its roots is a response to ecological rapaciousness and eco-political domination, has proved that this does not hold true any more.

For economic trade to flow smoothly, the logic of the future will need to be dominated by peaceful processes, and above all by processes not just of justice, but more so of reconciliation. Justice is often a necessary precondition for peace within and between nations, but sometimes justice does not prove sufficient. What is needed is to work towards deeper forms of consensus based upon reconciliation. Reconciliation requires creative visualization, because one needs to be able to retell or reinterpret the same story also from the sympathetic perspective of the 'other,' rather than purely from the more conventional, and often partisan, justice-oriented 'rights-duties' discourse. The 'Truth and Reconciliation Committee' experiment in South Africa, based more upon honest dialogue rather than incriminating discourse, provides us with a working model as to how this approach may better serve to bring about peace in our conflict-ridden world. Another example demonstrating the importance of this alternate logic of peace and reconciliation features in a joint letter framed by Archbishop Desmond Tutu and Amartya Sen with regard to the present political predicament in Myanmar:

> Now that Burma is on the [Security] council's agenda, we urge the passage of *a nonpunitive resolution* that will serve as a baseline for freeing political prisoners, ceasing attacks against Burma's ethnic minorities, and promoting a political dialogue that will lead to the peace and freedom the overwhelming majority of the Burmese people have demanded. (italics mine).[15]

This is because thinking in terms of punitive resolutions (especially extreme ones like the execution of Saddam Hussain) belongs to the logic of the past. This type of thinking, rather than resolving issues, only serves to fuel the cycle of violence.

The new age requires leaders quite different from the ilk of the Bushes and Bin Ladens of our time.

In this area of creative visualization, especially as applied to processes of reconciliation within and between nations, religion clearly has a pivotal role to play. Religious texts need to be interpreted in more benign and contemporary terms that match the ethos of the day and are more forward-looking, rather than serve to reinforce old prejudices against other communities. Those religions which are able to appropriately reinterpret themselves will also be able to attract more followers, while those that do not will either be marginalized, disregarded, or worse, gain pariah status. If religions have to survive they will need to learn how to relate well with other religious traditions as well as how best to contribute towards common human welfare by adopting the common mindset of collaborative solidarity.

Collaborative Solidarity

During the period of the Cold War there were more rigid power blocks, including that of the relatively powerless Non-Aligned Movement. Today global capitalism has allowed for and even necessitated the emergence of strategic relationships which break down such rigid power divisions. Thus it is quite possible (though not always easy) to have political alliances with one nation while at the same time pursuing economic relations with a nation which is politically hostile to the first. This is what makes the present eco-political situation more complex, but also far less polarized. Global trade has necessitated the pursuit of these transideological relationships.

But global trade will also necessitate the promotion of the well-being and success of the other, whether the other is the friend or the enemy. This is not just for magnanimous reasons, but for reasons of survival to begin with, and furthermore for reasons of one's own prosperity. For if the other person or community succeeds and is prosperous in life, this in turn will lead to the production of better economic and political opportunities for all. An enlightened globalization will not merely allow for the success of the other, but positively desire the success of the other. The present Indian government has realized, for example (beyond obvious politically strategic reasons), that if the country has to make progress, the most backward communities will simultaneously need to progress as well. Hence, based on the recommendations of the Sachar Commission Report, the present Government wants the Muslims of our country to be better educated and emancipated, so as to more suitably enter into and contribute towards the dynamics of nation-building.

This sense of partnership or collaborative solidarity is also called for in the area of interreligious relations. Religions have often arisen from quite different social contexts, and where they have arisen from the same context, they have sometimes had bloody pathways of separation. The time has come for the different religions (especially the mainstream ones) to learn to coexist together. The alternative is to live in disharmony–a state which should normally be antithetical to any religious tradition. This need for overcoming conflict and pursuing collaboration in interreligious relations is well brought out by the words of the summary statement of the 'International Conference on Religion and Globalisation' held at Chiang Mai, Thailand, in 2003:

> We in our respective religious communities can no longer afford to live in isolation, or with attitudes of exclusion or competition. We acknowledge the continuing need to reexamine our religious traditions and institutions, so that religion, rather than being part of the problem, can serve as a source of empowerment and enlightenment as we seek for solutions [to the world's problems].[16]

This partnership is an urgent need between religious believers who believe differently, but who need to work towards a more concerted effort in the resolution of global problems. The logic of superiority and domination needs to give way to the logic of partnership and solidarity. Furthermore, this solidarity needs to express itself not just in interreligious pathways, but more so in collaborative social action.

The various religions, with their vast international infrastructures, have the ability to radically alter the conditions necessary for economic prosperity. Amartya Sen is one of those economists who recognizes the role of non-governmental forces in the creation of better educational and health resources in order to foster long-term economic growth. In the words of Sen,

> As has been amply established in empirical studies, market outcomes are massively influenced by public policies in education, epidemiology, land reform, microcredit facilities, appropriate legal protections, et cetera; and *in each of these fields, there is work to be done through public action* that can radically alter the outcome of local and global economic relations. (italics mine)[17]

Rather than purely focus on the sacred and make religion purely an individualistic affair, religious leaders need to increasingly recognize the tremendous potential which religious organizations possess in terms of a contribution towards the economic welfare of the human family. This recognition, however, can only come about when one is open to develop a sense of transreligious and transnational responsibility, i.e., a sense of duty which does not terminate at the boundaries of one's religious or national community. When this happens, we will truly experience the full flowering of Teilhard de Chardin's 'noosphere' or global sense of interconnectedness.

Transnational Responsibility

Globalisation necessarily calls into question traditional political boundaries and juridical paradigms. What we will increasingly witness is a gradual reduction of the power of solely national legislative, executive and juridical processes in favour of a transnational and hence a more just global forum for the preservation and expression of human rights. It seems that we have indeed entered into this new age of critical co-responsibility for our world, or, in other words, the age of the global citizen. This is not as yet a structured political experience, but it is already an experience of the new global polis (the new global city), reflected by TIME magazine, when it nominated the 'Person of the Year 2006' to be 'YOU,' i.e., each and every citizen of the world. By doing this, TIME wants to make the claim that the makers of human history are no more primarily the leaders of the political or the business world, but average citizens who have access to the global communication network, and who thereby have the power to influence the direction of human history.

Political accountability, for one, is being considerably enhanced, because people are more free to 'blog' their views online, uncensored by restrictive governmental pressure and unfettered by mainline media propaganda and interests. This is tremendously helpful for NGOs who wish to network at the global level so as to put pressure on local governmental and business policies and practices. It is precisely such a network which can influence public opinion and lead to the denial of political status to tyrants who think they may adopt totalitarian or double standards in one country and get away with them in another. The denial of a visa to Narendra Modi to visit the U.S.A. is a good example of the power of this global network.[18] With its power to disseminate relevant and widespread information, the internet is beginning to function as a propitious shaming mechanism and needs to be put to full use towards this end, whenever necessary.

Globalisation will lead to the emergence of a democratic mentality, not because of the messianic missionary drive on the part of some powerful nations to colonize parts of the world in the name of democracy (which will more likely do a disservice to the spirit of democracy), but simply because democratic processes will increasingly be seen to be beneficial in terms of the common good. This is happening in India, especially in the cities, but also in the rural areas, when more and more citizens' groups are compelling state and metropolitan governmental authorities to be more accountable. The fructification and the optimal use of the RTI (Right to Information) Act is a good example of this emergence of the democratic spirit at the level of the ordinary citizen.

It is this process of the rapid and widespread dissemination of information that will bring about social transformation and accountability much more quickly than in the past. In his book,

Development As Freedom, Amartya Sen argues that no famine has ever taken place in the history of the world in a functioning democracy.[19] According to his analysis, economic disasters like famines more easily take place under the following circumstances: when government leaders and workers largely belong to the upper class, when there is less accountability of the leaders to the people they govern, when there is a greater centralization of authority, where there is a lack of an adequate political opposition, when there is rigid censorship which entails a lack of freedom of expression and freedom of the press, where there is a desire to fudge information, to conceal accurate data, and to misinform people. One can easily see how many of these factors can only survive when the dissemination of information and social analyses are limited and restricted. But this is not possible in our contemporary situation. Consequently, it will be more and more difficult for non-democratic governments to function in an irresponsible and autocratic manner. Even if countries are not technically democratic, they will increasingly become only nominally non-democratic republics, as is the case in China, where totalitarian practices are compelled to be less harsh, as compared to the past.

A greater sense of democratization has also resulted in greater corporate social responsibility on the part of a good number of TNCs, whereby corporations are increasingly recognizing the contributory role they need to assume in civic affairs. CSR (corporate social responsibility) has become the buzz word in many corporate offices, but for various motives. Some corporations use the opportunity for image building, while others only reluctantly and marginally enter into this process. A few, however, recognize that if business has to succeed, corporations need to get involved in the process of building up a better social and civic infrastructure.[20]

In this regard, what is remarkable is the establishment of the world's largest philanthropic endowment by the world's richest couple, viz., the Bill and Melinda Gates Foundation. What was even more consoling this past year was the fact that the second richest person, Warren Buffet, has added to the monetary volume of this already immense foundation. According to the official website of the Foundation, the mission statement reads as follows:

> Guided by the belief that every life has equal value, the Bill & Melinda Gates Foundation works to reduce inequities and improve lives around the world. In developing countries, it focuses on improving health, reducing extreme poverty, and increasing access to technology in public libraries. In the United States, the foundation seeks to ensure that all people have access to a great education and to technology in public libraries. In its local region, it focuses on improving the lives of low-income families.[21]

One of the reasons for engaging in such charitable ventures may be in order that business interests are strengthened rather than minimized in the future, because of a betterment of human standards of living, and hence better consumer education and buying power. But perhaps a deeper motivation is the realization of the sheer imbalance which constitutes contemporary global capitalism, which allows some people to make such obscene sums of money to be spent in vulgar opulence while others have to struggle to barely survive in hostile and subhuman conditions. It is a pity, however, that it is often (voluntary) charity and not forces of social and distributive justice which lies at the heart of such social projects.

Whether it is justice or charity which contributes towards the furthering of transnational responsibility, it is clear that transnational religions have a pivotal role in cultivating this virtue. As the sense of community within such religions is often transcontinental, there is a need to generate a concomitant sense of responsibility for the welfare of others within the community who need help in terms of integral welfare. Furthermore, while charity may begin at home, it ought not to end at home, but rather be extended to all, especially those who are in most need. Indeed, in an ideal global and virtual community, home is everywhere and everyone is a member of our home.

Over the past few years, the theologian Hans Kueng, along with others, has worked on the outlines of a 'global ethic' which would not only serve to unite believers and non-believers on the level of ethical theory, but, more importantly, serve to relate transcendent principles, whether religious or secular, with concrete projects connected with social development.[22] Whatever be the merits or demerits of such a project, it is the likes of such a mentality which is necessary to usher in a new consciousness more fitting for the new world of globalization. Such a mentality can only arise from minds and hearts which are dominated by the spirit of hope and optimism, rather than that of despair or cynicism.

Pro-active Optimism

Globalisation has little room for 'naysayers' and cynics. NGOs and religious believers sometimes take a bleak view of the transnational, globalizing corporate world, as if it is an inhuman monster about to devour whole peoples and civilizations. On the other hand, the corporate world and Governmental agencies often consider NGOs and religious-based ethical protest as an unnecessary hindrance on the sure pathway towards development. There is need to overcome this polarization and work together towards a common future. Constructive criticism while working together is not only welcome but necessary. But there is no room for pessimism, and worse, cynicism. Instead, what is needed is a realistic, optimistic and futuristic approach towards development.

A realistic approach enables one to sacrifice one's ideological presuppositions and prejudices if they are not consonant with new developments. For example, the struggle towards economic development in West Bengal is a good indication whether the State is ready to participate in the process of globalization or not. The Party which has claimed to best represent the interests of the workers and the proletariat is forced to do a tightrope walk between past ideology on the one hand and pressing concerns for present and future development on the other. Party leaders who have had the chance to visit neighbouring China are in a good position to rethink their priorities in terms of development. However, it is difficult to be inspired by the Chinese model (which is a top-down State-controlled one) when one has to work with the Indian model which is more democratic. That is why the State Government is under pressure to reconsider methods of landgrabbing as evidenced in the recent Singur and Nandigram peasant protests. The Chief Minister, while regretting the use of force on the part of the Government and party cadres, has however made it quite clear that a primary reliance on agricultural labour will only result in backwardness. Such an admission clearly favouring industrialization and globalization from a Communist leader would be unthinkable a few years ago. Today, however, it bears testimony to the power of globalization, and the necessity to reinterpret one's principles if one is to survive, or better, flourish, in such a world.

Similarly, with regard to language, some who are overly patriotic have resisted the use of English as a medium of instruction in India (this of course does not include those who hypocritically do so for politically convenient reasons). However, many Indians of the lowest social classes, especially in urban areas, seem to prefer an English-medium education if they can afford it, for the future of their children stands to gain if they can be educated in a globally-recognized and competitive medium. Ideological convictions are necessary, but one must be ready to reinterpret them in the light of new developments, if one is to make progress.

Where environmental development is concerned, the future is in some sense more important than the present. This is an area where unbridled global capitalism coupled with cheap technology and weak political resolve can cause havoc, and lead to dramatic climate change even in our own age, as is already happening worldwide. If realistic and futuristic measures are not adopted in a reasonable manner, the span and quality of human life (to say nothing of non-human life) will considerably reduce. Wisdom demands that sacrifices be made by all, not only by a few, so that future generations may profit. For example, while China is producing cheap goods for the West, but by using methods of primitive energy generation, it is imperative that both China and the West need to sacrifice–

China in terms of investing in better and ecologically safer technology both in terms of energy production and the manufacturing of goods, and the West by paying a coal tax (or energy tax in general) towards adequate monetary compensation for Chinese-manufactured goods, so as to partially cover these costs.[23]

Finally, with regard to the future, religion is one of those social institutions which are best suited to generate optimism and hope. All religions are based on narratives which end with some form of salvific or liberative situation. This is similar to other forms of developmental models, whether economic, political, cultural or educational. But religious myths, belief-systems, rituals and a sense of community place religion in a privileged and opportune position, both to generate hope among its adherents as well as to inject hope into the collective consciousness of humankind. What is needed is a conscious effort to relate religion with social development, so as to both guide the current forces of globalization in a proper direction, and to provide motivation to work towards social change, not only among believers, but together with all people of good will.

Conclusion

Globalisation is not a perfect example of social development, as numerous studies based on teleological and deontological considerations have demonstrated. However, whether we like globalization or not, as a social force it has come to stay, at least over the near future. We have to learn how to sublimate its productive energies into more salubrious channels and how to address and rectify its less integrally developmental dimensions.

Religion as a social force has a lot to offer in this regard. By cultivating relevant contemporary moral dispositions or virtues among its adherents (and I have focused on just five), believers can work along with people of other faiths and non-believers alike to make globalization a humane experience for all rather than a monstrous experience for a sizeable section of humanity. This ability of religion to be a resource for the cultivation of virtues for our contemporary age needs to be realized desperately today. If religion does not rise to this challenge, it will not be able to take its rightful place among the different social forces which are currently helping to shape human destiny. Not to be involved in human history towards this end is not to be true to one's sacred vocation. We live in the hope that the different religions will together rise to the occasion in the service of a global human family.

Notes

1. Virtue ethics is traditionally associated with the ethical approach of Aristotle, as compared to deontological ethics, which is associated with Kant and those who subscribe to some form of natural law, while teleological ethics is associated with the British Utilitarian philosophers.
2. See John Kline, *Ethics for International Business: Decision Making in a Global Political Economy,* Routledge, 2005, where the author discusses various aspects of globalization from an ethical perspective, especially from deontological and teleological concerns.
3. See my article, "Mutual Challenges to Religion and Globalisation," in Institute of Indian Culture Newsletter, Mumbai, July 2006.
4. *Making Globalisation Good: The Moral Challenges of Global Capitalism,* ed. John Dunning; Oxford University Press, 2003. In this work, there is an attempt to relate this process of globalization and global capitalism with primary ethical and religious movements and institutions. Specific Chapters are devoted to the relationship between globalization and the major religions, including 'Eastern Religions.
5. John Dunning, "The Moral Imperatives of Global Capitalism–An Overview," in Making Globalisation Good, p. 12.
6. *Ibid.,* p. 13.
7. Joseph, Stiglitz, "Towards a New Paradigm of Development," in Making Globalisation Good, p.76. Stiglitz is a Nobel Laureate in Economics, who famously stepped down as the Chief Economist and Senior Vice-President of the World Bank in 2000. His books include Globalisation and Its Discontents, W.W. Norton, 2001, and more recently, Making Globalisation Work—the Next Steps to Social Justice, W.W. Norton and Allen Lane (Penguin), 2006.

8. See the document, *Globalisation and Marginalization–Our Global Apostolic Response*, brought out by the Jesuit Social Justice Secretariat in Rome, 2006, which argues towards this end.

9. The terms MNC (multi-national corporation), TNC (trans-national corporation), MNE (multi-national enterprise) and 'supranational companies' are used to describe the same reality, viz., business interests and projects which span nations and continents in order to produce and distribute goods and services mainly for profit.

10. A good example of exaggerated rhetoric leading to futile action is the war in Iraq. It was ostensibly based on the claim of weapons of mass destruction, which the 'embedded' American media rhetorically supported right from the inception of the bellicose discourse, systematically obfuscating the truth. This war in Iraq is one of the more pressing international hindrances towards global development, with not only economic but even interreligious overtones of disharmony.

11. See *Globalisation and its Victims–As Seen by its Victims,* Michael Amaladoss, S.J. (ed.) Delhi, Vidyajyoti/ISPCK, 1999, for a broad analysis of how irresponsible globalization has the potentiality to generate a wide variety of 'victims.

12. J. Orstrom Moller, "Wanted: A New Strategy for Globalisation," The Futurist, Vo.38, Jan 2004. p.20ff. Moller was Ambassador of Denmark to Singapore, and is one who argues that globalization is resulting in a greater divide between the haves and have-nots and, if unbridled, will result in an ascendancy of nationalism (to safeguard local interests) rather than internationalism.

13. See Amartya Sen, *Identity and Violence: The Illusion of Destiny,* London, Allen Lane (Penguin), 2006.

14. A good example is *Wikipedia,* the free (and perhaps fastest-growing) online encyclopedia started in 2001, to which anyone is free to contribute. But besides this, there are numerous medical and engineering problems which are placed on the internet eliciting responses and solutions, to say nothing of chatrooms and blogsites which allow free expression and interaction on almost every aspect of human existence.

15. Archbishop Desmond Tutu received the Nobel Peace Prize in 1984, while Amartya Sen received the Nobel Prize for Economic Science in 1998.

16. The full summary statement of the "International Conference on Religion and Globalisation" is edited by Ruben Habito, and may be found in Buddhist-Christian Studies, 24 (2004) 241ff. This statement covers the most significant areas which relate the promise and the problems of globalization on the one hand with the power and the limitations of religious resources on the other.
17. Amartya Sen, "How to Judge Globalism," *The American Prospect*, Vol. 13, Issue. 1 (2002) p. 2ff.
18. Narendra Modi will go down in history as the Chief Minister who was primarily responsible for the pogrom against the Muslims in his state. Indeed, his strategy of communally divisive politics has been poignantly referred to as the 'Gujarat experiment,' perhaps intended to be the precursor of a Nazi-like 'final solution' of some of the minorities in India.
19. Amartya Sen, *Develcpment as Freedom*, Oxford University Press, 2001.
20. See, for example, the DNA (Daily News and Analysis), Mumbai, report of December 15, 2006, p.1, which is titled, "Private Sector Wants to Maintain City–Corporations Will Adopt Municipal Wards and Help in Their Upkeep."
21. *http://www.gatesfoundation.org/MediaCenter/FactSheet/*
22. *See http://astro.temple.edu/~dialogue/Antho/kung.htm for an outline of this global ethic project.*
23. See "The Coal Trap," *Newsweek*, January 15, 2007, in which this point is argued.

5

The Voice of the Marginal and the Poor: Responsibility, Ethics and Development in Emmanuel Levinas

Roger Burggraeve SVD

The starting point for this reflection is the suggestion of Ananta Kumar Giri[1] that we should broaden and deepen development ethics with the thought of Emmanuel Levinas[2]. For this purpose we begin with his famous idea of the face of the other as the source of responsibility. Insofar as the face of the other displays a radical alterity, it puts us on the track of the vulnerable other, which Levinas likewise calls "the poor, the widow, the orphan and the stranger". This vulnerability, which manifests itself in an extreme manner in its mortality, reveals at the same time its mastership, which is from the very beginning an ethical mastership, meaning an appeal to responsibility. Not only will we lay bare the foundation of this responsibility but likewise make explicit its different major lines. Concretely speaking, we will demonstrate how the responsibility to which the vulnerable face appeals to us displays a multi-dimensional character. It indeed takes place as a responsibility for the responsibility of the other. And in its turn this implies a double line of responsibility. Firstly, there is an emancipatory aspect, namely a responsibility for the responsibility of the other–the poor, the widow, the orphan and the stranger–for oneself. And then there is likewise a strong ethically provocative aspect, namely the responsibility for the responsibility of the other for others.

The Mastership of the Marginal and the Poor

The core of Levinas' thought consists in that he does not primarily link the vulnerability of the marginal and the poor with their factual condition of poverty or exclusion, but with the essential and radical alterity of the other, that is to say with the epiphany of the other as 'other' or as 'face'. Hence we commence our search for the link between development ethics and Levinasian thought with a description of this alterity. The poor is not in the first place a poor person, but an other who as other directs oneself towards me.

The 'I', that by means of its capabilities and knowledge draws the world to itself, becomes as it were frightened by the epiphany of the other, precisely insofar as the other manifests itself as the *radically other*. The other presents itself to me as a 'withdrawing' and 'transcending movement', and this not only factually and temporarily but essentially and definitively. The other derives its meaning not integrally and wholly from the world surrounding it, nor from evolution, history, a system of totality. The other surpasses all historical, sociological, psychological and cultural origin of meaning. The other presents itself as the unique one, that radically goes beyond all belonging to kind, race, family, tribe, ethnicity and people - which already implies a condemnation of all racism (VA 98). The other is already infinitely more than the images, photographs, representations, evocations and interpretations that I design or am able to design. Of course the other is visible; of course the other appears and evokes all sorts of impressions, images and representations, whereby the other is describable. Of course we can come to know much about the other on the basis of what the other allows to be seen somatically, psychologically and sociologically. But the other is always more than, and irreducible to, its photograph. This not only coincidentally or factually, but also in principle: the other can never be adequately represented and contained in one or the other image. I can never encase the other in, or equate the other with, its graphic form (EI 90-91/86-87). Even though the other has its own physiognomy and character, and thus a recognisable estimable feature, still its face precisely consists in breaking through and surpassing its own image and appearance time and again (AE 109/86). In so doing the other essentially escapes all typology, characterisation, diagnosis and classification–in short all attempts at knowing and understanding the other totally. The other makes all inquisitiveness ridiculous (TI 46/ 73-74). This implies that the other is not constituted by me as a supplement to my deficiency, and likewise not as my mirror image, alter-ego or 're-issue of myself' (TA 75/83). In short, 'the other is invisible', as Levinas expresses it provocatively (TI 4/34). The face continually belies its own countenance, meaning to say its own visibility and describability. It is literally '*retraite*' or '*anachore-sis*', withdrawal. Its epiphany is always a breaking through, and a confounding of, this epiphany, whereby the other always remains enigmatic and thereby precisely intrudes as the irreducible one, the separate and different, the foreigner–in short, as the pre-eminently different or as radical alterity.

If we relate this to the marginal and the poor (dalits, proletarians, elderly, mentally disabled persons...), then this means that they definitely have a biologically determined origin, but also that they transcend this origin infinitely. Poor persons always transcend their past and milieu. They never coincide with their appearance, family, psychology, sociology. They are always different from what their background appears to be or would lead us to suspect. They do not only remain a mystery factually but also principally. In this aspect poor persons are–no matter how visible or tangible–invisible. That means that they are irreducible to their tangible or descriptive characteristics. Sociology, psychology and other human sciences can most certainly make a contribution to 'define' the marginal and the poor, but they will never coincide with these descriptions. (Later on we will see how on the ethical level they *may* never be reduced to these descriptions). The poor as the radically other will always escape and show themselves different from the 'foreseen'. Poor and marginal people will continue to surprise those who take care of them as the ones who are ultimately new and other!

This rather negative description of the alterity of the other in general, and of the poor in particular, however, has a clearly positive meaning. The basis for its in-visibility, un-knowability and un-predictability is indeed its 'manifestati-on *kath'auto*' (TI 37/65). The face breaks through its form in order to show itself out of itself. It is pure and simple 'expression' (TI 37/66). This self-expression occurs in a concrete manner in the word and glance of the face. The other is the one who looks at me straight in the eye and also directly addresses me: we stand '*face-to-face*' with each other. Its glance and word make it present without any detours or intermediary stages. I need not reason out, starting from the fact that a glance or word comes toward me, in order to decide that someone lies behind this expression. The word and the glance of the other make it immediately, ineluctably and almost obtrusively present (LC 41/20). Moreover, the primary, most fundamental content or message of its self-expression is nothing else than the essential quality of the other, namely its absolute alterity and irreducibility. It is not *what* the face expresses that is of importance here, but *that* it expresses itself. The *fact* of its expression is the announcement of its very presence, of its appearance *as* other, whatever the content of its expression may be (TI 170/196).

In terms of the marginal and the poor this means that they can never be an object for the ones who take care of them or approach them. The marginal other will always be a face that speaks directly to them. The poor person is not an object, but a subject: someone who gazes at me, touches me and speaks to me with the authority of an other who comes to me. In this respect the poor person is always the one who literally comes to us: the poor comes from elsewhere, from itself–its alterity–as someone over whom we have no power (nor can we exercise power over it, as we will explain from an ethical position later). Maybe we can even say that the poor are 'strong as death', in the sense that through their gaze and (often wordless) word, they break into our existence and from within their alterity address us directly. The face of the poor is an ultimate heteronomous experience that we have not foreseen or could not predict. We therefore have no control over it. It is an experience that comes from an other who addresses us!

That is also why Levinas labels the expression of the other as *teaching*. This can in no possible way be reduced to one or other form of (Socratic) maieutics or midwifery that only draws out that which was already contained within. The expression of the face comes to me 'from elsewhere'. It introduces more into myself than that which I already contain slumbering within me, namely, the real 'message' or 'revelation' of the presence of the other (TI 22/51): "the absolutely new is the other" (TI 194/219). The other manifests itself in its face as a strong alterity that from its height or loftiness directs itself immediately and authoritatively towards me (TI 175/200). In that sense Levinas can say that the other is my *master*: "The absolutely foreign alone can instruct us" (TI 46/73). By means of its very appearance, the other teaches me about its irreducible alterity without my having already contained this teaching within the depths of my being. In this regard, the fundamental teaching of the face is not without any imposition, not without any form of unassailability and a 'self-sufficiency' that is to be taken literally (a teaching that is sufficient in itself). Levinas even speaks of a "cold splendour" (TI 175/200). I am not able to let the teaching of the face bubble up from within me. I cannot foresee or predict the word of revelation of the face; I do not have it at hand in any way whatsoever. I am not the one who designs, but the one who receives, who listens, and who, by means of listening, obeys (TI 41/69, 73/99).

Continuing in this line we can say that the marginal and the poor are elevated above us, not because they are more powerful, but because as irreducible others they are our master and teacher. Mostly we assume that the poor is lesser than us, precisely because he or she is small and vulnerable. But thanks to Levinas it becomes clear how we are in an asymmetrical relationship to the poor, in the sense that the poor is more than us, and we are less than the poor. We do not first teach and instruct the poor. First the poor has to speak to us and teach us. Every relationship of helping the poor has therefore to begin – every time again – with a form of humility and obedience to the poor as our teacher. We are talking here about a different life from what in Greek tradition is called self-knowledge: "know yourself" ("gnothi seauton"). In relationship to the marginal and the poor, as in every relationship to the other, I do not learn by descending into myself and discovering in my innermost being wisdom over all things, but by going out of myself and being open to the other as the other reveals him or herself to me. The relationship to the poor as the ultimate other is no autonomous or heteronomous happening that rests on the realisation of my not-knowing. In the relationship to the poor I am not the one who designs and determines, but the one who has to receive and accept what the other 'teaches' me. In this respect the alterity of the poor as the starting-point for my learning is not only exterior, but also anterior and superior. As the radical other the poor brings me towards laying down all pretensions and to approach her or him with a certain meekness, so that the face of the poor can in all liberty reveal its alterity to me, and this on the basis of the authority of this alterity.

In this way, Levinas turns around the usual, traditional vision of 'caring for the marginal and the poor'. We are not in the first place the helping persons who pass on their insights, wisdom and convictions to the 'receiving' poor. It is the poor themselves who come first in assistance: the radical priority of the other. The face of the poor that speaks, is and becomes the first teacher of the 'assistant' person. As the radical other the poor establishes its mastership in all works of aid and assistance. In this way the face of the poor also establishes the learning process of all kinds of (professional) people and organisations 'assisting' the poor, and this not just for once, but time and again.

The Vulnerability of the Marginal and the Poor

With this turning around of mastership in 'assisting the marginal and the poor', we arrive at the ethical relationship to them. For the marginal and the poor do not only reveal their mastership in terms of their radical alterity, but through their alterity they appeal to us to recognise, respect and enhance their alterity. For the explication of the concrete content of this ethical relationship to the marginal and the poor, we return once again to the general insight of Levinas about the appeal to responsibility that comes to us in and through the face of the other.

Upon closer inspection, the mastership that ensues from the alterity of the face appears to be a very exceptional mastership. It is a mastership that rests on the vulnerability of the other whereby the mastership of the face becomes precisely an ethical mastership. The face, according to Levinas, is the remarkable fact that a being touches me not in the indicative but in the imperative (LC 44/21).

In order to understand how this functions, we must reflect more deeply on the phenomenology of the appearance, or rather the non-appearance, or epiphany, of the other. This we began above. The strong alterity of the face, insofar as it presents itself as its irreducibility to one or other 'countenance', photograph or representation, has a reverse side. It has an extreme vulnerability. Levinas calls this also "strangeness-destitution" (*l'étrangeté-misère*) (TI 47/75) or the 'nudity of the face' (EI 90/86). As a *countenance* the other is vulnerable. It can quite easily be reduced to its appearance, its family, its social position and environment, its accomplishments, its health and clinical picture. As 'in-visible', that is as being irreducible to its face, the other appears by not appearing. In short the other appears as the one who does not belong in my organised world – a world that I begin to organise precisely as 'my world' on the basis of my natural 'care for myself'. The face of the other eludes not only my foresight, literally my 'pro-vidence', it also falls outside of it. It finds itself literally in 'extra-territoriality' and 'u-topia' or 'non-place'. Precisely for that reason is the face so vulnerable: "The transcendence of the face is at the same time its absence from this world into which it enters, the exiling of a being, his condition of being a stranger, destitute, or proletarian. The nakedness of the face extends into the nakedness of the body that is cold and that is ashamed of its nakedness. Existence *kath'auto* is, in the world, a destitution" (TI 47/75). "The face in its nakedness presents to me the destitution of the poor one and the stranger" (TI 188/213). The gravity of the other's nakedness, destitution, or hunger, freezes all laughter. In its 'height' (supra), the other reveals also an extreme 'humility' - not as a virtue but as a condition (TI 174/ 200). And this condition of defencelessness is revealed most sharply in its mortality and suffering unto death (EN 166-167/ 124-125).

Levinas characterises this humility in an evocative manner by referring to the biblical terms "widow, orphan, stranger, poor" (TI 5078). However, we must be careful in the use of these terms. We could consider them as kinds or genres or groups of people with certain social characteristics, which distinguish them from others. But then we would indeed go beyond the true meaning of Levinas' use of the terms. After all it is not on the basis of their qualities and thus not on the basis of their differences that these people are bearers of the radical, vulnerable alterity, which is Levinas' main concern (VA 97). The question, however, is why does Levinas give a certain preference to these categories of people? Upon closer inspection, he is not so much interested in their qualities as in their essential vulnerability. By means of their social 'condition' they make visible and tangible the vulnerable nakedness of the other (although alterity itself is not visible and tangible). By means of their poverty, rejection and exile they stand closer to death than the others. Their mortality is more evident and notable. And that is precisely Levinas' main concern when he concerns himself with the nakedness of the other. By using the metaphorical reference to the biblical groups of those 'rejected' and 'naked', Levinas wants to make clear that he is concerned with the vulnerability of the other, which manifests itself unto the body. It is about their 'nearness to death', their mortality, the coming closer to their suffering unto death. They 'display', or rather they evoke the essential vulnerability of every face, of every other. It involves the 'precarious' character of the other, namely its assailable nakedness. Hence the use of qualifications like fragility, nudity, suffering, destitution, and especially 'mortality', to be understood as being under threat and exposure to death: "Exposure, pointblank, extradition of the beleaguered, the tracked down–tracked down before all tracking and all beating for game. Face as the very mortality of the other person" (EN 206/160). In this manner, a relationship arises between me and the other, which situates itself beyond all rhetoric: a relationship that qualifies all flattery, and even all poetry, about the other as ridiculous, or rather as repulsive, inappropriate and despicable.

This relationship, however, displays a remarkable character. Upon closer inspection it is precisely the appearance of the face as vulnerable (unto death) that invites me, as it were, to reduce the other to be a function of my own being. In this respect, Levinas takes the paradoxical position that the other presents itself to me as the 'temptation to kill' (EI 90/86). The nudity of the face is not only an 'uncomfortable' nudity–one that testifies to an essential destitution, as we said–it is also a 'touchable' nudity. By its destitution it invites me, as it were, to violence. By the condition of its humility the face seduces me to 'integrate' or to imprison the other in my self-interested effort of existing (AE 113-115/89-91). It is thanks to the essential vulnerability of the face that I, in my attempt at being that strives for happiness and meaning, am tempted to draw the other to myself and do it violence. This happens concretely by attempting to make the other subordinate to me, to take it in service, to consume and to use it in one way or another. For that purpose I often make use of the wealth and power that I have accumulated for myself out of my expansionistic vitalism. I can use, or rather abuse, all possible means in order to reduce the other to myself, to blackmail, to intimidate or to bribe it, in short to subjugate it–without giving the direct impression of a brutal tyranny or slavery. In its extreme form, this will to power flows from the denial of the other. Of this, murder as the total negation or annihilation of the other, is the physical incarnation (TI 172/198).

What can we deduce from this position of the 'attraction to kill' with respect to the ethical relationship to the poor? It leads us to recognise that violence in relationships between people, is a realistic possibility and may not be seen as an exception related to perverse and sadistic persons. Precisely on the-basis of the nakedness and vulnerability of the poor the possibility for violence is real. Violence displays many faces. The extreme cases of the physical violence of murder and all kinds of abuse are not alone. There is also hate, tyranny, intimidation, blackmail, bullying and the refusal to give recognition, or exclusion and neglect. There is subjection, manipulation, oppression and slavery. Violence includes all forms of both direct and more subtle forms of indifference. There is the violence that flows from approaching the poor on the basis of perception and knowledge. It is precisely in the daily perception and exploration of the poor that the greatest risk for violence lies, in the sense that it does not take much to reduce the poor to its appearance, that means to its situation and reality of destitution.

The Heteronomous Responsibility for the Other Begins as a Prohibition

In this very temptation to kill lies the ethical significance of the face. At the moment in which I am tempted to reduce the other to a means of my own existence, I simultaneously realise that that which can be, actually must not be. This is the core of the fundamental ethical experience beginning from the face of the poor as the other (LC 44/21-22). In my self-sufficient effort at existing, which on the ground of perception and representation aims to become the expression and realisation of individual freedom, I am not merely limited from the outside but in my deepest being. I am–in the very principle of my freedom–shaken and called into question (EI 129/120). In the face I discover myself as the potential murderer of the other. In this sense, through the destitution of the other I stumble once again upon its substantial strength. I come up against a radical resistance against my egocentric, reducing avarice. The face appears as the *opposite*: it takes up a position *before* me as a radical and immediate 'stop' or *no*, as an absolute opposition to all my capabilities (TI 173-174/198-199). The *logos* of this 'no', the first wordless word that ensues from the face of the other, namely the poor, is then also a prohibition: 'You shall not kill' (EN 48/30). You shall not make the other into a means for yourself. Moreover, this resistance against the denial and instrumental reduction of the other is in no way coincidental or accidental. Indeed, it does not rest on a free decision of the other but on its essential alterity itself, which as vulnerability is at the same time an unparalleled protest against every grasp of this vulnerability by the 'I' and its attempt at being that is concerned for itself (HS 141/93-94).

From all this appears something very paradoxical. The ethical relationship with the other, the poor as the other, begins as a shock experience, namely, the possibility *and* the prohibition to do violence to the other in any way whatsoever. This implies that the ethical relationship with the poor does not begin with a positive commandment that determines what I *must* do, but rather with a negative intervention, a prohibition that questions the straightforward-without-beating-about-the-bush movement of the attempt at being. At the same time, it concerns an external law, which does not come up from within the dynamism of the 'living being' itself. The fundamental ethical sensitivity that is aroused by the external prohibition against violence is a remarkable form of fear. Not the fear or concern for oneself, but the fear of being after the blood of the other. Levinas in this regard also speaks of the scruple. Literally, the word 'scruple' means a 'pebble in one's shoe'. It becomes impossible to stand still, and instead moves or incites one to take another step. A scruple, therefore, is a disquiet that works its way through the soul obstructively. The scruple can likewise be understood as a form of shame and discomfort: I am apprehensive about the other, namely the poor, as to its irreducible being-other, whereby it is surrendered to me to seize and to do violence, to violate, to pest, to maltreat, to abuse, to deny or to destroy, in short to 'kill' in one way or the other and to do it injustice (DVI 254/169). We can then label this first ethical movement before the vulnerable other as an "apparently negative movement of restraint" (NLT 96/126). Confronted with the principal assailability *and* vulnerability of the other, I am called to restrain myself and to pull back – in other words, to *not* do something. The ethics towards the poor as the radical other begins as the paradox of 'restraint', curtailment or 'self-contraction' in the midst of the unabashed and energetic way with which our caring for ourselves rushes forward without looking right or left, without seeing the 'corpses' it leaves aside. Or to put it in different terms, the ethical relationship towards the other begins as a hesitation, a shame over oneself, as a movement of withdrawal and self-questioning. I may feel inclined to ask myself questions along the lines of: "Am I perhaps too 'vehement', too self-assured and insouciant, only concerned about my own happiness, future and meaning? Do I perhaps 'kill' (i.e. not allow space for others to be) simply by being myself?" The appearance of the poor as the other touches and traumatises me to the very core of my heart, so much so that I am "suffering in my skin" (AE 66/51).

All of this implies that the ethical responsibility for the marginal and the poor has to begin with the respect for the commandment: 'You shall not kill'. No form of violence towards poor people is acceptable, whether in the context of daily life, economics, or society. The demand for strict non-violence is the primary ethical task of people working with the poor. It is such a fundamental ethical duty, that it precedes all other ethical approaches to the poor. Its fundamental character is simultaneously utterly paradoxical. By not killing or by not using any form of violence one has in effect not yet done anything. Through obedience to the commandment not to kill the preconditions are created in which things still need to be done.

The fact in itself that we have in our societies the prohibition 'You shall not kill', 'You shall not commit violence towards the marginal and the poor', indicates not only the unacceptability of this violence, but also the fact that violence towards the marginal and poor other is not that strange or exceptional. There would not be an ethical prohibition as expression of practical ethical wisdom if there had been no violence towards people in general, and against the marginal and the poor in particular. Human civilisation exists precisely in recognising the potential of factual violence towards the poor (and all vulnerable others) so that something can be done about it, through sanctioning, for example, where the prohibition of violence is not respected.

By means of the prohibition and the ethical scruple or restraint awakened in me, the radical ethical asymmetry or 'non-reciprocity' between me and the other, namely the poor, becomes visible. In contrast to Buber's idea of the reciprocity between 'I' and 'Thou', Levinas speaks about "the 'curvature' of the intersubjective space" (TI 267/291). Through the prohibition the 'I' and the other or the poor are not only radically separated from each other, they are also distinct. And, note well, this discrepancy does not depend on their respectively distinct characteristics or on their coincidentally unequal psychological dispositions and moods during the encounter (TI 190/215). It lies in the 'I-other-conjunction' itself: through its demanding, prohibiting, character the face of the vulnerable other stands above me as an *authority* that comes upon me from its ethical 'height' making demands and claims. We can label this as the 'sacred' and 'divine' character of the face of the poor. As such the marginal as the other then is not my equal, but my *superior*: not only my master who reveals something radically new, as we have seen above, but also my 'lord' who as a 'Thou' commands me unconditionally from its eminently ethical height (TI 74-75/100-101). That is precisely the paradox of the epiphany of the face of the poor: as the factual inferior, the poor as the radical other is ethically my superior. In this way it refers to the sublime awe and majesty of God. Thus the mastership of the marginal and the poor as the other sketched above, is reinforced, or, rather, ethically qualified.

The Emancipatory Dimension of Heteronomous Responsibility

Only through obedience to the prohibition of violence is space created for a positive filling in of a respectful responsibility that allows the poor and the marginal to unfold and raise their voice: the voice of the irreducible, exalted other. This responsibility is more than not killing or not making use of any violence. It is an attitude of acknowledgement and respect for the being-other of the poor. And it does not stop at this. It unfolds itself even further. It must be *more* than the 'appreciative respect'. It must develop into a responsibility 'in deeds and actions', meaning to say into a responsibility that expresses itself in concrete deeds of care that are directed towards the well-being of the other, namely the poor. Responsibility is thus neither the sentimentalism nor the naïve romanticism of being moved by the miserable and marginalised poor. Its affectiveness must turn into effectiveness, its dedication to the other into 'works' of care for the other (HAH 40-44/90-93). Without incarnation the responsibility for the other is hollow and empty. Stronger still, it is a lie and denial of oneself. How can one be concerned for the other if one performs no concrete deeds as the expression of this concern? Or to put it in a rabbinical way: it is not enough to love the other with our heart and soul, when we do not also love the other with our money, and even more so, with our hospitality. It is so that when you let the naked into your house he makes the floor mat dirty. In short, our yes-word must become flesh–in and through our body–and that in economic-earthly, appropriate forms (AS 81).

Applied to the responsibility for the marginal and the poor, this means that one must take up concrete care for the 'being' of the other, in this case the poor and excluded other, meaning to say for their life and 'well-being' (to be understood literally as the tangible unfolding of being). As a bodily other, the poor is in the first place a needy and finite and thus vulnerable creature, who needs others for its survival and good life. This flows forth directly from one's essential nakedness and vulnerability, that expresses itself in an extreme manner in one's mortality, as was sketched above. Or to put differently still: the essential alterity of the other takes place and reveals itself in the other's factual shortcomings and injuries of one's 'conatus essendi'. "The other's hunger–be it of the flesh or of bread–is sacred; there is no bad materialism other than our own" (DL 12/XIV). It would be a hypocritical form of spiritualism if in the responsibility for others, namely the poor, one would not take up any care for their nourishment and clothing, their protection against heat and cold, disease and accidents, "as if the entire spirituality on earth did not reside in the act of nourishing" (DL 12). The unrelenting suffering, that incarnates in a concrete way the essential nakedness of the poor and the marginal other, requires what Levinas calls "the severe seriousness of goodness" whereby the fate of the misery that the other meets loses its inhuman character (TI 175/200). Hence Levinas cites in this context the 'hard' words of the Jewish Rabbi Jochanan: "To leave men without food is a fault that no circumstance attenuates" (TI 175/201). Towards the hunger of people, our responsibility is unrelenting! In this regard, the 'rich' are objectively and fully responsible for the elimination of poverty. The ethics of heteronomous responsibility of the one for the other has a very 'worry-some' and disturbing meaning, namely to confront the 'well-to-do' with the vulnerable, marginal and poor others. To relieve the others with food and drink is not a question of non-committal or gratuitous charity, meaning to say of good intentions and good resolutions, but an inescapable duty of justice. And this duty to responsibility goes so far, says Levinas, that when giving food and drink no longer helps, one still does not leave the other to its fate in its irreversible suffering and dying. Herein lies the most tangible and ultimate criterion of the responsibility for the other, and thus of human civilisation: "facing the face, in its mortality" (EN 206/160). This even leads Levinas to formulate a new categorical imperative: "You shall not let the other alone, be it in the face of the inexorable" (EI 128/119).

There is more, however, than this incarnation of the responsible care for every other, in particular the marginal and poor other. Not only do we have to answer for their bodily being and well-being, but also for the unfolding of their 'attempt at being' into an independent and free existence. Oftentimes, the poor–especially when the excluded are concerned–avail of only a very limited freedom, which they only are able to receive and develop thanks to the responsibility of others in society. In that sense, the promotion of the poor into independent and active persons does not contradict the heteronomous responsibility for the other; the responsibility for the self-unfolding of the other flows forth directly from heteronomous responsibility. The responsibility by and for the other sees to it that 'mastership', which was discussed above in our description of the radical alterity of the face of the poor, acquires its true ethical form. By means of our responsibility for the naked and sidetracked poor, we effectively make possible their ethical mastership. The responsibility for the poor after all implies essentially the care for their becoming independent and mature. Stronger still, without the asymmetrically responsible care by-and-for-the-other, the marginal and the poor cannot even grow into active, able persons. The heteronomous responsibility for the poor as the radical other is the condition of possibility for the development of that poor other into a subject responsible-for-oneself. According to Levinas this is precisely the paradox of the heteronomous responsibility for the poor: it is a strongly concrete responsibility, in the sense that it is geared towards the being and self-development of the other. To take heteronomous responsibility for the poor concretely means to create space and possibilities for the growth of the poor to independence and responsibility for itself. This means anything but a negative or suspicious approach to the weak and the poor in their attempts to take their own responsibility. If the poor and marginal person is not an object, but an other, a subject, then we have to treat the poor as a full human person. When necessary, we will make critical remarks, so that poor and marginalised people can adjust their active responsibility and develop it better.

Furthermore, the heteronomous responsibility for the poor also means that one should pay attention to the many hurts that alienate marginalised persons from themselves so that, through caring closeness, they can heal sufficiently from these wounds. In this way a poor person can become the best possible responsible 'I': a responsible self that not only asserts itself, but also acts and speaks from within itself. In this sense, we are responsible for the responsibility poor and marginal people should have for themselves. With Levinas we can here even go further and speak of a substitute responsibility. During the decisive moments of growth and development, and from within our own task of responsibility, we take the lack of responsibility of the vulnerable, the weak and the poor unto ourselves. In this way, too, responsible ones for others recognise and promote the uniqueness of the poor and marginal other. We can call all of this the emancipatory aspect of each and every responsibility by and for the poor other: the possibility to enable and promote the responsibility of the poor for and by itself and through which it becomes an active responsible agent. In this manner, the marginal and poor others are no longer reduced to 'target groups' and 'objects', meaning to say to 'beneficiaries of development', but are transformed into 'subjects' and agents of their own development. The marginal and the poor are not only 'recipients' of development aid; they are also responsible for their own development.

Responsible for the Responsibility of the Marginal and the Poor for Others

We do wish to go even one step beyond Levinas' philosophical vision of heteronomous responsibility, though we remain indebted to him for our inspiration. We wish to turn around the asymmetrical responsibility by and for the other and look at it from the perspective of the responsibility of the marginal and the poor for others. We call this a chiastic responsibility, in the sense that we are speaking of two types of responsibility that cross one another. Our responsibility for others, namely for the marginal and the poor, is only integral if it grows into the responsibility for the responsibility of poor people, not only for themselves (cf. supra) but also, and especially for, others. If we then only apply the idea of responsibility for the other to the people taking care of the poor and the marginal, our analyses is lacking. It will give rise to a partiality that leads to disastrous results.

It is very well possible that people caring for the marginal and the poor, with all their commitment and energy, end up in an egocentric result with the ones they take care. The caring responsibility for the other can be very altruistic and unselfish, but this can imply that the other–the object of this care–is promoted into a self-complacent life, wherein only the care for oneself is important. To put it in paradoxical terms, the altruism of the one can lead directly to a promotion of the egotism of the other. We should not be blind to the fact that hunger, poverty and exclusion, in short all sorts of forms of deprivation and need, drive people to a hard and unrelenting 'struggle for life'. Poverty brings back the person to one's 'natural existence', in the sense that by means of one's fragile and finite being one is incited in 'life and limb' to be concerned about one's own being. The more acute the needs, even more the needy person becomes an 'impassioned' person, meaning to say a creature that is concerned for its own being and sees everything and everyone in the light of the satisfaction of its own needs. With Levinas we can label this as an unavoidable, natural selfishness, in the sense that the poor - precisely as poor - approach everything and everyone out of themselves and their own survival. In this regard poverty manifests itself as 'animal existence'. This 'banal' approach of poverty, that throws back the needy to the (at times fanatic) care for their own being, implies a direct critique on the idea of 'self-actualisation', which in Western late-modern thought was developed by a number of authors (Rogers, Maslow, ...). The link between poverty and the egocentric struggle for life unmasks the thought on self-unfolding as naïve, stronger till as typically Western, in the sense that it expresses *and* justifies the Western context of wealth and welfare. That is why the manner in which Levinas speaks about the natural striving of humans to be ('conatus essendi') seems more honest and more realistic than the 'romantic' discourse about an 'aesthetics of Self-Cultivation' (Foucault).[3] Therefore, the emancipatory promotion of the poor, sketched above, into a free self-determining and creative agent should never have the final word. The heteronomous responsibility by and for the other must go further. It must not only be an expression of the self-transcendence in the caring person, but also in the one taken care for, namely the poor. In society we are responsible for the responsibility of the marginal and the poor, in the sense that they must invite and provoke them into responsibility for others, and not only into responsibility for themselves. The one being responsible for the other is faced with the task to take up in such a manner its heteronomous responsibility for the other so that the other is guided and stimulated likewise to acknowledge, to take up and to develop its heteronomous responsibility by and for the other. When this does not take place, heteronomous responsibility contradicts itself. It even destroys its own dynamism and meaning: out of an extreme attention to the one affirmed as the radical other, that other is then brought to a place in a central position, at the cost of others.

This also concretely implies that in society the marginal and the poor are confronted with a number of boundary rules. Of these, 'You shall not kill' is the most fundamental. It is the minimal but strictly necessary condition for humane social life and for the creative development of the responsibility for the other, to which the poor must precisely be appealed. In a humane society we have the ethical mission to initiate and to introduce everyone, and therefore also the marginal and the poor, into the major importance of this prohibition, and also into a fundamental respect for it. All that was said above about the prohibition to violence can be applied without hesitation to the marginal and the poor as active agents. To put it in the words of Levinas: "The *vital* life, the natural life, perhaps begins in a naiveté and in repugnancies agreeing with ethics; it ends in compliance with loveless debauchery and looting erected into a social condition, into exploitation. *Human* life begins where this vitality, innocent in appearance, but virtually destructive, is mastered by interdictions. Does not authentic civilization, whatever be the biological echoes or the political defects it brings to pass, consist in holding back the breath of naive life and thus awakening 'for posterity and to the end of all generations'?" (NLT 25-26/61-62). All persons, without exception, must be guided in order to transcend their natural, vitalistic existence towards the other and for the sake of the other: a limitation through which life awakens from its somnambulant spontaneity, sobers up from its nature, and interrupts its centripetal movement, to open itself to the otherness of the other (NLT 23/60). When this is neither the goal nor the result of interpersonal and social responsibility, then we fail in our task. Taking of the marginal and the poor even ends up in an anti-society, in spite of all the possible means and forms whereby the marginal and the poor are made capable of leading a happy and prosperous life as active agents. Then they have not yet grown beyond the level of their natural urge-to-be and urge-to-live into the level of humane civilisation. In short, a humane, ethically qualified society consists in this that we appeal to the responsibility of the marginal and the poor, not only for the cooperation in the unfolding and possible healing of their own freedom and attempt at being, but also, and especially, in order to take upon themselves, and creatively substantiate, the responsibility for other.

Finally, if the idea of the marginal and the poor as responsible and active agents is disconnected from the concept of the heteronomous responsibility for others but itself, it will flow into all sorts of conflict, aggression, threats and violence. If the free exercise of independence is left to its own, and so can not be inspired from within by the responsibility for the other, it easily becomes a insolent demand for freedom that thrashes about wildly and actively terrorises others. Only an inspired freedom, that is, a freedom that allows itself to be inspired by the other, is able to transcend self-centredness and to enter into true humane relationships with others. This is also the case for the marginal and the poor in all their interpersonal and social relationships.[4]

Conclusion

To re-imagine and reinvent development as a transformative practice, Giri proposes to "reconstitute development as responsibility, which can provide a self-critical and transformative supplement to the contemporary definitions of development as freedom".[5] We have attempted to demonstrate how the ethical thought of Levinas about the other and the heteronomous responsibility for the other, achieves this in an eminent manner. However, so that this responsibility would not lapse into the one-sidedness of the old altruism, whereby the marginal and the poor would only be the objects of personal or organisational aid, we have developed out of Levinas' thought itself the idea of an emancipatory responsibility. The responsibility for the development of the marginal and the poor other essentially implies the idea of self-unfolding and thus of responsibility for oneself. But in order that this emancipatory responsibility in its turn would not turn into a new and disastrous one-sidedness, we have indicated with Levinas how the heteronomous responsibility for the other implies a responsibility for the responsibility of the other. Only by applying Levinas' idea of heteronomous responsibility to the marginal and the poor as well, is full justice done to the thesis that they are not only objects but likewise subjects of responsibility.

Notes

1. See among others his study "Rethinking the Imperative of Responsibility: Development Ethics, Aesthetics, and the Challenge of Poverty," in A.K. GIRI, *New Horizons of Social Theory. Conversations, Transformations and Beyond,* Jaipur/New Dehli/Bangalore/Mumbai/Hydrabad, Rawat Publications, 2006, p. 199-221, esp. pp. 207-211.

2. The cited studies of Levinas are listed below in alphabetical order. Citations in our text are indicated with an abbreviation of the original French edition, along with the cited page or pages. The cited page from the available English translation is indicated after the forward slash (/). Abbreviations used:

   AE: *Autrement qu'être ou au-delà de l'essence,* La Haye, Nijhoff, 1974. [English translation (ET): Otherwise than Being or Beyond Essence, translated by A. Lingis, The Hague/Boston/London, Nijhoff (Kluwer), 1981.];

   AS: *Autrement que savoir* (Interventions in the discussions and Débat général), Paris, Osiris, 1988;

   CPP: *Collected Philosophical Papers,* translated by A. Lingis.

Dordrecht/Boston/Lancaster, Kluwer/Nijhoff, 1987;

DL: *Difficile Liberté ; Essais sur le Judaïsme,* Paris, Albin Michel, 1976 (2nd ed.).

ET: *Difficult Freedom. Essays on Judaism,* translated by S. Hand. Baltimore, The John Hopkins University Press, 1990.];

DVI: *De Dieu qui vient à l'idée, Paris,* Vrin, 1982. [ET: Of God Who Comes to Mind, translated by B. Bergo, Stanford, University Press, 1998;

EI: *Éthique et Infini. Dialogues avec Philippe Nemo,* Paris, Fayard & France Culture, 1982. [ET: Ethics and Infinity. Conversations with Philippe Nemo, translated by R.A. Cohen, Pittsburgh, Duquesne University Press, 1985.];

EN: *Entre nous. Essais sur le penser-à-l'autre,* Paris, Grasset 1991. [ET: Entre nous. Thinking-of-the-Other, translated by M.B. Smith and B. Harshav, London/New York, Continuum, 2006];

HAH: *Humanisme de l'autre homme,* Montpellier, Fata Morgana, 1972. [ET: The three essays are taken up in CPP, respectively "Meaningful Sense" at pp. 75-107, "Humanism and Anarchy" at pp. 127-139, and "No identity" at pp. 141-151.];

HS: *Hors sujet, Montpellier,* Fata Morgana, 1987. [ET: Outside the Subject, translated by M.B. Smith, London, Athlone, 1993.];

LC: "Liberté et commandement" (suivi de "Transcendance et hauteur "), Montpellier, Fata Morgana, 1994. [ET: "Freedom and Command," in CPP, pp. 15-45.];

NLT: *Nouvelles lectures talmudiques,* Paris, Minuit, 1996. [ET: New Talmudic Readings, translated by R.A. Cohen, Pittsburgh, Duquesne University Press, 2000.];

TA: *Le temps et l'autre, Montpellier,* Fata Morgana, 1979 (2nd ed.). [ET: Time and the Other, translated by R.A. Cohen, Pittsburgh, Duquesne University Press, 1987.];

TI: *Totalité et Infini. Essai sur l'extériorité,* La Haye, Nijhoff, 1961. [ET: Totality and Infinity An Essay on Exteriority, translated by A. Lingis, The Hague/Boston/London, Nijhoff, 1979.];

VA: "La vocation de l'autre" (interview with E. Hirsch), in: E. HIRSCH, *Racismes. L'autre et son visage,* Paris, Cerf, 1988, p. 89-102.

3. A.K. GIRI, Art. Cit., pp. 207-208.

4. This requires the further elaboration of the social, economic and political dimension of the Levinasian concept of the heteronomous responsibility by and for the other. For that purpose we refer to our studies: 'The Other in Me: Interpersonal and Social Responsibility in Emmanuel Levinas', in Revista Pörtuguesa de Filosofia, 62(2006), pp. 631-649; *The Wisdom of Love in the Service of Love. Emmanuel Levinas on Justice, Peace, and Human Rights*, Milwaukee, Marquette University Press, 2002, 2003 (2nd ed.), 213 p.
5. A. K. GIRI, Art. cit., p. 208.

6

Amartya Sen and Paul Ricœur on Participative Development and Freedom

Kuruvilla Pandikattu SJ

Current development theories have been dominated by what can be called the 'human development school',[1] widely popularised by the annual Human Development Reports[2] of the United Nations Human Development Programme, and whose conceptual roots are to be found in the works of the economist and Nobel Prize winner Amartya Sen. "Development can be seen, it is argued here, as a process of expanding the real freedoms that people enjoy."[3] So opens *Development as Freedom*. He identifies two reasons for viewing freedom as central to the process of development. First, there is an evaluative reason, for "assessment of progress has to be done primarily in terms of whether the freedoms that people have are enhanced." And second, there is the instrumental reason, for "achievement of development is thoroughly dependent on the free agency of people."[4]

Despite the fact that Amartya Sen is an agnostic, and his theory of development has built up itself in purely secular circles–indeed, Sen remains deeply traumatised by religion and the bloody conflicts between Muslims and Hindus he witnessed as a child in Bengal–,there are intriguing similarities between his capability approach and Catholic social thinking. I will illustrate that both show many similarities at a superficial level. However, when one goes into a deeper examination of Sen 's capability approach, one discovers a fundamental different anthropology which will have important consequences for the way poverty is conceived and the way it is tackled.

These insights of Sen, which are valuable to our exploration of freedom and development need to be at times complemented by that of Paul Ricœur, whose theistic and existential perspective complements and enhances Sen 's analysis. So in this paper it is not meant to be comparative but primarily philosophical. I try to look at some of the issues related to freedom and indicate discourse as a means of enhancing freedom. Since this paper is explicitly philosophical and open to both religious and non-religious, no theological ideas are brought in and God is bracketed out of our discussion.

First, I examine Sen 's understanding of poverty as lack of freedom. Then I study his profound understanding of development as freedom. This demands us to go beyond unfreedom and to make ourselves capable of wellbeing both as individual and social beings. Thirdly at the philosophical level, borrowing from Ricœur, we analyse the human fallibility which is a crucial issue while discussing freedom and which is intimately related to the various forms of unfreedom. Finally from an agnostic point of view, we see Sen 's and Ricœur's suggestion that creative discourse could be a means to befriend human fallibility and cultivate freedom both as a means and an end. Such a notion of freedom as well as development fits in very well with Gandhian notions of them.

Poverty as Lack of Freedom

Since its emergence, development theory has been concerned with the achievement of better human lives, but, Sen argues, by focusing on the possession of commodities, development theory has failed to include the very nature of human living and has failed to take into account the fundamental aspects of the life that a human being succeeds in living.[5]

Sen 's capability approach characterises human well-being in terms of what people are or do (like being healthy, reading or writing, taking part in the life of the community), which Sen calls functionings. And more specifically, as he considers freedom as one of the most basic aspects of human life, well-being is to be assessed not as much in what people are or do, but in what they are *able* to be or choose to do (like being able to be healthy, being able to read and write, being able to participate in the life of the community), which Sen calls capabilities. A capability is "a person's ability to do valuable acts or reach valuable states of being," it "represents the alternative combinations of things a person is able to do or be."[6]

While functionings are distinct aspects of the living conditions or different achievements for living a certain type of life, capabilities are the real notions of freedom and reflect the real opportunities people have to lead or achieve a certain type of life. Sen often refers to the example of the fasting monk and the starving child. While both show similar level of functioning (nutritional deficiency), the fasting monk has the capability to be adequately nourished (he could eat should he choose so), while the starving child does not have that capability. Poverty is thus seen as lack of freedom, as an unfreedom. In this sense development can be regarded as "the removal of various types of unfreedoms that leave people with little choice and little opportunity of exercising their reasoned agency."[7] Development is a matter of liberating people from what makes them unfree, from what prevents them to live a life the they would have the reason to choose and value.[8]

Thus, for Sen 's capability approach, human freedom is the aim of development, and poverty prevents people to reach their full human freedom. For example, a clever tribal teenager may dream of going to go to the university and be a doctor, but her freedom to live such a life is crippled by the poverty of her family who cannot pay for her going to school and by the inability of the government to offer free education for all.[9]

Freedoms, Choices and Capabilities

But what does Sen really mean by 'freedom'? Sen defines freedom as a "real opportunity that we have to accomplish what we value."[10] He maintains that what is important in the process of development is not so much the quality of life that people are actually living, but the quality of life that they *choose* to live among an available set of functionings–a capability being "a set of vectors of functionings, reflecting the person's freedom to lead one type of life or another [...] *to choose from* possible livings."[11] As Sen summarizes it, "This approach focuses on the substantive freedoms that people have, rather than only on the particular outcomes with which they end up. For responsible adults, the concentration on freedom rather than only achievement has some merit, and it can provide a general framework for analysing individual advantage and deprivation in a contemporary society."[12]

It is interesting to note that, in this matter, Sen 's capability approach has many resemblances with the utilitarian consumer theory, with the focus on the freedom to choose to consume a particular bundle of functionings rather than on the preference to consume a particular bundle of market goods. The aim of development policies is to provide people with as many different functioning bundles as possible so that people can have the choice to pick some of them up, should they choose to do so.[13]

Capabilities as not Closed

Séverine Deneulin notes that Sen deliberately avoids identifying the capabilities that are valuable to promote (Deneulin 2007). Development is a matter of promoting the freedoms that people have reason to choose and value. It is up to the democratic processes in each society to work out what this 'reason to choose and value' means. Sen insists that his capability approach does not claim to contain an exhaustive evaluation of what is relevant for well-being. Eventually the choice of relevant capabilities that public policies ought to pursue has to be related to the underlying social concerns and values within a particular society. Sen calls this the "fundamental reason for incompleteness" of his approach. And even if it would not be a mistake to find a complete ordering of human well-being, we could not identify it in practice; this is what Sen calls "the pragmatic reason for incompleteness."[14] Despite the incompleteness of the capability approach, Sen argues that it still has a "cutting power", "both because of what it *includes* as potentially valuable and because of what it *excludes* from the list of objects to be weighted as intrinsically important."[15] Even though it is impossible to determine quality of life in an exhaustive and precise way, Sen concludes in two famous quotes that, "it is better to be vaguely right than precisely wrong,"[16] and that "babbling is not, in general, superior to being silent on matters that are genuinely unclear or undecided."[17]

Individual Freedom and the Common Good

The thrust of Sen 's capability approach to the development is that it be judged in terms of the expansion of substantive human freedoms. These substantive human freedoms are "seen in the form of individual capabilities to do things that a person has reason to value."[18] By situating the evaluative space of the quality of life in what individuals are able to be or do, Sen 's capability approach to development implies that the individuals are to be considered as the very subjects of development, but it does obviously not consider them as detached from the social setting in which the individuals breathe and live. Sen emphasises that the individuals are "quintessentially social creatures."[19] The freedom that each individual enjoys is "inescapably qualified and constrained by the social, political and economic opportunities that are available to us."[20] Institutions or societal arrangements are of central importance for promoting the freedoms of individuals. The development and the expansion of freedoms cannot occur without the presence of key institutions such as the market, public services, the judiciary system, political parties, the media, etc. As Sen puts it, such "a freedom-centred view [of development] calls for an institutionally integrated approach."[21]

Even if social arrangements or institutions are seen as very important elements in enhancing or impeding individual freedoms, they are still to be "investigated in terms of their contribution to enhancing and guaranteeing the substantive freedoms of individuals."[22] Sen does not ignore the importance of intrinsic social goods in the evaluation of human well-being, like for example democratic freedom. It is "a significant *ingredient*–a critically important *component*—of individual capabilities."[23] However, the importance and value of democratic freedom are only relevant to the extent that they enter as a component of individual human well-being, to the extent that it makes the lives of individuals better. Sen is very reluctant to approach development with a supra-individual subject. He underlines that all actions finally bear upon their effects on the lives that human beings live, lives which are only lived by the individuals and not by some meta-subject.[24]

The position according to which states of affairs should be evaluated only according to their goodness or badness *for* individuals is known as ethical individualism. The individual subjects are to be the unit of moral concern. However, ethical individualism leads to an excessive focus on the existing individual lives and directs attention away from the examination of the social structures and the historical explications of these structures, which are responsible for the conditions of life of the individuals today. It does not suffice to evaluate institutional arrangements by looking at their effects, positive or negative, upon individual dispositions such as individual freedoms. There is a strong case for assessing development in terms of these structures themselves and not only upon their consequences upon individual freedoms.

The Structures of Living Together

The idea of the common good is very close to the idea of 'structures of living together' put forward by the philosopher Paul Ricœur. He defined them as structures which belong to a particular historical community, which provide the conditions for individual lives to flourish and which are irreducible to interpersonal relations and yet bound up with these.[25] The common good could be seen as the sum of these structures of living together. It is irreducible to interpersonal relations. It is something that emerges from the life in common, from the 'living together' in human communities. Identifying the common good is a matter of identifying the set of all these structures of living together which provide the conditions for the individual lives to flourish. Among these structures, one finds for example the country's power structure, its social norms, its national identity or its political and democratic history.

To sum up, while Sen 's capability approach focuses on individuals, and then looks at institutional arrangements to promote the well-being of the individuals, which is a common good approach to development, focuses on the institutions themselves, as well as on the individuals, because it is precisely within these institutions that the individuals are formed and nurtured. Because the institutional fact is constitutive of a person's individuality, it is not only the well-being of individuals which is to be secured but also the well-being of these institutions. But how is this common good to be fostered? How to promote these structures of living together which sustain the good life in common?

Political Participation and Capability Approach

One of the most foundational building blocks of Sen 's capability approach is "the ability of people to help themselves and to influence the world."[26] Throughout his works, Sen emphasises that people should not be seen as the passive spoon-fed patients of the social welfare institutions, but "have to be seen as being actively involved in shaping their own destiny."[27] In that respect, the capability approach grants a fundamental role to the public debate and democratic decision-making, or in more generic terms, to the ability to participate in the life of the community and to take decisions in matters that affect one's own life and the life of fellow-human beings. This ability "to do something not only for oneself but also for the other members of the society" can even be considered as "one of the elementary freedoms that people have reason to value, [...] even among people who lead very deprived lives in material terms."[28]

Democratic freedom or the ability to participate in the life of the community, has three fundamental roles in the capability approach to development.[29] First, it is of the fundamental intrinsic worth to human well-being, it is "a significant ingredient, a critically important component"[30] of the capabilities that the individuals have reason to choose and value. Second, given the open-endedness and the plurality of the different capabilities that people have reason to choose and value, "there is a strong methodological case for emphasizing the need to assign explicitly evaluative weights to different components of the quality of life (or of well-being) and then to place the chosen weights for open discussion and critical scrutiny."[31] The democratic freedom plays a crucial role in specifying and choosing the capabilities that are worthwhile to be promoted. It is essential in specifying a society's underlying values and in choosing the capabilities that are valuable and worthwhile to be pursued. Referring to the choice between cultural tradition and poverty on the one hand and modernity and material prosperity on the other hand, Sen writes: „ If a traditional way of life has to be sacrificed to escape grinding poverty or minuscule longevity, then it is the people directly involved who must have the opportunity to participate in deciding what should be chosen."[32] The role of participation also extends to the choices of the means that will bring about the chosen priorities, and hence to the kind of policies required to promote the chosen capabilities. Third, the democratic freedom is also of constitutive importance in value formation. It clarifies and constructs a society's values and priorities, builds consensus and achieves compromises that prevent conflicts.

One might object that such an emphasis on political participation to promote social justice, or even that equating political participation with commitment to the common good, is very naïve. Political participation obviously occurs in a context of power inequalities with conflicting interests. The world ideological systems and the world configuration of political power impose their constraints. Along with these power imbalances with the outside world, which affect a country's margin of manoeuvre, one has also to include the power imbalances within the political community itself in which political freedom is exercised. Although every person might formally have an equal political voice, those who command more resources and education are likely to better be able to influence the decisions to their own advantage.

Drèze and Sen are not ignorant of the influence of socio-economic inequalities upon inequalities in political participation. They note that these inequalities "give disproportionate power to those who command crucial resources such as income, education and influential connections."[33] This has much to do with the tension that Sen has pointed out but little explored, namely the tension between the freedom to participate in the market economic exchange and the freedom to participate in the life of the political community. Among the capabilities that people have reason to choose and value in Sen 's capability approach, lies not only the fundamental capability to shape one's own destiny by participating in the life of the community, but also the fundamental capability to participate in the markets: "We have good reasons to buy and sell, to exchange, and to seek lives that can flourish on the basis of transactions. To deny that freedom in general would be in itself a major failing of society."[34] People should have the fundamental „right to interact economically with each other", and failing to grant that right would be a significant "social loss".[35]

Sen warns however that the freedom[36] in markets should go hand in hand with the freedom in other institutions, so that extensive freedoms of some in the markets do not override the freedoms of others in participating in the life of the community: "While emphasising the significance of transaction and the right of economic participation (including the right to seek employment freely), and the direct importance of market-related liberties, we must not lose sight of the complementarity of these liberties with the freedoms that come from the operation of other (non-market) institutions."[37] This is particularly important because, although the freedom to pursue market transactions lead to efficiency results, they may also result in greater inequalities, and corrective measures will need to be taken so that the freedom of all in the different institutions, market and non-market, may be guaranteed. For example, extensive freedoms in market transactions may result in environmental loss or in reduced lower access to health or educational facilities by lower income groups. Sen emphasizes however that the remedy to correct the unfreedom that the market freedoms might generate "has to lie in more freedom–including that of public discussion and participatory political decisions."[38]

Drèze and Sen insist that the presence of inequalities cannot justify the authoritarian regimes that would provide a more equal basis for exercising political freedom. Even if a perfectly benevolent dictator would provide all the fundamental human freedom (so that no member of that political community would be lacking of food, shelter, health, education, etc.), it would violate an important aspect of human well-being if it deprived the members of the community, say in the organization of the community. This is why Drèze and Sen insist that the *only* route that can be taken to promote human freedom is enhancing the political power of the unprivileged,[39] so that they can exercise their political freedom on the same equality basis as the more privileged.

Drèze and Sen propose two ways for enhancing the political power of the underprivileged and for responding to the problem of the poor people's claims being trumped by the claims and interests of the more powerful.[40] Firstly, the capability of the underprivileged for self-assertion must be enhanced through offering incentives for them to organize in political organizations through which they will gain sufficient power to counteract the power of the privileged. Secondly, a sense of solidarity must be created between the most privileged and the underprivileged (e.g. intellectuals and higher social classes speaking on behalf of the underprivileged and defending their interests).

But the question remains how to bring about these two crucial factors that Drèze and Sen point out are needed. If a country is driven by powerful elites who are not sensitive to the needs of the less privileged, and if powerful elites who are directing policy decisions impede the poor from organizing themselves politically (for example by maintaining low educational standards, by not improving the public education system), one can have legitimate doubts about how these changes are ever to emerge in unequal societies.

Sen, a Smithian liberal by inspiration, gives prime importance to freedom as an ideal and process and not a product and so he relates freedom to the struggles of the people in search of collective well-being and development. He acknowledges that development is a multifaceted and at the same time integrated goal (Maliekal 2002: ch 1). The themes of autonomy, agency, freedom, resistance to ultimate injustice and deprivation are found often in Sen 's writings.

Influenced by Adam Smith, Robert Malthus, David Ricardo, Karl Marx and John Stuart Mill, Sen acknowledges that the natural interdisciplinary perspective of the classical political economy is profoundly important for analyzing economic problems,"[41] like hunger. He has adopted a broad perspective on issues like hunger and poverty, class conflict, ideological alienation, etc. We limit out treatment to development as freedom, wellbeing, capability and entitelement.

Development as Freedom

The notion development as freedom is the sum total of many an analytical framework developed by Sen, while grappling with several burning issues of the Third World. Issues that he has dealt with–famine and endemic hunger, rampant poverty and growing unemployment, population explosion and missing women–are indications of persistent inequalities and multiple alienations suffered by the exploited, many unfreedom fettering them.[42]

In his vision of economics as the science of human welfare, Sen departs from the classical standpoint, that lays importance on wealth and its creation. He is also at odds with the neo-classical approach to income, whether personal or national, which is regarded as the sole measuring rod of this wealth. He looks beyond wealth and to freedom as the end and means of development, laying stress both on the individuals as well as on the communities in the process of development (Sen 1999a: 7-14). Various freedoms can be viewed from under the aspects of opportunities (e.g., longevity of life, financial security, sound health, peaceful and crime-free environment, etc.). They can also be viewed from under the aspect of the process of attaining freedom (i.e., participation in the political process, deliberating regarding collective decision making and social choices) (Sen 1999a: 11).

Freedom, being not only the primary end of the development, but also its principle means, has to be understood in its links to various other kinds of freedom. Political freedom, like free speech and election, helps to promote economic security. Social opportunities, in the form of education and health facilities, augment economic freedom. According to Sen, economic freedom in turn can create personal wealth and public resources, which are needed for social development. Such mutually enriching and synergetic dimensions of freedom has its implications for our understanding of development as freedom.[43]

Freedom involves the need to assess the requirements of removing various unfreedom, which the members of the society may suffer from. This process is intimately related to the process of economic growth and accumulation of physical and human capital, but its reach and scope go beyond the different types of income. Thus there is no one homogenous and immutable criterion for well being. There are varied aspects in the process of development, each of which requires attention and will have various weight and ranking. They will help us to overcome the various unfreedom to varying degrees and will collectively foster freedom both for the individual and the community.

Such freedom has both an instrumental and constitutive character. If we recognize freedom as development, it is both instrumental in overcoming unfreedom and constitutive, in empowering oneself and others. Thus the various freedoms are interrelated and mutually advancing.[44]

The process of human development corresponds to these multiple nterconnected freedoms, and involves multiplicity of institutions and mechanism in the society involving private initiatives and public arrangements. The people are to be not the means of developments but the end of the process of it and are actively involved in shaping their own destiny. So they are active participants and not passive recipients of the process and programmes of development. The state and society play their extensive roles of strengthening and safeguarding such human capabilities for the promotion of freedom. But theirs is essentially a supportive role and do not provide the people with the finished products and projects.

4. Freedom as Enabling the Other

Thus for Sen freedom is essentially both individual and social. It is here that we can draw more the insight of Ricour on the necessary philosophical relation between oneself and the other. Following Emmanuel Levinas, and to some extent Martin Heidegger, Ricœur would hold that the other is constitutive of oneself, not merely ontologically but also existentially . This explains the title of one of his famous books: *Oneself as the Other!*.[45]

Therefore E. Levinas[46] calls for a universal responsibility towards the other. He refers to "the Face"as real expression of the person, avoiding by this way any economic, social or cultural context, and using the traditional ancient vision of the other' singularity. In this context the social interactions with the others have to be ethical. If this feature disappears, then the person becomes an abstract entity and any destructive excess may happen, for instance the Shoal, the gulags, genocide, etc. The specificity of the person is, therefore, to be embedded in a set of normative relationships. Setting the primacy of ethics, he differs from the usual phenomenological view, which only analyses intention and the rights-obligations interaction. This ethical social relationship with the other has to be described through the wording of the infinite or absolute since "it allows to think far ahead from what it is possible to think". Therefore, it opens the way to transcendence and commitment.

The other, as a person, i.e. a human being autonomous, is able to decide in a rational and responsible way, but still remains vulnerable due to weaknesses in his capability set. The feeling of solidarity, and then of responsibility, come from the confrontation to this vulnerability, and to the suffering that may result of it. It is an absolute and sudden responsibility for the well-being of the other. This ethical relationship that is suddenly generated when encountering the other's *face* has nothing to do with the evaluated responsibility based on consequences and benefits as referred to the utilitarian view. It implies the capacity to imagine the situation of another and to have compassion for that situation, then to feel responsible of the well-being happiness of the other and to help him/her increase his capacity to live a decent life[47]. Such an ethical behaviour relates to a transcendental attitude.

For Levinas, which refers to the *face* of the other as an absolute, the priority is always given to the other and it may be necessary to sacrifice personal freedom to ensure the happiness of the others. This is the extreme case of an infinite responsibility. However this ethical vision brings two key elements extremely useful to ensure social sustainability. First, he introduces and explains in absolute terms that the other is also a person that requires all attention, second, it gives to everyone an infinite responsibility for the well-being, and the happiness of others, those who are near as well as those who are far away, or have not come yet. As he said : "All men [and women] deserving such a name are responsible towards the others."[48]

Freedom and Fallibility

Why there are so many unfreedoms? Why is it that as a community we are not always interested in the development of freedom for ourselves and for the society. In this section, consciously I do not have recourse to a religious response in terms of sin, reconciliation and redemption.

Description of Human Fallibility

The fact that human being can be observed from various different perspectives, all of which may be justified but not always compatible with each other, is puzzling. Added to it is the phenomenal fact of the existence of evil in the human society. The good that we know we should do and the freedom that we can foster are not always attended to. While the rational basis of Amartya Sen's philosophy does not answer this problem, the existential and symbolic basis of Ricœur addresses this problem.

Though it is very difficult to give any explanation to human fallibility, which causes the various unfreedom, Ricœur accepts the situations where people do not always choose decisions that will remove the many unfreedom. So he affirms: "Evil is something that is and that should not be, but of which one cannot say why it is. It is what it should not be" (Ricœur 1988 60-2). The vulnerability or fragility of political communities is precisely the locus by which human responsibility emerges: "We are rendered responsible by the fragile," adds Ricœur (Ricœur 1996: 28)[49] Since the structures of living together is rendered fragile by fallibility, Ricœur invites us to think about the crucial role of moral principle given below: "Because there is evil, the aim of the 'good life' has to be submitted to the test of moral obligation, which might be described in the following terms: Act solely in accordance with the maxim by which you can wish at the same time that what ought not to be, namely evil, will indeed not exist" (Ricœur 1992: 218). In other words evil forces us to be responsible and to be moral.[50]

The analysis of the fundamental possibility of human will in Ricœur's *Le volontaire et l'involontaire* has shown that there is a break, a wound, a non-agreement within human person himself or herself. This non-agreement makes it impossible for him to see himself transparently. Ricœur is not satisfied just with this analysis. The fundamental structure of the will, which he has traced out, is only a preliminary result in view of the fact of human failures and fallibility. Since it is an absurd fallibility, it cannot be captured though the description of its own nature. Furthermore it presents an alien object which can be philosophically approached only through concrete experiences.

Thus human fallibility provides us an understanding of the possibility of evil for human freedom without implying its necessity. As such fallibility is a concept open to elaboration from a purely reflective basis. Fallibility as the possibility for evil is taken as a primary characteristic of human existence. With this concept of fallibility human existence is the place or possibility for the manifestation of evil.[51]

In two different ways Ricœur tries to capture and describe this *fallibility*. The transition from innocence to guilt can be understood only in concrete expressions of human experiences, that is, through the act of confession, or avowal *(Bekenntnis)*, which later leads him/her to take responsibility for human actions. In *La symbolique du mal*, he examines therefore the symbolic language of the experiences of guilt. But before that he studies the breaking point of the evil. Thus he continues his description of the fundamental human possibilities, which he had begun and executed in a preliminary and abstract form in *Le volontaire et l'involontarie* by interpreting the structures of the will as fallible. The fallibility describes a weakness which makes the evil possible. It lies in the "structure of mediation between the poles of finite and infinite nature of man".[52]

Interpretation of Fallibility

Ricœur has sought to show the situation of the human being as being in between the finite and the infinite, as having a certain *in-betweenness* or *disproportion*, all of which is constitutive of his fallibility or the possibility for the Rupture. Thus in relation to knowledge there is a disproportion of *finite perspective* and *infinite word;* in relation to willing there is a disproportion between finite *character* and infinite *well-being* and in relation to feeling there is a disproportion between *pleasure* and *happiness*. This could be illustrated as follows:

	Infinite Orientation	*Finite Fulfilment*	*Mediation*
Knowing	Infinite Word (Verb)	Finite Perspective	Pure Imagination
Willing	Well-being	Character	Respect
Feeling	Happiness	Pleasure	Mind
	Original Affirmation	Existential Difference	Human Mediation

The fallibility is exposed through evil. Otherwise we can say that fallibility is the condition or the potential for evil. Thus fallibility has double sense. It is the breaking point of the evil, so to say, the weak point in the chain. In this sense fallibility is the original situation, from which evil emerges. The evil in fact points to an original situation of innocence. The *depravity* of human beings lies in a longing for a non-guaranteed perfection. The original situation of innocence is nowhere present. It can be imagined of through the existing situation determined by the evil and set apart from it. So one can imagine this original situation of innocence, as happens in the myths. Thus the myths of fall are always connected with the myths of creation and those of innocence.

Over and above, fallibility means not just the breaking point of the evil, but also the capability to sin and to commit evil. It requires only one step to move from the vulnerability to the *actuality* of evil. "To say that man is fallible is to affirm at once that the limitation of one being, that does not fall with itself, is the original weakness out of which evil emerges. Further, the evil can emerge out of this weakness only because it dares."[53] Such a daring demands from us responsibility.

Conclusion: Responsibility by Discourse[54]

In spite of some legitimate and some exaggerated criticisms of postmodernity, I hold that collective and creative discourse can be the crucial means, if not only means, to go against such dehumanising tendencies towards unfreedom.

All humans seek freedom and development. Still there is a collective rapture expressed in terms of exploitative and exploiting structures of social sins and personal fallibility. Therefore in conclusion plead for a culture of discourse as a collective corrective against such inherent tendencies that further unfreedom.

P. Ricœur does not admit the rule of infinite responsibility, which can be accepted and internalised by very few people, as suggested by Levinas and Jonas.[55] He does not admit either the short-term egoistic view of utilitarianism, since he also refers to the inalienable right person. He defines, as a primary capability, the capacity of a person to impute responsibility on the current actions. This capacity is called "imputatio" and expresses the ability to freely assume finite actions and to recognise the corresponding impacts on the others[56]. More generally, he shows that obligations have to be mostly fulfilled first, much before associated rights can be exercised. This demonstrates the relevance of his "imputatio" theory of responsibility and, by the way, its "multiple realisability"[57] in various contexts.

Evaluation of development and freedom is vast and therefore there is no one distinct model for dealing with the problem of the results of the various development models. Since the need for development is part of the process of decision-making of the politicians and consumers, both politically and personally it obviously has something to do with the morals and responsibility.

Amartya Sen 's and Paul Ricouer's answer to this question is a concept of (moral) responsibility by *discourse*. In his *The Argumentative Indian*, he pleads for such a culture of discourse. If one agrees to the thought that moral responsibility is aimed at the idea of improving social relationships, then responsibility has to be construed in a way which takes into consideration the needs, rights, or interests of all affected parties. For this it is necessary to hear the affected parties beforehand in a real discourse. Responsibility *ex post* is in this setting only of interest in so far as it affects future actions. The objective of the discourse is the clarification of the validity claims (*Geltungsansprüche*).[58]

These validity claims, it may be remembered, do not only concern moral norms but they are concerned as well with the clarification of the perception of situations. This concept of responsibility overcomes the philosophy of consciousness and realizes a philosophy of communication. It is an ethical notion which does not try to force substantive morals on anybody; it is not, however, an empty concept. The problem of the moral solipsism is overcome and at the same time no particular moral action is unjustly favoured (Cf STAHL 2007).

The moral responsibility, as it is understood here, has to be actively assumed by those who act. This fact underlines the pragmatic character of responsibility and simplifies the understanding of the fact that the responsibility as discourse has the future as its temporal horizon. The future as focus of responsibility is also a plausible thought considering the usual understanding of responsibility. Whenever we hold somebody responsible for something that has happened, we do so with a perspective of avoiding future mistakes. Ricœur affirms that it is the meaning of responsibility to accept something that will happen as the result of one's action as a representative of oneself.[59]

The pragmatic character of responsibility is ascribed reflexively also answers the question of the need for God. In this case there is no need for an external agency like God or some personal or societal construction. Also the discourse is a guarantor of publicity, which has been widely recognized as a requirement for ethics.

The realization of this principle has to be imagined as follows: A person who wants to be responsible realizes that he/she is about to make a decision which affects the rights or interests of others. Before acting he is now obliged to start a discourse with others. The topic of this discourse is the reality of the situation one is in as well as the norms which are to be applied. In the ideal case all participants of the discourse reach a consensus and the right action to take becomes clear. The consensus, this has to be noted, is always a temporal one. Under the impression of new the facts or perceptions the result of the discourse can be the topic of the next discourse.

Such idea of responsibility may appear to be almost simplistic. The numerous problems arising from the implementation as well as the implied conditions were not discussed here. Nevertheless I do not think that this concept is either trivial or without relevance to moral philosophy or to human development. Given that a consensus or a strong majority decision is achieved, there is a strong assumption that this consensus has a higher legitimacy than anything any philosopher in his/her study or any engineer at his/her workplace could have come up with. Furthermore, the result of the discourse takes all points of view into consideration. This leads to one central advantage of the discourse which takes into consideration the concerns and knowledge of the affected parties which is a prerequisite of responsibility.[60]

Another advantage of discourse is the possible inclusion of the three described methods of dealing with development and its results. Furthermore, it opens a perspective of the responsibility of the collectives. While individuals are losing the ability and the knowledge to deal with development paradigms, those abilities are taken over by collectives such as corporations, NGOs or bureaucracies. The conventional notion of responsibility does not allow these entities as the subjects of responsibility. Our notion of responsibility would render such an imputation possible, without which the notion of responsibility does not seem to be of any use in the modern society.

Coming to our contemporary Indian context when we reflect on the development we have to take seriously the "call for responsibility"[61] specially towards the weaker sections of our nations, including the tribals, dalits, women and rural poor.[62] The development is possible only when we can enter into a discourse with them at different levels including their own humdrum lives. Development implies that we regard them as constituting our own identity and self. Thus a healthy, creative and respectful dialogue interlocutes the participative and progressive freedom and development. A prospect Mahatma Gandhi would have loved, had he been alive today!

Notes

1. I am indebted to two excellent articles by Séverine Deneulin "Poverty: Amartya Sen Compared to Catholic Social Thinking" accessed from internet *www.theology-centre.org/leuven28_04.doc. And Séverine Deneulin "A Freedom-centered view of development in RICŒUR's ethics" accessed from www.st-edmunds.cam.ac.uk/vhi/rioeur/papers/deneulin.pdf.*
2. It is to be noted that Human Development Index (HDI) for India is 0.611, which gives India a rank of 126th out of 177. See *hdr.undp.org/hdr2006/statistics/countries/country_fact_sheets/*

cty_fs_IND.html. In 2004 and 2005 the position was 127. The HDI is a comparative measure of life expectancy, literacy, education, and standard of living for countries worldwide. It is a standard means of measuring well-being, especially child welfare. It is used to determine and indicate whether a country is a developed, developing, or underdeveloped country and also to measure the impact of economic policies on quality of life. See *http://en.wikipedia.org/wiki/Human_Development_Index*. However one may disagree with the procedure followed with HDI, India that claims to be an economic power just cannot remain complacent.

3. Sen (1999a:3).
4. All quotes are from Sen (1999a:4).
5. See for example Sen (1985 a,b, 1987 a,b, 1988, 1992, 1993, 1999a).
6. Sen (1993:30).
7. Sen (1999a:xii).
8. Poverty as a lack of freedom has been at the core of Catholic Social Thinking. For example, one reads in *Gaudium et Spes*:

   "Only in freedom can man direct himself towards goodness. Our contemporaries make much of this freedom and pursue it eagerly; and rightly to be sure. [...] For its part, authentic freedom is an exceptional sign of the divine image within man. For God has willed that man remains 'under the control of his own decisions'." (GS §17).

   "Human freedom is often crippled when a man encounters extreme poverty, just as it withers when he indulges in too many of life's comforts and imprisons himself in a kind of splendid isolation." (GS §31).
9. Deneulin (2007a).
10. Sen (1993:30).
11. Sen (1992:40). Italics added.
12. Sen (2002:83).
13. Sev criticises this approach of Sen: Such a capability approach remains however a theory of individual choice, which has little to offer for guiding collective choices. First, collective choices, such as the government's actions to provide its population with the conditions for them to live long and healthy lives through the provision of public health services, cannot be assessed at the

level of each individual's freedom to choose that particular functioning but will have to be assessed at the level of each individual's achievements and not each individual's freedoms. There are areas of human life, such as health and education, which cannot be left up to 'people's choices'. Public actions will often have to be guided by the concern of making people function in one way or another rather than by the concern for giving them the opportunities to function should they choose so. This is particularly the case where externalities are involved. For example, when dealing with environmental problems, it is more relevant that policies ensure that people do live in a non-polluted environment, rather than make them able to do so, should they choose or not. Given that individual choices have important consequences upon other people's lives, and given that an individual never lives alone and that human choices are deeply interconnected with other people's lives, the focus on individual capabilities rather than functioning as political goal may lead to important losses in well-being.

This is why the freedoms or capabilities that development policies should promote are to be understood as good states of doings or beings rather than possible states of beings or doings, should one choose to exercise these states or not. The freedoms that the capability approach should speak about are best considered as excellences, as fundamental properties of human life which have to be perfected. But it is not only in its conception of freedom as choice that Sen's capability approach betrays its commitment to liberalism, it does so even more by considering the good human life as freedom.

14. Sen (1992:49).
15. Sen (1992:49).
16. Sen (1987a:6).
17. Sen (1992:134).
18. Sen (1999a:56).
19. Sen (2002:81).
20. Sen (1999a:xii).
21. Drèze and Sen (2002:20).
22. Sen (1999a: xiii).
23. Sen (2002:79).

24. Sen (2002).
25. Ricœur's (1992:194) original definition refers to institution: "By institution, we understand the structure of *living together* as this belongs to a historical community, a structure irreducible to interpersonal relations and yet bound up with these."
26. Sen (1999a:18).
27. Sen (1999a:53).
28. Drèze and Sen (1995:106).
29. See Sen (1999b).
30. Sen (2002:79).
31. Sen (1999a:81).
32. Sen (1999a:31).
33. Drèze and Sen (2002:28).
34. Sen (1999a:112).
35. All quotes in the sentence from Sen (1999a:26).
36. Sen tends to use the term 'freedoms' frequently. In this paper, I limit to the use of 'freedom' as a singular entity.
37. Sen (1999a:116).
38. Sen (1999a:123).
39. Drèze and Sen (2002:376).
40. Drèze and Sen (2002:29).
41. Maliekal (2002).
42. For this section I am dependent on the excellent work of Jose D Maliekal, An Enquiry into the *Religious Consciousness of the Dalit Madigas of Konaseema in Encounter with Catholicism*, PhD Dissert. Chennai, University of Madras, 2002.
43. Sen (1999a: 10-11).
44. Sen (1999a: 33-37).
45. Ricœur (1992).
46. Lévinas E., 1983, *Le temps et l'autre,* PUF, Paris.
47. Lévinas E., 1974, *Autrement qu'être ou au-delà de l'essence,* Nijhoff, La Haye.
48. Cited in Dubois & Mahieu (2007).

49. According to Ricœur, we are "rendered responsible by the fragile" since by an "appeal" or "injunction" another "declares us responsible" or "calls us to responsibility" (Ricœur 1996: 16, 17). Ricour adds further: "Responsible for what, one may ask? For what is fragile, one is henceforth inclined to answer. ... one becomes responsible for harm because, first of all, one is responsible for others." (Ricœur 2000: 29).
50. Cf. Deneulin (2007a).
51. Pandikattu (1998: 63).
52. Pandikattu (1998: 68-70).
53. Pandikattu (1998: 68-70).
54. Bernd Carsten Stahl, "Responsibility for Technological Development by Discourse" *http://www.cse.dmu.ac.uk/~bstahl/publications/2000_Resp_tech_dev.pdf.*
55. Levinas calls for a universal responsibility towards the other. He refers to "the Face"as real expression of the person, avoiding by this way any economic, social or cultural context, and using the traditional Ancient vision of the other' Lévinas E., 1983, *Le temps et l'autre,* PUF, Paris. Further, already in 1979 Hans Jonas raises the issue of the responsibility towards the future generations. Faced with the depletion of natural resources, only a decision of responsibility expressed by "precautionary principles" can set the priorities. It ensures that future generations won't suffer from any decision taken by the current generation. Jonas, H., 1979, *Le principe responsabilité,* Cerf, Paris. See *http://www.ethiclaw.dk/publication/consumersfoodethics.pdf.* accessed in July, 2007.
56. Ricœur P., 1995, *Le Juste,* Esprit, Paris.
57. Nussbaum M., 2000, *Women and Human Development: The Capabilities Approach,* Cambridge University Press.
58. With Habermas, on whose theory of communicative action (HABERMAS 1981) this model is built, one can differentiate three claims of validity: truth ("*Wahrheit*"), (normative) correctness ("*Richtigkeit*"), and veracity ("*Wahrhaftigkeit*").
59. Ricœur (1990, 341). Jonas even goes so far as to see responsibility as a moral complement of our ontological condition of being in time.
60. Cf Stahl (2007).
61. Franz-Xaver Kaufmann (1992) *Der Ruf nach Verantwortung,* Freiburg im Breisgau.

62. An excellent survey of caste and freedom is found in Swami Dharmathertha, *No Freedom with Caste: The Menace of Hindu Imperialism,* G Aloysius (ed.) Delhi: Media House 2004.

References

Deneulin, Séverine (2007a), "Poverty: Amartya Sen Compared to Catholic Social Thinking" and accessed from *internet www.theology-centre.org/leuven28_04.doc on June, 2007.*

——— (2007b), "A Freedom-centered View of Development in Ricœur's ethics" Accessed from *www.st-edmunds.cam.ac.uk/vhi/ Ricœur/papers/deneulin.pdf.*

Dubois, Jean-Luc and MAHIEU, François-Regis (2004), "Institutionalizing Solidarity and Responsibility," Forum on Faith and Development: Practice and Theory Seminar *26th - 27th November 2004,* Von Hügel Institute, St. Edmund's College, Cambridge

Drèze, Jean, and Sen, Amartya (1995), *India: Economic Development and Social Opportunity.* Delhi, Oxford University Press.

——— (2002), *India: Development and Participation.* Delhi, Oxford University Press.

Habermas, J. (1981), *Theorie des kommunikativen Handelns I.* Frankfurt a. M.

Jonas, H. (1979), *Le principe responsabilité,* Cerf, Paris.

Kaufmann, Franz-Xaver (1992), *Der Ruf nach Verantwortung,* Freiburg im Breisgau.

Levinas E. (1974), *Autrement qu'être ou au-delà de l'essence,* Nijhoff, La Haye.

——— (1983), *Le temps et l'autre,* PUF, Paris

Maliekal, Jose D. (2002), *An Enquiry into the Religious Consciousness of the Dalit Madigas of Konaseema in Encounter with Catholicism,* PhD Dissert. Chennai, University of Madras.

Nussbaum, M. (2000), *Women and Human Development: The Capabilities Approach,* Cambridge University Press.

Pandikattu, K. (1998), *Idols to Die, Symbols to Live: Dynamic Interaction between Language, Reality and the Divine,* Intercultural Pub, New Delhi.

Ricoeur, Paul (1988), Philosophie de la volonte, vol 1. Le volontaire et l'invollontaire, Philosophie de l'espirt, Paris, Aubier, 1950, reprint 1988.

——— (1995), *Le Juste*, Esprit, Paris.

——— (1996), 'Fragility and Responsibility' in R Kearney (ed) *Paul Ricœur: The Hermeneutics of Action*. London: Sage.

——— (2000), 'The Concept of Responsibility' in *The Just*. Chicago: University of Chicago Press.

——— (1992), *One Self as Another*. Kathleen Blamey, Trans., Chicago: University of Chicago Press. Translation of Ricœur, Paul (1990): *Soi-même comme un autre*. Paris

Sen, Amartya K. (1985a), *Commodities and Capabilities*. Amsterdam: North-Holland.

——— (1985b), 'Well-Being Agency and Freedom: The Dewey Lectures 1984'. *Journal of Philosophy*. 82/4: 169-221.

——— (1987a), *On Ethics and Economics*. Oxford: Basil Blackwell.

———(1987b), *The Standard of Living*. Cambridge: Cambridge University Press.

——— (1988), 'The Concept of Development'. In Behram and Srinivasan 1988, eds. *Handbooks of Development Economics*. Vol. 1. Elsevier: North-Holland. 3-23.

——— (1992), *Inequality Re-examined*. Oxford: Clarendon Press.

——— (1993), 'Capability and Well-Being'. In M. Nussbaum and A. Sen . *The Quality of Life*. Oxford: Clarendon Press, 30-53.

——— (1999a), *Development as Freedom* Oxford: Oxford University Press.

——— (1999b), 'Democracy as Universal Value'. *Journal of Democracy*. 10/3: 3-17.

——— (2002), 'Symposium on Development as Freedom: Response to Commentaries'. *Studies in Comparative International Development*. 37/2: 78-86.

——— (1995), Argumentative Indian, Penguin: London.

Stahl, Bernd Carsten (2007), "Responsibility for Technological Development by Discourse", *http://www.cse.dmu.ac.uk/~bstahl/publications/2000_Resp_tech_dev.pdf*

7

Amartya Sen's Development as Freedom: An Inter-disciplinary Appreciation

Binoy Pichalakkatt SJ

Introduction

The Nobel laureate Amartya Sen introduces a new way of looking at the multifaceted problems of poverty and injustice through his ideas of development as freedom.[1] The most original and creative characteristic of his thinking is to see development from the perspective of the poor and suffering and to respond to this vision by searching for effective grass root strategies to transform the oppressive structures existing in different parts of the world. In this way, Sen opens the door toward bringing about a just society where there are enough opportunities for all the people to develop their capabilities. Should the Church take into account the insights from individuals like Amartya Sen in its official teachings on Justice and development? Can the Church be open to secular theories on development? If so how far or to what extent? The scope of this paper is to find out how Amartya Sen and Catholic Social Teaching together can contribute to bring forth justice and development in society. We start with the harsh realities of our times, which is followed by a brief account of Amartya Sen's view on *Development as Freedom*.[2] Next we expose the important milestones in the history of the Catholic social teaching of the Church. Both lead to the emergence of an interdisciplinary approach to development without undermining justice and human rights. This holistic approach to development ensures the importance of political participation and democratic freedom for the common good and individual good.

Context: Forms of Unfreedom

It is true that we live in an era of scientific advancement and technological development. The different regions of the globe are now more closely linked than they have ever been. And yet we also live in a world with remarkable deprivation, destitution and oppression. More than one out of four human beings are living on the earth in absolute poverty. Forty million persons die each year from hunger or hunger related problems. Fourteen million persons die every year before the age of five. One–fourth of the world's population, posses five-sixths of its riches. The richest fifth of the world's population enjoys 150 times the income of the poorest fifth. More than two million deaths a year are linked to polluted water and poor sanitation. 37.4 million acres of forests are destroyed every year. 13 million acres of land yearly lose their productive topsoil and are turned into wasteland. Many biologists fear that 25 percent of the world's remaining species will be wiped out within the next fifty years.[3] The fact of suffering is very often the result of human decisions. Those who have power decide to do harm to other human beings. The realities of injustice and victimization nurture the dreadful spectre of physical and ecological suffering. The internal and external wars in Lebanon, Palestine, Iraq, Sri Lanka, and Kashmir are evident of this fact. Very many people across the world suffer from varieties of unfreedom. Famines continue to occur in particular regions, denying to millions the basic freedom to survive. Undernutrition affects very large numbers of vulnerable human beings around the world. Great many people have little access to health care, to sanitary arrangements or to clean water often succumbing to premature mortality. The richer countries too often have deeply disadvantaged people, who lack basic opportunities of health care, or functional education or economic and social security. Further inequality between women and men afflicts the lives of millions of women and severely restricts the substantive freedoms that women enjoy. A great many people in different countries of the world are systematically denied political liberty and basic civil rights. Corruption, nepotism, religious antagonism, political decay and unbearable chaos have become the order of the day. It is in the context of various forms of unfreedom that Sen introduces his *Development as Freedom*.

Development as Freedom

Overcoming the contextual problems is a central part of the exercise of development. To counter the contextual problems we face, we have to see individual freedom as a social commitment and a social product. According to Sen Development consists of the removal of substantive unfreedom and substantive freedom is constitutive of development. So opens *Development as Freedom*. Amartya Sen identifies two reasons for viewing freedom as central to the process of development. First, there is an evaluative reason, for "assessment of progress has to be done primarily in terms of whether the freedoms that people have are enhanced." And second, there is the instrumental reason, for "achievement of development is thoroughly dependent on the free agency of people."[4] In an instrumental perspective there are five distinct types of freedom: Political freedom, economic facilities, social opportunities, transparency guarantees and protective security.[5] Each of these helps to advance the general capability of a person. Political freedoms refer to opportunities that people have to determine who should govern and on what principles, and also include the possibility to scrutinize and criticize authorities. Economic facilities refer to the opportunities that individuals respectively enjoy utilizing economic resources for the purpose of consumption or production or exchange. Social opportunities refer to the arrangements that society makes for education; health care and so on which influence the individual's substantive freedom to live better. Transparency guarantees deal with the need for openness that people can expect which means the freedom to deal with one another under guarantees of disclosure and lucidity. It has a clear role in preventing corruption and financial irresponsibility. Protective security implies the need to provide a social safety net for preventing the affected population from starvation and death.

Both in evaluative reason and instrumental reason attention is given to the "capabilities"[6] of persons to lead the kinds of lives they value. These capabilities can be enhanced by public policy and the public policy can be influenced by the effective use of participatory capabilities by the public. The two-way relationship is central to freedom. Further the freedom centred perspective has a specific concern to quality of life, the ability to survive rather than succumb to premature mortality. Development as freedom requires an integral approach to economic, social, and political activities, involving a variety of institutions (the state, the market, the legal system, the media, public inertest groups and public discussion forums) and many interactive agencies with a view to enhance the substantive freedoms of individuals. What people can positively achieve is influenced by economic opportunities, political liberties, social powers, and the encouragement and cultivation of initiatives. The institutional arrangements of these opportunities are also influenced by the exercise of people's freedoms, through the liberty to participate in social choice and in the making of public decisions that impel the progress of these opportunities.[7] This is the basic approach of Amartya Sen to development. Freedoms are not only the primary ends of development; they are also among its principal means.[8] The expansion of freedom is viewed as both. They can be called respectively the "constitutive role" and the "instrumental role".[9] The constitutive role of freedom relates to the importance of substantive freedom in enriching human life. The instrumental role of freedom concerns the way different kinds of rights, opportunities and entitlements contribute to the expansion of human freedom in general and thus to promoting development. Development, in this view, is the process of expanding human freedoms.

Choices of Excellence as Freedom

According to Amartya Sen what is important in the process of development is not so much the quality of life that people are actually living, but the quality of life that they choose to live among an available set of functioning. Development is a matter of promoting the freedoms that people has reason to choose and value. Poor people are given he choice between having political freedoms and fulfilling economic needs, they will invariably choose the latter. So there is a contradiction between the practice of democracy and its justification .It is up to the democratic processes in each society to work out what this 'reason to choose and value' means.[10] Since people have reason to want to eliminate economic deprivation and misery, they have reason enough for not insisting on political freedoms, which would get in the way of their real priorities. Amartya Sen observes that authoritarian rulers, who are themselves rarely affected by famines tend to lack the incentive to take timely measures to promote individual freedom to choose.[11] On the contrary democratic governments have strong incentives to undertake measures to avert famines and other such catastrophes. No famine has ever taken place in the history of the world in a functioning democracy be it economically rich or relatively poor.[12] Famines have occurred in ancient kingdoms and contemporary authoritarian societies, in primitive tribal communities and in modern technocratic dictatorships. Hence the freedoms that the developmental approach speaks about are best considered as choices of excellence, as fundamental properties of human life, which have to be perfected. Such a developmental approach remains however a theory of individual choice, which has little to offer for guiding collective choices.

Underdevelopment as Capability Deprivation

The best example for underdevelopment is poverty. According to Amartya Sen poverty must be seen as a deprivation of basic capabilities rather than merely as lowness of incomes.[13] But the perspective of capability does not involve any denial of low income since lack of income can be a principal reason for a person's capability deprivation. In the opinion of Amartya Sen poverty can be sensibly identified in terms of capability deprivation, which concentrates on deprivations that are intrinsically important.[14] It should be acknowledged that the instrumental relation between low income and low capability is variable between different communities and even between different individuals. What the capability perspective does in poverty analysis is to enhance the understanding of nature and causes of poverty and deprivation by shifting primary attention away from means to ends that people have reason to pursue and, correspondingly to freedoms to be able to satisfy these ends.[15] There are influences on capability deprivations other than lowness of income. The capability deprivation takes into account the inequality of freedoms.[16] The problem of inequality gets magnified as the attention is shifted from income inequality to the inequality in the distribution of substantive freedoms and capabilities. Inequality has an important role in the development of famines and other severe crises. Fundamentally various forms of capability deprivation including low income and inequality originate from lack of freedom. Poverty as lack of freedom has been at the core of Catholic Social thinking too. For example, in *Gaudium et Spes* we see: "Only in freedom can man direct himself towards goodness."[17] "Human freedom is often crippled when a man encounters extreme poverty, just as it withers when he indulges in too many of life's comforts and imprisons himself in a kind of splendid isolation."[18] Now we understand that poverty, underdevelopment and capability deprivation and lack of freedom are interconnected as a web. For Sen's developmental approach as for Catholic Social Thinking, human freedom is the aim of development, and poverty prevents people to reach their full human freedom. Having viewed Amartya Sen's concepts of *Development as Freedom* we move on to the important milestones in the history of the social teaching of the Church during the past decades with a view to develop an integral and interdisciplinary approach to development.

The Important Milestones in the History of the Social Teaching of the Church

The history of the social teaching of the modern Church is generally recognized to have begun with Pope Leo XIII (+1903) and his encyclical Rerum Novarum (1891). An early phase of social teaching, the first seventy years form Leo XIII to the end of Pope Pius XII's pontificate (+1958), can be clearly distinguished from a later phase from Pope John XXIII (+1963), the second Vatican Council (1962-1965) and Pope Paul VI (+1978) to the present day. During the first phase Catholic social teaching developed into a coherent body of teaching deriving from Christian doctrine about the dignity, nature and destiny of the person and the family. In the later phase we detect a changed approach beginning with the encyclicals of Pope John XXIII and the second Vatican Council and the liberationist perspective formally adopted by the Latin American Bishops at their conference in Medellin(1968). Catholic social teaching adopted, reconstructed and consolidated a number of radical modern ideas and was acknowledged as an essential form of evangelization to the modern world.[19]

During the first phase two central themes were constantly present. First, there was a considerable concern for the workers, particularly those in the industrial areas, and for the poor and the powerless in society, and also marked criticism of the political and economic systems, both liberal capitalism and socialism. The second principal theme was a consistent defense of certain basic human rights, such as private property, a just wage and a better working condition. In his encyclical *Rerum Novarum,* Pope Leo XIII insisted that the Church had a duty to intervene in social matters, while the state had a responsibility to intervene to defend those who suffered from the economic system. He reasoned that the structures and institutions of industry were themselves responsible for the wrongs in society. He believed that only and organized effort on behalf of all could bring about such a fundamental change in society. The new encyclical remained a kind of *Magna Carta* for subsequent social teaching for decades. In the midst of the social and economic crises of the 1920s and 1930s, Pope Pious XI took up the cause of the workers and the poor in society in his encyclical *Quadragesimo Anno*(1931). It rejected socialism as anti-Christian and searched for a middle path (120) calling to reconstruct the social order.[20] It developed the teaching on the common good of society and o the obligation of the state to champion the temporal well being of every sector of society. The encyclical upheld the Principle of Subsidiarity that emphasized people's rights to care for each other in an atmosphere protected by just laws and just governments acting for the common good. It also introduced the concepts of social charity and social justice.

In 1961 on 70th anniversary of *Rarum Noarum* Pope John XXIII formulated the encyclical *Mater et Magistra* (1961) which focused on underdeveloped countries and the global common good.[21] In 1963 he brought out *Pacem in Terris* which focused on a new world order rooted in justice, love, equality and dignity of the human person. Gaudium et Spes of the second Vatican Council(1965) affirmed the Church at the service of the world and developed a theology of human development. It relativized private ownership and insisted on participation of labour. In 1967 Pope Paul VI exposed *Populorum Preogressio* which development as the development of whole man and of all men.[22] Taking into account the after effects of nationalism and colonialism introduced a new phrase as "Preferential option for the poor". Through his encyclical *Octogesima Adveniens* in 1971 Paul VI highlighted the environmental problems for the first time in the history of Catholic social teaching. In the same year the Synod of Bishops in Rome recognizing the struggle of the oppressed for freedom put forward the document on *Justice in the World*. It envisaged the idea of interdependence in the establishment of a just society. The encyclical *Solicitudo Rei Socialis* by John Paul II in 1987 aimed at reexamining the concept of development and explained Structural Sin based on global economic injustice. It took into account the impact of consumerism and ecological issues.[23] Through *Centesimus Annus* in 1991 he called for a shared responsibility for all humanity in promoting development. He insisted o the importance of morality in economic transactions. In the encyclical *Ecclesis in Asia* John Paul II made a systematic analysis of the socio-cultural, religio-political and economic realities of the Asian context. It enhanced the promotion of justice and peace for all especially to migrants, tribal peoples, women, children and refugees. The social encyclical *Deus Caritas Est* (2005) of Pope Benedict XVI made an attempt to dialogue with modernity. He pointed out the direct role of politics in the establishment of a just social order and acknowledged the indirect role of the Church in the same.

In a brief outlook we see that justice and development has been the concern for the Catholic Church for the past hundred and more years. Catholic social teaching of the Church included economic, social, cultural, and religious issues of respective times. It took in to account the right of man to work, the right of individuals to own property, just wage, the duty of the government to work for the common good of all citizens, the duty of companies, factories and larger agencies to respect the principle of subsidiarity; and the right to freedom of worship. A grave concern was expressed in issues of corruption, injustice, consumerism, environmental problems, violation of person's dignity and human rights. It is true that these encyclicals and related documents responded constructively to the signs of the times. But we cannot make a genuine claim that they have succeeded in addressing the inner dynamics of those issues in every respect. From a specific perspective *Rerum Novarum* upheld*s* a poor analysis of social systems and restricted itself to the framework of capitalism. In *Quadragesimo Anno,* to a great extent, the Church is perceived above the world. *Pacem in Terris* has made poor political analysis of then times. The aspect of power is overlooked in *Laborem Exercen, which* ignores the problem of unemployment especially of the third world. *Centesimus Annus* is predominantly Euro-centered having only passing reference to third world. In a deeper analysis *Deus Caritas Est* is sociologically and anthropologically weak. So we can can to the conclusion that there are areas ignored in the encyclicals or issues not authentically addressed. At certain junctures Church finds herself incompetent in analyzing and responding to the root cause of the structural problems proper. Even if addressed through the encyclicals they could not bring out the expected outcome. I think here lies the relevance of the Church to be open to the secular theory of Amartya Sen's *Development as Freedom*. In his work Sen has made a brilliant attempt in analyzing the root cause of the problems from the perspective of the down trodden and the marginalized and put forward practical suggestions to overcome the stumbling blocks for sustainable development.

Do We Need An Interdisciplinary Approach to Development?

While we try to make an interdisciplinary approach to development based on the Church documents and the secular theory of Amartya Sen, it is not our aim to trigger out which is the best out of two approaches. Rather we would prefer a holistic and interdisciplinry approach, which is the blend of both. The developmental theory of Amartya Sen and Catholic Social thinking would pave the way for the emergence of an interdisciplinary approach. Catholic Social Thinking has a word "common good"[24] for the structures that are necessary for 'integral human development'. The central idea of the common good is that it is a good shared in by all those who are forming a certain community. While Sen's developmental process focuses on individuals, and then looks at institutional arrangements to promote the well-being of individuals. The common good approach of the Church to development focuses predominantly on the institutions themselves because it is precisely within these institutions that individuals are formed and nurtured. Since the institutional fact is constitutive of a person's individuality, it is not only the well-being of individuals, which is to be secured, but also the well-being of these institutions. But how the well-being of these institutions is ensured? What are the practical ways with which common good to be fostered? How to promote these structures of living together which sustain the good life in common? I feel the inner dynamism of these questions regarding common good are not sufficiently addressed in the Church documents. Hence the Church needs to understand the importance of political participation in the developmental process as Amartya Sen puts forward. Only this interdisciplinary approach can ensure "common good" and individual freedom. It is the blend of both the secular and the sacred.

Political Participation in Amartya Sen's Developmental Approach

Amartya Sen advocates democracy based political participation in view of development. Developing and strengthening democratic system is an essential component of the process of development. The significance of democracy lies in three distinct virtues: its intrinsic importance, its instrumental contributions, and its constructive role in the creation of values and norms.[25] We must acknowledge the importance of democratic institutions in the process of development. Public debates and discussions, permitted by political freedoms and civil rights, can also play a major part in the formation of values. Just as it is important to emphasize the need for democracy, it is also crucial to safeguard the conditions and circumstances that ensure the range and reach of the democratic process. There is also the need to examine the ways and means of making it function well, to realize its potentials. The achievement of social development and social justice depends on effective practice of democracy.[26] Indeed the absence of democracy is in itself an inequality. According to Sen the challenge of development includes both the elimination of persistent, endemic deprivation and the prevention of sudden, severe destitution.[27]

One of the most foundational building blocks of Sen's developmental approach is the ability of people to help themselves and to influence the world. Throughout his works, Sen emphasises that people should not be seen as passive spoon-fed patients of social welfare institutions, but have to be seen as "agents"[28] being actively involved in shaping their own destiny." The freedom centred understanding of the process of development is very much an agent-oriented view. By the term "agent" Sen means someone who acts and brings about change, and whose achievements can be judged in terms of one's own values and objectives. He believes, with adequate social opportunities individuals can effectively shape their own destiny and help each other. In this respect, the developmental approach grants a fundamental role to the public debate and democratic decision-making, or in more generic terms, to the ability to participate in the life of the community and to take decisions in matters that affect one's own life and the life of fellow-human beings. This ability to do something not only for oneself but also for other members of the society can even be considered as one of the elementary freedoms that people have reason to value, even among people who lead very deprived lives in material terms.

Democratic freedom plays a crucial role in specifying and choosing the capabilities that are worthwhile to be promoted. It is essential in specifying a society's underlying values and in choosing the capabilities that are valuable and worthwhile to be pursued. Referring to the choice between cultural tradition and poverty on the one hand and modernity and material prosperity on the other hand, Sen writes: If a traditional way of life has to be sacrificed to escape grinding poverty or minuscule longevity, then it is the people directly involved who must have the opportunity to participate in deciding what should be chosen.[29] The role of participation also extends to the choices of the means that will bring about the chosen priorities, and hence to the kind of policies required to promote the chosen capabilities. The democratic freedom is also of constitutive importance in value formation.[30] It clarifies and constructs a society's values and priorities, builds consensus and achieves compromises that prevent conflicts. In this sense individual freedom becomes a constructive choice and a social product.

Political Participation as Commitment to Common Good

For Catholic Social thinking, the very idea of the common good generally implies that every individual, no matter how high or low, has a duty to share in promoting the welfare of the community as well as a right to benefit from that welfare. One could even affirm that commitment to the common good is synonymous to solidarity. The social encyclical, *Sollicitudo Rei Socialis* defines solidarity as "this firm and constant determination to work for the common good; that is, for the good of all and each because we are all responsible for all."[31] The encyclical goes on stating that freedom and solidarity are intrinsically linked and that none of both can be sacrificed for each other: "In order to be genuine, development must be achieved within the framework of solidarity and freedom, without ever sacrificing either of them under whatever pretext."[32] The human being is fully free and human to the extent that he or she is responsible for others. When political participation is low, the common good is low as well, and people have less freedom to determine the conditions of the life they share together. A low political participation confines people to pursue the good they can in their private lives. Official Catholic Social Thinking, as manifested in the papal encyclicals, hardly speaks of the importance of political participation and democratic freedom in promoting the common good. It goes at length about the virtue of solidarity. But few Catholic theologians have been linking this emphasis on solidarity with political participation. This is a domain where Amartya Sen's developmental approach can make a significant contribution to Catholic Social Thinking.

Challenges Posed

The developmental approach of Amartya Sen primarily understands freedom as choice, and that is, in a way, an insufficient way of conceiving freedom when poverty is at stake. He gives too much stress on the enhancement of individual freedom. Moreover, Sen's developmental approach refrains itself from specifying the various lacks of 'freedoms' with all their nuances that constitute poverty. This causes problems when the developmental approach is put into practice. For Sen's approach, development is a matter of expanding the freedoms of individual human beings. In contrast, Catholic Social Thinking has emphasised the importance of the common good, of the good of the community as a whole and not only of its individual members. Whether one conceives development as the expansion of individual well-being or of the common good will have important implications for poverty reduction. In a deeper exploration we understand that both the Church documents and the secular developmental theory, at times, experience their limitations in addressing issues of justice, poverty and development. Amidst these limitations, it is widely accepted that the Church concept of common good and the secular concept of individual freedom have argued for the need to go beyond the unjust structures and less-freedom based approach to development. If traditional Catholic Social Teaching sees the common good as the nucleus of its social ethics, Amartya Sen emphasizes the issue of political participation as central to social ethics. This is certainly an area where Catholic Social Thinking has still to make further progress. This is most probably the area where the Church can have an important role and be key players in strengthening political participation and in increasing the political power of the less privileged. In many developing countries, churches have more authority than traditional political parties, and benefit a much greater trust from the population and there lies a significant potential for political renewal.

The Church had been long contented itself with drawing a strong separation between the temporal and spiritual order. For Christians, political involvement had become a matter of infusing the political sphere with their religious values. By being members of a faith community, we learned certain values like loving one's neighbour as one self, and tried to apply these values to decisions that are taken in the public sphere. Moreover, it was some how imprinted in the conscience that it was the particular duty of the laity, and not members of the clergy and religious orders, to be involved in civil society as political actors. The call for political participation as part of the Church's commitment to the common good seems to put these assumptions into question. It is the Church as a whole, who is called, to be a political actor of social change. What the Church need today is a new political consciousness. In this regard the Church faces two challenges: first, the capability of the underprivileged for self-assertion must be enhanced through offering incentives for them to organize in political organizations through which they will gain sufficient power to counteract the power of the privileged. Second, a sense of solidarity must be created between the most privileged and the underprivileged.[33] I believe that the Catholic Church must be able to respond constructively to these challenges by way of being open to the secular dimensions of capability building, political participation and democratic freedom.

Conclusion

From our study we may draw the conclusion that to bring forth justice and peace on earth the Church should take into account the insights from individuals like Amartya Sen in its official teachings on Justice and human rights. Each approach in itself is limited but the blend of both is promising. For me, it seems that the theological and ethical reflections in Amartya Sen's writings and in Catholic social teaching is an apt hermeneutic key to interpret the lives of the people in the same situation of poverty, oppression and suffering in the whole world. The main proposal of Sen for the development of the underprivileged poor people is to enhance individuals by way of helping them to develop their capabilities, while Catholic social teaching is very much insisting on the sharing aspect of the Christians. We can understand Catholic social teaching by historically and critically analysing the social documents of the Church in a special way from the perspective of mediation proposed by Amartya Sen to develop strategies to uplift the downtrodden and show that the Catholic social tradition becomes significant when it finds its meaning in the light of the realities of our times. In this regard I would like to conclude this paper highlighting a few requisites of a new global political economy. In the light of the interdisciplinary approach to development I would recommend that the Catholic social teaching and secular theories should be directed toward a new global political agenda for development. According to Leonardo Boff, the liberation theologian, the new global political economy includes a minimum of humanization, citizenship, equity, human and ecological welfare and cultural reciprocity and openness to complementarity.[34] A Minimum of humanization means that all human beings should have the basic right to existence This means that they should be able to at least one meal a day, have a roof over their heads, and be helped with basic heath care. Most of the present development programme today does not focus on whole persons but only on their work efforts. It is a challenge for us to nourish genuine love and friendship for human persons beyond their ethnic, religious or cultural attributes. Citizenship implies that socio-political system should not tend to exclude people. All people should feel themselves to be potentially citizens of the world, thinking globally and acting locally. Equity seeks a greater realization of the political ideal of equality. Solidarity among groups and nations alleviates the harshness of social inequalities. Human and ecological welfare ensures quality of life to make life truly human. It is possible by developing the capacity to communicate with the deepest subjectivity of other persons, and all other entities, including the otherness of other created beings and the absolute otherness of God. It is not sufficient to recognize otherness. Along with we need to develop reciprocity, which is the exchange of experience and understanding. It means one person or culture can complement the other. In conclusion development is the expansion of human life and freedom.

In the context of underdevelopment, lack of freedoms, capability deprivation and unjust politics we need to keep our hope alive towards sustainable development. As Sebastian Kappen says we need to sustain our hope in the New Humanity.[35] The New Humanity is the definitive suppression of all barriers consisting of excusive claims and privileges (Mk 3: 31-35). What is envisioned here is a new community that transcends all bounds set up by kinship, religion or race. In the New Humanity all the children of God will gather around to sit at table with Jesus in total love and self giving (Mt 11:19).

It includes "the little ones"(Mk 9:42), "the humble"(Mt 25:40), the simple as opposed to the wise, the uneducated, and the ignorant. The New Humanity is the flock Jesus gathered around him and for which he gave his life (Lk 12:32, Jn 10:14-15). "I tell you this: tax-gatherers and prostitutes will enter the Kingdom of God, and not you"(Mt 21:31). We need to keep our hope alive in the New Humanity, which is the Kingdom of God. To lose hope is to die, is to lapse into nonbeing. Where hope has withered away, families disintegrate, political systems collapse, and the educational systems come to stand still. Hope is a constituent of development. Let us be hopeful that the interdisciplinary approach to development would enhance human freedom and capabilities toward the establishment of New Humanity. The scope of this paper was to find out how Amartya Sen and Catholic Social Teaching together can contribute to bring forth justice and development in society. We started with the harsh realities of our times, which then followed by a brief account of Amartya Sen's view on *Development as Freedom*. Then we exposed the important milestones in the history of the Catholic social teaching of the Church with a view to develop an interdisciplinary approach to development which is a blend of both the sacred and the secular.

Notes

1. I am grateful to Dr. P.T. Mathew S.J., the dean of the faculty of Theology, Regional Theology Centre Kalady, Kerala, for his valuable insights on the topic of concern.
2. Refer Amartya Sen, *Development as Freedom*, Anchor, New York, 1999. He looks at the problems of poverty and injustice through his ideas of development as freedom.
3. Paul F. Knitter, *One Earth Many Religions*, Orbis, Maryknoll, New York, 1995, p. 62, 65.
4. Amartya Sen, *Development as Freedom*, Anchor, New York, 1999, p. 4.
5. *Ibid.*, p. 38.
6. *Ibid.*,p. 18. A person's "capability" refers to the alternative combinations of functioning that are feasible for one to achieve.

Capability is thus a freedom: the substantive freedom to achieve alternative functioning combinations.

7. *Ibid.*, p. 5.
8. *Ibid.*, p. 52.
9. *Ibid.*, p. 36.
10. Amartya Sen, *Development as Freedom*, Anchor, New York, 1999, p. 148-149.
11. *Ibid.*, p. 149-151.
12. *Ibid.*, p. 149.
13. *Ibid.*, p. 87.
14. James E. Foster and Amartya Sen, *On Economic Inequality*, Oxford University Press, 1997, p. 211.
15. *Ibid.*, p. 90.
16. *Ibid.*, p. 119.
17. *Gaudium et Spes*, no.17.
18. *Ibid.*, 31.
19. Gregory Baum and Robert Ellsberg (ed.), *The Logic of Solidarity, Commentaries on the Encyclical on 'Social Concern' by Pope John Paul*, Orbis, Maryknoll, N.Y., 1989, pp. 100-126.
20. *Quadragesimo Anno*, No. 120.
21. *Mater et Magistra*, Nos. 78-80.
22. *Populorum Preogressio*, Nos. 7, 14,76.
23. *Solicitudo Rei Socialis*,. Nos. 28,34,36.
24. Refer David Hollenbach, *The Common Good and Christian Ethics*. Cambridge: Cambridge University Press, 2002. p. 81. The common good is "the good realized in the mutual relationships in and through which human beings achieve their well-being."
25. *Ibid.*, p. 157-158.
26. *Ibid.*, p. 159.
27. *Ibid.*, p. 188.
28. *Ibid.*, p. 11.
29. *Ibid.*, p.38.
30. *Ibid.*, p. 158.

31. *Sollicitudo Rei Socialis,* No. 38.
32. *Ibid..,* No. 33.8.
33. Refer article by Séverine Deneulin on *Poverty: Amartya Sen Compared to Catholic Social Thinking, www. http://www.theology-centre.org/leuven28_04.doc.*
34. Leoardo, Boff, *Ecology and Liberation-A New Paradigm,*Orbis, Maryknoll, New York,1995, p. 128-130.
35. Sebastian, Kappen, *Jesus and Freedom,* Orbis, Maryknoll, New York, 1977, pp. 153-160.

References

Sen, Amartya (1999), *Development as Freedom,* Anchor, New York.

Foster, James E. and Sen, Amartya (1997), *On Economic Inequality,* Oxford University Press.

Henriot, Peter *et. al.,* (1989), *Catholic Social Teaching-Our Best Kept Secret,* Orbis.

Pennock, M. (2000), *Catholic Social Teaching-Learning and Living Justice,* Ave Maria.

Dorr, Donald (1983), *Option for the Poor: A Hundred Years of Vatican Social Teaching,* Orbis.

Curran, Charles (2002), *Catholic Social Teaching,* Georgetown Univ. Press.

Boff, Leoardo (1995), *Ecology and Liberation-A New Paradigm,* Orbis, Maryknoll, New York.

Deneulin, Séverine (2004), *Poverty: Amartya Sen Compared to Catholic Social Thinking,* in *www.http://www.theology-centre.org/leuven28_04.doc,* Von Hügel Institute, Cambridge.

Baum, Gregory and Robert Ellsberg (ed.) (1989), *The Logic of Solidarity, Commentaries on the Encyclical on 'Social Concern' by Pope John Paul,* Orbis, Maryknoll, N.Y.

Paúl F. Knitter (1995), *One Earth Many Religions,* Orbis, Maryknoll, New York.

Kappen, Sebastian (1977), *Jesus and Freedom,* Orbis, Maryknoll, New York.

Hollenbach, David (2002),*The Common Good and Christian Ethics.* Cambridge: Cambridge University Press.

8

The Understanding of "Development" in Some Christian Documents

Jose Thayil SJ

Introduction

The question of development is a complex issue: who decides what development means and for whom. The idea of 'development' has undergone change and development over the years. The first part of this article deals with the attempts at development in India. This will give us the context in which the growth in the understanding of development in four major Church's magisterial documents of the past fifty years is discussed.

Initially, the term 'development' was used mainly to denote economic development. Thus, many social activists tried to bring about development by introducing modern methods of agriculture and other economic activities to improve the standard of living of the rural poor. According to them, lack of capital was the cause of underdevelopment. "The solution, therefore, was to promote economic growth by an infusion of capital, which would lead to industrialization and eventual prosperity."[1]

But those third world countries which adopted this model ended up with 'economic stagnation coupled with political and social unrest'.[2] The main reason for this was the unjust trade relations between the developed and the underdeveloped nations.

Many of these projects were funded by the government and some foreign funding agencies. But since these activities failed to achieve the desired aim, the need was felt to give importance to the fields of health and education. Again, the rapid rate of population growth hindered any attempt at development. So family planning programmes were also introduced as part of the process of development.[3]

Now we are slowly moving away from and beyond purely economic development to social development. "The concept of social development is inclusive of economic development but differs from it in the sense that it emphasises the development of the totality of society in its economic, political, social, and cultural aspects."[4] Social development basically means an integrated development of the whole person. This concept does not accept that economic development is the basis of other forms of development. It stresses the simultaneous development of the different areas.

Development in India

A country like India is on the road to becoming a developed nation and its GNP is going up rather rapidly. At the same time a large number of people in our country continue to remain below the poverty line. Due to the effects of globalisation and other similar trends many have lost their jobs and remain unemployed or underemployed. Hence, a small percentage of people are becoming very rich at the expense of the development of the majority.

India is said to be a rich country with poor people residing in it. India has very rich resources, but somehow these resources are not well utilized. The 'mixed economy' policy did not bear the desired result. "Coupled with these economic problems were the mismanagement of funds, consecutive elections, corruption of high magnitude at all levels, inefficiency, clamour for higher wages not backed by productive increase, high military expenditures, and expenses on populist programmes."[5] Due to large scale corruption the facilities meant for the poorer sections often ended up in the hands of the well-off people. When India requested the IMF help to recover from the economic crisis, we had to accept their conditions of economic liberalization and Structural Adjustment Policies (SAP). These policies include 'encouraging greater participation of the private sector, disinvestments in state owned public sector enterprises, deregulation of industries, liberalisation of foreign trade and foreign investment and changes in fiscal policy'.[6]

The consequences of liberalisation are very damaging to the general public. A large number of people have lost their jobs under the names of 'Golden Handshake' and the 'Voluntary Retirement Scheme'. "Between 1991-94 it is estimated that about 75,000 in the public sector and 1,25,000 in the private sector have been sent out."[7] When more and more people are losing their jobs, even if the industries make profits, this cannot be seen as integral development. In order to keep them economically viable, Industries have to go in for modern technologies with less employees. The agriculture sector will not be able to employ many more people if it has to run profitably. "Therefore, the unorganised sector, with its large scope for self-employment, must expand rapidly in order to create the additional jobs."[8]

One sign of economic development is the movement of the labour force from the unorganised to the organised sector, where they form their own unions and their interests are taken care of. But in India, due to the New Economic Policies, the reverse process is taking place creating more and more casual labourers. Among the casual labourers, the number of women and children are on the increase. "Multinational companies are keen in exploiting such cheap labour by sub-contracting the various production processes."[9] The developed countries are making use of India for their continued wealth accumulation.

The Church and Development

Till the middle of the 20th century, the Church was involved in preaching the gospel to those who had never heard of Jesus and in the work of charity, education and health care. To be concerned about developmental activities was not considered part of its mission. Today the Church accepts developmental activities and promotion of justice as part and parcel of its evangelising mission. The synodal document, 'Justice in the World', considers "action on behalf of justice and participation in the transformation of the world as a constitutive dimension of the preaching of the Gospel".[10] In the recent past the Church has been very active in Northeast India with a view to evangelisation. Along with evangelisation, the Church was very active in the apostolate of human development.[11]

Though many Church documents deal with the topic of development, I like to restrict myself to the study of only four documents: Vatican II's Pastoral Constitution on The Church in the Modern World (*Gaudium et Spes*), the encyclical of Pope Paul VI on The Development of Peoples (*Populorum Progressio*) and his Apostolic Exhortation on Evangelisation in the Modern World (*Evangelii Nuntiandi*) and the encyclical of John Paul II on Social Concern (*Sollicitudo Rei Socialis*).

Magisterial Teaching on Development

Gaudium et Spes

Gaudium et Spes of Vatican II (1965) seems to give the impression that 'development' would be able to solve the problems of poverty. Many of the bishops and experts at the Council might have believed that the best way to promote international social justice and overcome poverty was to opt for a Western-style development. The assumption behind this approach is that Western-style 'development' can be imitated. Developing nations could follow the same path of development as the developed nations during the last two centuries.[12] Yet this may only lead to the creation of a Fourth or even a Fifth World.

The responsibility for development of the underdeveloped nations is laid both on the developing as well as on the developed nations. Developing nations need to be concerned about the complete human fulfilment of all their citizens as the explicit goal of progress. "Let them be mindful that progress begins and develops primarily from the efforts and endowments of the people themselves. Hence, instead of depending solely on outside help, they should rely chiefly on the full unfolding of their own resources and the cultivation of their own qualities and tradition."[13]

The document also points to the responsibility of the developed nations. "The development of any nation depends on human and financial assistance... The developing nations will be unable to procure the necessary material assistance unless the practices of the modern business world undergo a profound change. Additional help should be offered by advanced nations, in the form of either grants or investments."[14]

Gaudium et Spes (GS) recognizes that a major source of injustice in international trade is the inequality in power between trading partners. In order to regulate this inequality, the document calls for the setting up of effective institutions to promote a just economic order.[15] "Let adequate organizations be established for fostering and harmonizing international trade, especially with respect to the less advanced countries, and for repairing the deficiencies caused by an excessive disproportion in the power possessed by various nations."[16]

GS is not content with a conversion in the mentality and attitudes of peoples, but also calls for reforms in the socio-economic realm. "Numerous reforms are needed at the socio-economic level, along with universal change in ideas and attitudes."[17] The Council says that in many situations there is urgent need for a reassessment of economic and social structures.[18] The term 'reassessment' suggests that the Council does not identify itself with those who fight for the overthrowing of the existing structures. But what is significant is that the Council Fathers did not shy away from calling for a reassessment. They did not start with the assumption that any fundamental restructuring is unnecessary, nor did they rule it out on the ground that it might lead to some confusion in society.[19]

GS also cautions against sudden technical solutions at the cost of the priceless heritage of the non-Western cultures. "But nations must beware of technical solutions immaturely proposed, especially those which offer man material advantage while militating against his spiritual nature and development. For, 'Not by bread alone does man live, but by every word that comes forth from the mouth of God' (Mt 4:4). Each branch of the human family possesses in itself and in its worthier traditions some part of the spiritual treasure entrusted by God to humanity, even though many do not know the source of this treasure."[20]

GS speaks of deep compassion for the poor, but gives no clear indication of solidarity with them. It seems to be more concerned about doing something for the poor rather than being with the poor. GS presents poverty as an urgent problem which is to be overcome mainly by 'development'.

Populorum Progressio

Populorum Progressio was issued on 26th March 1967 by Pope Paul VI barely sixteen months after the Council Document, *Gaudium et Spes*. This shows his great commitment to the problem of development. This encyclical deals with the relationship between rich and poor nations. Pope Paul VI is concerned about the problem of poverty and he wants to find out its basic causes before he suggests any solution. He points out that the main causes of poverty are the negative effects of colonialism in the past, neo-colonialism and the huge difference of wealth and power between nations.[21] Though he speaks of the negative effects of colonialism as one of the reasons for poverty, he mentions that colonialism has also done some good to the people by way of diminishing ignorance and sickness. He is of the opinion that colonialism has also brought better communications and improved the living conditions of the people.[22]

The Pope is of the opinion that the social problems cannot be solved at the national level alone. PP deals with the challenge of integral development. He condemns unbridled liberalism. "However certain concepts have somehow arisen out of these new conditions and insinuated themselves into the fabric of human society. These concepts present profit as the chief spur to economic progress, free competition as the guiding norm of economics, and the private ownership of means of production as an absolute right, having no limits, nor concomitant social obligations."[23]

He emphasizes the role of the Church in the process of development and gives a Christian vision of development. The Pope envisages a well integrated development of everyone. "What must be aimed at is complete humanism. And what is that if not the fully rounded development of the whole man and of all men?"[24] The development of a nation is to be judged by the level of development of the last and the least. This calls for a commitment to justice and equality for all the citizens. "This commitment is to the historical project of the poor, whereby the non-persons become persons and agents or subjects of their own history and cease to be objects of exploitation and manipulated history."[25] The development of every person is mediated by the option for the development of the last and the least.

Jesus is our model for commitment to the development of the poor and the marginalized. Jesus came to proclaim the good news of the Kingdom of God to the poor. He had a preferential love for the poor and this was shown by his close association with them. His personal life and ministry were directed towards the liberation of the oppressed and the downtrodden. He reinterpreted the Sabbath for the benefit of the poor and the heavy burdened. Jesus' commitment to everyone was mediated through his preferential option for the poor.

He suggests economic planning and aid to promote development.[26] He concludes by terming 'development' the new name for peace, and exhorts all Christians to strive for true development. "For if the new name for peace is development, who would not wish to labour for it with all his powers?"[27] He feels that revolution is not the right means to bring about human development, but he points out that if the interests of the poor people are not given proper importance, they may be forced to have recourse to violence.[28] At the same time he also mentions that a revolutionary uprising will only produce new injustices, imbalances, and disasters.[29] The Pope is quite optimistic when he says that despite all its failures, the world is in fact moving towards greater brotherhood and an increase in humanity.[30]

We cannot expect integral development to take place from the top. "We have a tendency to consider the poor as the problem: the fact is that they are emerging as the solution!"[31] Many groups are slowly emerging all over the world which challenge the oppressive forces. We need to look up to these groups and support them so that they may bring about meaningful changes in the society.

Evangelii Nuntiandi

In *Evangelii Nuntiandi* (1975), Pope Paul VI deals with the controversial theological question raised by the document of the Synod on 'Justice in the World', when it said that action on behalf of justice is a constitutive dimension of preaching the Gospel.[32] According to EN, the Church is a community of believers gathered 'in the name of Jesus so that they may together seek the Kingdom, build it up and implement in their own lives'.[33] Building the Kingdom is not confined to the so called 'religious' or 'spiritual' activities. It also requires secular activities such as working for the integral development of people and struggling against the oppressive and inhuman structures in the society.

In *Gaudium et Spes* and *Populorum Progressio* the main emphasis is on development rather than liberation. Starting from the Medellin documents there is a shift from development to liberation. Pope Paul in writing *Octogesima Adveniens* in 1971 was very cautious in his use of the word 'liberation'. In EN he provides a thorough theological analysis of the concept of liberation. He writes that the main purpose of the coming of Jesus was to proclaim the Good News of the Kingdom of God. He summarises the content of the Good News: "As the main point and the very centre of his Good News, Christ proclaims salvation; this is the great gift of God which is liberation from everything that oppresses people, particularly liberation from sin and the Evil One..."[34] It is not possible to preach the Good News without questioning the dehumanising structures of society. The Good News about the risen Lord is the news of liberation from poverty, oppression and injustice. Even though the word liberation goes beyond economic and political liberation, it cannot replace the word 'salvation'. Salvation is a gift of God. It begins in this life but is fulfilled only in eternity.

The Pope gives an overall vision of evangelisation, one that transcends any division such as 'religious versus secular' or 'spiritual versus temporal'. All the same the mission of the Church should not be reduced to merely a temporal project.[35] If that were not the case, the Church would have nothing more to offer than the social activists or political movements. EN understands evangelisation as bringing "the Good News into all the strata of the human race so that by its power it may permeate the depths of humanity and make it new".[36] There is a need for inner transformation. External transformation brought about by force will not be lasting unless it is supported by love and concern for fellow human beings. It means "affecting the standards by which people make judgments, their prevailing values, their interests and thought-patterns, the things that move them to action, and their models of human living".[37]

Preaching of the Good News is to be done by all Christians. This task involves working for an integral development and liberation of all peoples. Every Christian has to use his special God-given talent and charism for the betterment of the whole society. Every one is called to contribute his/her might for the building up of the Kingdom of God, which Jesus came to establish.[38]

Sollicitudo Rei Socialis

Dated December 31, 1987, published in February 1988, the encyclical *Sollicitudo Rei Socialis* by Pope John Paul II commemorates the 20th anniversary of *Populorum Progressio.* Its purpose was to re-examine attempts made in the field of development during the intervening twenty years. The Pope comes to the conclusion that the efforts at development failed in many areas. The Pope says that education and easy access to information are among the most positive means of achieving development. He also feels that there is a need for radical political reforms in order to achieve them. He finds the conflict between East and West of over forty years has been a cause for the Third World to remain underdeveloped. The resources that could have been used for the development of the Third Word countries were used for the accumulation of weapons.[39]

The Encyclical points out that integrated development can take place only in a culture which promotes initiative. Of course the Pope has in mind the situation of the Eastern block, which was suppressing personal initiatives. Democratic forms of government seem to be the best for true development of all people. The people become the subjects rather than the objects of development.[40] In order to get participation of the general public, they have to be somehow made participants in decision making and implementation. The Indian government's attempt at *panchayati raj* is a good starting point. At the same time it is very difficult to get the support of all the people due to various reasons. "In India, the existence of religious minorities and the claims of regional linguistic loyalties have created difficulties at the national level and the differentiation based on caste has vitiated local regional politics."[41] Because of the very low percentage of literacy, the illiterate masses tend to believe in the false promises made by politicians for their own political advantage.

The Pope gives a broad meaning to development and he says that the poor as well as the rich need development. Along with economic and social development there is a need for moral development. This means that the attitudes of people have to be changed along with the external manifestations of development. It is a pity that underdevelopment goes hand in hand with superdevelopment. Those who enjoy superdevelopment become slaves of their possessions and they cultivate a culture of consumerism and 'throw-away'.[42] Pope John Paul II uses the term 'solidarity' in order to explain the duty of the developed nations to come to the aid of the developing nations and to treat them as their 'neighbours' and 'helpers'.[43] The Pope insists that one's neighbour is ' the living image of God the Father, redeemed by the blood of Jesus Christ and placed under the permanent action of the Holy Spirit'.[44] Solidarity also implies that the material goods as well as the products of human industry should belong to everyone without distinction.

Conclusion

There has been a slow progress in the understanding of 'development' in the Church as well as outside. Initially the emphasis was more on economic development. Gradually the emphasis shifted to integral development or social development. Through social analysis we came to know that poverty in the world is purposely maintained by the vested interests of a few wealthy individuals or nations. Hence, development alone will not be able to address this issue of poverty and underdevelopment. There is a need to work towards liberation, which involves a fight against oppression, injustice and the unjust distribution of wealth.

There are various forces working against the integral development of individuals and nations. Faulty religious beliefs and practices, wastage of money in prestigious programmes, exaggerated defence expenses, structural adjustment policies, new economic policies, globalisation, invasion of multinational companies, voluntary retirement scheme, utter selfishness, large scale corruption, unequal treatment of women, high illiteracy rate, lack of health facilities for the poor, unemployment, underemployment, child labour, etc. are some of the factors which hinder the growth process. India as a nation is moving towards becoming a developed nation, but wealth is concentrated in the hands of the top ten per cent of the people. As a result the gap between the rich and the poor is steadily increasing. The politicians, who are supposed to be living exemplary lives, are often leading scandalous lives and as a result they do not have any moral authority to lead the country to be a prosperous nation.

The Church in India has been successful to a great extent in its attempts at education and health care. After Vatican

Council II, it is moving in the direction of identification with the poor, conscientizing the marginalized, integral development of the masses, etc. Since there are many landlords and politicians who are opposed to education and development, the Church personnel are facing strong opposition by way of persecution, false legal cases, intimidation, etc. The Church needs to involve itself in a more scientific manner. Though some have done studies in social work, more people need to be equipped with the tools of social analysis and organizing people.

Notes

1. Mary Hembrow Snyder, "Development," in *The New Dictionary of Catholic Social Thought,ed. Judith A. Dwyer* (Minnesota, The Liturgical Press, 1994), 279.
2. Mary Hembrow Snyder, "Development," in *The New Dictionary of Catholic Social Thought, ed. Judith A. Dwyer* (Minnesota, The Liturgical Press, 1994), 279.
3. Gore M. S., *Social Development* (Jaipur, Rawat Publications, 2006), 7-8.
4. Gore M. S., *Social Development* (Jaipur, Rawat Publications, 2006), 20.
5. Shanti K, "Development with a Human Face," *Jeevadhara*, Vol. XXX, No. 175, Jan. 2000, 30.
6. *Ibid.*
7. Shanti K., "Development with a Human Face" *Jeevadhara*, Vol. XXX, No. 175, Jan. 2000, 31.
8. *Ibid.*, 33.
9. *Ibid.*
10. Justice in the World, 6.
11. George Palamattam, "Church and Development," *Indian Missiological Review*, December 1990, 188.
12. Donal Dorr, Option for the Poor: A Hundred Years of Vatican Social Teaching (New York, Orbis Books, 1985), 124.
13. GS 86.
14. GS 85.

15. Donal Dorr, *Option for the Poor: A Hundred Years of Vatican Social Teaching* (New York, Orbis Books, 1985), 124.
16. GS 86.
17. GS 63.
18. GS 86.
19. Donal Dorr, *Option for the Poor: A Hundred Years of Vatican Social Teaching* (New York, Orbis Books, 1985), 125.
20. GS 86.
21. P. 7-9.
22. P. 7.
23. P. 26.
24. P. 42.
25. S. Arokiasamy, "Sarvodaya through Antyodaya – The Liberation of the Poor in the Contextualisation of Morals," *Vidyajyoti*, Nov. 1987, 547.
26. Henriot J Peter, *Catholic Social Teaching: Our Best Kept Secret* (New York, Orbis Books, 1988), 58-59.
27. P. 87.
28. P. 30.
29. P. 31.
30. P. 79.
31. R.V. Mathias, "The Potential Agents of Development and the Task of the Church," *Vidyajyoti Journal of Theological Reflection*, August 1997, 544.
32. JW 6.
33. EN 13.
34. EN 9.
35. EN 32.
36. EN 18.
37. EN 19.
38. Cf. Paul Puthanangady, "Evangelii Nuntiandi: Reflections on some of its Salient Points" *Indian Missiological Review*, Jan. 1984, 85.

39. SRS 22.
40. SRS 44.
41. Gore M.S, *Social Development* (Jaipur, Rawat Publications, 2006), 26.
42. SRS 28.
43. SRS 39.
44. SRS 40.

9

Poverty, Peace and Development in an Era of Globalisation

Indunil Janaka Kodithuwakku

Robert J. Schreiter in "The New Catholicity, Theology between the Global and the Local" divides the evolution of the Church's modern missionary activity into three periods namely;

1. The period of Expansion (1492-1945)
2. The period of Solidarity (1945-1989)
3. The period of Globalisation (1989-)[1]

Accordingly, since 1989 the world belongs to the history of globalisation. Thus, local problems, whether socio-economic, political, or religious, in the last analysis often have global or international roots. The Message of Pope Benedict XVI for the celebration of the World of Peace, 1 January 2009 entitled "Fighting poverty to build peace" situates the social problem of poverty in a wider context, namely globalisation. Besides, he analyses the link between poverty and conflicts and shows how as a vicious cycle, "these conflicts fuel further tragic situations of poverty" (n. 1). He thus identifies poverty as one of the grave threats to peace in the modern world. "The gap between rich and poor has become more marked, even in the most economically developed nations" (n.1) A growing divide between the haves and the have-nots has left increasing numbers, especially in the Third World, in dire poverty, living on less than a dollar a day. [2] Pope Benedict XVI highlights: "All the indicators of relative poverty, in recent years, point to an increased disparity between rich and poor" (n. 7). Joseph E. Stiglitz is correct when he says: "If globalisation has not succeeded in reducing poverty, neither has it succeeded in ensuring stability."[3] Moreover, poverty sows the seeds of conflicts, fundamentalisms and extreme nationalism. Pope Benedict XVI, referring to Pope Paul VI, underlines that peace is development (cfr. n. 6). In other words, lack of development contributes to multiple conflicts. Furthermore, the soul-searching question of Joseph E. Stiglitz has a direct impact on the mission of the Church. "What could we do about the 1.2 billion people around the world living on less than a dollar a day, or the 2.8 billion people living on less than $2 a day–more than 45 per cent of the world's population?"[4] The president of the Pontifical Council for Justice and Peace Cardinal Renato Martino says that "Poverty and, above all, the growing inequality between areas, continents and countries,... constitutes the most dramatic problem facing the world today."[5] Thus, the fertilizing factors for extremism in the world are inequality, despotism, stereotyping, poverty, sense of insecurity, disappointment from peaceful means, humiliation. Besides, Archbishop Migliore at the 3rd Committee of the 63rd session of the U.N. General Assembly on the promotion and protection of human rights noted that "The current global economic collapse highlights and will surely exacerbate the plight of the so-called 'bottom billion,' a figure which due to the present aggravating conjuncture is on a constant rise".[6] Thus, the present global financial crisis adds fuel to the fire and thereby worsens the problem of poverty.

Positive Impact of Globalisation and Poverty

Pope Benedict XVI recognizes the positive potentialities of globalisation to remedy the malaise of the world including poverty. "Globalisation eliminates certain barriers, but is still able to build new ones" (no. 8), "Effective means to redress the marginalization of the world's poor through globalisation if people everywhere feel personally outraged by the injustices in the world and the concomitant violations of human rights" (no. 8). "In the field of *international commerce* and *finance,* there are processes at work today which permit a positive integration of economies" (n. 9). Thus, globalisation represents both a peril and a promise to our world.

Pope John Paul II points out that "Globalisation, *a priori,* is neither good nor bad. It will be what people make of it. No system is an end in itself, and it is necessary to insist that globalisation, like any other system, must be at the service of the human person; it must serve solidarity and common good."[7] The same Pope insisted upon the need for "globalisation without marginalization."[8] Pope Benedict XVI points out that globalisation "needs to be managed with great prudence" (n. 13). Thus, if globalisation is guided in the right path it is capable of bringing the following benefits to humankind.

Humanity	*Globalisation*
Geographical/cultural/ethnical economical/political/ religious divisions to	Sense of common humanity/ universal human family leading to unification (n. 8)
Race/caste/creed/colour/ culture discrimination to	Human dignity/human rights/ universal ideals
Particularism leading to conflicts	Universalism in diversity leading to unity
Abuse of law/genocide/ human rights violators to	International penal tribunals
Abuse of political power/ corruption to	Global governance
Isolated local issues to	Global attention/publicity/solidarity
From particular ethics to	Search for Global Ethics or common code of ethics (n. 8)
Religions as closed up groups to	Religions as collaborating groups
Local social problems	Help/advice/proposal from International organizations
Local markets to	Global market/foreign investments/ new economic opportunities (n. 9)
Issues related to local education/ health/welfare	Aid/training/medicine/advances in science and technology
Restrictions on migration to	International migration of people

As Pope Benedict XVI affirms, "in this sense globalisation should be seen as a good opportunity to achieve something important in the fight against poverty, and to place at the disposal of justice and peace resources which were scarcely conceivable previously" (n. 14). Even though, globalisation has the potentiality to contribute to peace and development, the empirical evidence often goes contrary to it.

Negative Consequences of Globalisation

It is true that globalisation today is contributing to the progress of human family in various ways. Besides, it is wrong to blame globalisation for all the evils in our society, which can stem from a variety of causes and cultural factors. Nonetheless, globalisation poses serious questions not only for the universal human family but also to the whole planet.[9] Analyzing different social issues generated directly or indirectly by globalisation, Pope Benedict XVI mentions how it has contributed to global poverty and instability, child poverty (n. 5), current food crisis (no. 7), lack of equal opportunities of access to the world market, without exclusion or marginalization (n. 9) short-term economic goals and the importance of ethical approach to economics, politics and participation (n. 12). *Ecclesia in Asia* (EA) affirms, "Globalisation has also worked to the detriment of the poor" (EA n.39). It further explains how globalisation tends to convert people thus: "a cultural globalisation, made possible by modern communications media, which is quickly drawing Asian societies into global consumer culture that is both secular and materialistic" (EA n.39). The prophetic views of Pope Paul VI are valid even for today. He stated that unless the developed world becomes more sensitive to third world poverty, Marxism's "social messianism" would become attractive and provoke "a violent revolution."[10] With a little modification, we can say that today globalisation in some countries has generated religious/ethnic fundamentalism,[11] extreme nationalism and the reincarnation of Marxism's "social messianism."[12] Moreover, according to "*Populorum Progressio*" of Pope Paul VI, the Christian idea of progress is not merely material or technological. It necessarily embraces the entire human person in his social, moral, cultural and spiritual dimension as well. Pope Benedict XVI emphasized that "increasing *per capita* income cannot be the ultimate goal of political and economic activity; it is still an important means {...} of the fight against hunger and absolute poverty" (n. 11). Hence, it is logical to argue that "Without reform, the backlash that has already started will mount and discontent with globalisation will continue."[13] The same concern is expressed thus by Pope Benedict XVI: "giving priority to the needs of the world's poor, and overcoming the scandal of the imbalance between the poverty and the measures which have been adopted in order to address them" (n. 13). If we want to have a globalisation with a more human face, it is indispensable to reform the international agencies which govern it. Pope Benedict XVI voiced the same concern against the world hunger earlier. "Certainly, the structural causes linked to the system of government of the world economy, leading the major part of the world resources of the planet to a minority of people, needs to be eliminated. {...} It is necessary largely to "convert" the global model of development. It is required today not only because of the scandal of hunger but also because of the environmental and energy crisis."[14]

Global Solidarity and Alleviation of Poverty

Pope Benedict realistically proposes a global agenda to fight the ills of globalisation. "One of the most important ways of building peace is through a form of globalisation directed towards the interests of the whole human family. In order to govern globalisation, however, there needs to be a strong sense of global solidarity {...}" (n.8). How can we bring about necessary structural changes to globalisation in order to build a world in which people can live truly human lives, freed from servitude imposed on him by other men or by natural forces (Cfr. PP n. 47)? The Catholic social teaching proposes the solidarity of humankind as a solution since the human person has a natural vocation to community. "God did not create man as a solitary. ... For by their innermost nature human beings are social, and unless they relate themselves to one another they can neither live nor develop their gifts" (GS n. 12). How can this human solidarity be realized? The Council indicates that Christ "clearly outlined an obligation on the part of the sons of God to treat each other as brothers." It is an illusion to believe that dialogue alone is the panacea for mismanaged globalisation and a host of evils it has produced. The leaders of Sunni Muslims and Catholic leaders, in a statement issued after a meeting, observe that dialogue is not enough to combat religious extremism but integral development must also be promoted.[15]

How can solidarity of humankind overcome the "local and global structural sins? Jawaharlal Nehru once said, *"Without a revolution within there cannot be a revolution without."* Pope Benedict XVI also identifies that the root causes of poverty are harboured within the human heart, like greed and narrow vision (cfr. n. 13). Vatican Council II also affirms it thus: "at a deeper level, economic, political, and social problems come from selfishness and pride (cfr. GS n. 25). Thus, structural sin is identified as originating from personal sin. Pope Paul VI, in *Evangelii Nuntiandi* (EN), deals with the notion of personal reform and structural change. EN observes, "The best structures and the most idealized systems soon become inhuman if the inhuman inclinations of the human heart are not made wholesome, if those who live in these structures or who rule them do not undergo a conversion of heart and of outlook" (EN n.36). Pope Benedict XVI in his message for the World Day of Peace 2008, citing *Centesimus Annus,* notes the importance of "a change of life-style, of models of production and consumption, and of the established structures of power which govern societies" (n. 15). Is the Catholic social teaching moralizing or creating the impression that if each person becomes more loving and generous, then social problems will fade away? The changes are neither easy nor automatic. We are not sheer spectators of this drama of globalisation and the evil it generates. The Lord Jesus has entrusted a mission to his Apostles: "*Vos date illis manducare*–Give them something to eat yourselves (LK 9:13) (n. 15). We must take responsibility for the direction our society takes. As Christians, we believe that each of us has a specific vocation and a mission to fulfil. In this light, solidarity of humankind against all exploitative and oppressive structures and false values signifies doing our part to bring about the kingdom of Christ in human society. "Building a just and civil order, wherein each person receives what is his or her due, is an essential task which every generation must take up anew" (*Deus Caritas Est* n. 28).

Global Ethic for Universal Family and Mission

If the context of mission in the 21st century is globalisation and if proclamation is at the centre of Christian mission, then naturally, today two forms of proclamation are more specific.

1. Denouncing of the idolatrous use of religious concepts by economic globalisation to legitimate its activity in quasi-religious fashion. This reveals the false gods being presented as absolute and the inevitable.
2. Solidarity and resistance: solidarity with the excluded to reaffirm the dignity of each person and resistance to the dehumanizing forces of globalisation.[16]

Pope Benedict XVI "extends to every disciple of Christ and to every person of good will a warm invitation to expand their hearts to meet the needs of the poor and to take whatever practical steps are possible in order to help them" (n.15). The other religions are also opposed to these egoistic and exploitive structures and their members also are victims. Yet, collaboration had become difficult due the clash of religious/ cultural fundamentalisms.[17] Since the extremist elements whether religious or cultural are a minority albeit powerful, there are rays of hope. The "Spirit of Assisi" is the best way to pull the world out of its present crisis. The Church as a sign and means of reconciliation is called to form the new people of God. In the 21st century, reconciliation has become a new paradigm of mission.[18] Globalisation is thus not a part of the problem but a part of the solution. "The present reality of global interdependence makes it easier to appreciate the common destiny of the entire human family, and makes all thoughtful people increasingly appreciate the virtue of solidarity."[19]

According to the book of Genesis, God is seen as the origin of all that exists. The original harmony in creation was tarnished by sin. Yet, God did not abandon fallen human persons, but rather initiated a project to save all. God promised a kingdom of peace and harmony on earth and Jesus realized it by his passion, death, and resurrection. The risen Lord entrusted his disciples with the mission of bringing harmony to all nations. Thus, the mission of the Church is to work towards restoring peace and harmony among all nations until the full realization of the Reign of God with the Second coming of Lord Jesus. Besides, the following similarities help the human person to grasp the common human destiny.

God/Ultimate reality	Global
Universal human family	Global
Sin/evil	Global
Human quest for universal moral law	Global
Human thirst for salvation/liberation	Global
Mission of world religions building just and peaceful society based on transcendental values	Global
Eschatological vision	Global

From the above illustration, we can *roughly* infer that if humanity has a common origin (God), a common search (spiritual/material), a common pilgrimage (kingdom of God "already and not-yet"), a common end (integral liberation/salvation "here" and "after"), common problem (sin and evil manifested in diverse ways), then this commonality ought to lead humanity to common solutions. Pope John Paul II notes that "an element common to all religion is "a profound respect for conscience and an obedience to conscience which teaches all of us to seek the truth, to love and to serve every person and all people," to respect, protect and promote human life, to overcome selfishness, greed and the spirit of revenge."[20] The declaration of the Parliament of World's Religions in Chicago (1993) proposes four irrevocable global ethics: (1) You shall not kill! Or in positive terms: Have respect for life! (2) You shall not steal! Or in positive terms: Deal honestly and fairly! (3) You shall not lie! Or in positive terms: Speak and act truthfully! (4) You shall not commit sexual immorality! Or in positive terms: Respect and love one another.[21,22] Pope John Paul II in his address to the Papal Academy of Social Sciences on 27 April 2001 supported the universal search for a common ethical code for humankind. The World Council of Churches, at its Eighth General Assembly in Harare in 1998, called for fundamental shared ethics. Pope Benedict XVI also calls upon people to formulate a "common code of ethics" "rooted in the natural law inscribed by the Creator on the conscience of every human being" (cf. Rm 2:14-15) (n. 8). Besides, today humanity needs a conversion to realize (1) Stability without stagnation, (2) Freedom without anarchy, (3) Development without ecological catastrophe, (4) Creating one world without losing our individual identities, (5) Conflict resolution in a non-violent way without war and aggression, (6) Human dignity for all people by human rights for all people.[23]

Conclusion

It is no exaggeration to say that we inhabit a divided world. The way the globalisation operates today, seems to divide as much as it unites the world. Thus, there are both winners and losers, the included and the excluded. Catholicism privileges those who lack voice and resources by making a preferential option for the poor. This preferential option for the poor gives the Catholic Social teaching a bias for the victims of history because in the poor the Church sees Christ (cf. n. 15). Moreover, Pope John Paul II notes that the ultimate winner of the process of globalisation must be "humanity as a whole, and not just the wealthy elite that control science, technology, communication and the planet's resources to the detriment of the vast majority of its people".[24] Besides, the emerging global culture must be moulded by global ethics. As Cardinal Alfonso Lopez Trujillo observes that global ethics are needed because, "There is a very close relationship between globalisation and attempts by the most economically developed countries to arrogantly impose prevailing pseudo-values".[25] To create a just globalisation, the slogans ought to be "Trade for People, not People for Trade"; "People not profit"; "Our world is not for sale"; and "Another world is possible".[26] The same globalisation, with global ethic and global solidarity is capable of bringing peace and a new world order. Yet, until the human person overcomes the greed, craving, and insensibility in his heart, peace will be a mirage and integral development a nightmare. It is the duty of the disciples of Christ, with all people of good will to work together to fight poverty to build peace.

Notes

1. Robert J. Schreiter, The New Catholicity; Theology between the Global and the Local, Orbis Books, Maryknoll, NY 1997, 122-126.
2. Martin E. Marty-R. Scott Appleby (eds.), Accounting for Fundamentalisms, Chicago University Press, Chicago 1994, 32.
3. Joseph E. Stiglitz, Globalisation and its Discontents, W. W. Norton & Company, New York, 2003, 6.
4. *Ibidem*, 25.
5. *http://www.Zenit.org (02.09.2008)*
6. *http://www.Zenit.org (29.10.2008)*
7. Pontifical Academy of Social Sciences, Acta 7, Globalisation Ethical and Industrial Concerns, the Proceedings of the Seventh Plenary Session of the Pontifical Academy of Social Sciences 25-28 April 2001, Vatican City, 37-39.
8. John Paul II, "Message for the World Day of Peace", (1st January 1998), 3: AAS 90 (1998), 50.
9. The first commandment of the 21st century has become the adaptation to climate change. "Who will ride us to rescue? Even at Davos, where the chieftains of world politics and industry gather on Wednesday (24.01.2007) for the World Economic forum, a worry is creeping in that nobody is really in charge." International Herald Tribune, Wednesday, January 24, 2007, 7.
10. Cfr. Paul VI, "Nel X anniversario del C.E.L.AM, Esortazione Pastorale Per il Lavoro Apostolico Nell'America Latina", (23 novembre 1965), Insegnamenti, (1965), III, 653-669.
11. "These are: anti-globalism, ethnification, and primitivism. Each of these chooses certain strategies to reassert the local in the face of the global." See, Robert J. Schreiter, The New Catholicity, Theology between the Global and the Local, 20 See also, Martin E. Marty-R. Scott Appleby, Fundamentalisms Comprehended, University of Chicago Press, Chicago-London, 1995.

12. "In Latin America, where the disastrous import-substitution development model of the 1970s gradually gave way to a 1990s consensus on economic opening, the enthusiasm that accompanied the taming of inflation gave way to anger over growing income disparities and poverty. Hugo Chávez of Venezuela emerged to lead the anti-market, anti-Washington charge with his missed-a-century cry of "Socialism or Death." Bolivia, Ecuador, Nicaragua and, of course Cuba got nostalgic and liked the sound of that." Roger Cohen, "Since the Cold War, a world of vast change", International Herald Tribune, Saturday-Sunday, February 17-18, 2007, 2.
13. Joseph E. Stiglitz, Globalisation and its Discontents, 248-249.
14. Pope Benedict XVI, "Angelus Domini", 12 November 2006, L'Osservatore Romano (Editione Italiana), Lunedi-Martedi 13-14 November, 2006 (Translation from Italian). "Although no one has been able to measure this exactly, the general estimate is that approximately 20 per cent of the world's population benefits from globalisation, while 80 per cent find their position worsened. If the poor has become central to an understanding of mission during the Cold War period, their situation cries out even more for action today." Robert J. Schreiter, "Globalisation and Reconciliation, Challenges to Mission" in Robert J. Schreiter (ed.), Mission in the Third Millennium, Orbis Books, Maryknoll, NY 2001, 125-126.
15. "Yet dialogue alone is not sufficient to overcome extremism; there is always need for attention to basic aspects of society: family life, education, social development, the influence of the mass media, promotion of justice and solidarity within countries and on an international scale." See, Annual report (the committee for dialogue of the PCID and Permanent committee of al-Azhar for dialogue with Monotheistic Religions), Pro Dialogo 110, (2002/2), 228.
16. Cfr. Robert J. Schreiter, "Epilogue, Mission in the Third Millennium", in Robert J. Schreiter (ed.), Mission in the Third Millennium, Orbis Books, Maryknoll, NY 2001, 157.
17. "Globalisation has heightened the sense of the local, but also the sense of loss of control over the local, immediate environment in which people live. People then turn to religion to find some surer footing in the midst of the maelstrom that globalisation creates. The result is that religion becomes invested with the means to create a more secure social space....Other religious traditions are then extirpated from that space. Christians have

often become victims of this kind of interreligious violence...Such violence is further formented by the fact that Christianity, given its colonial past, is identified with the alienating forces of globalisation arising from the West.", Robert J. Schreiter, "Epilogue, Mission in the Third Millennium", in Robert J. Schreiter (ed.), Mission in the Third Millennium, Orbis Books, Maryknoll, NY 2001, 150-151.

18. Robert J. Schreiter, "Reconciliation as a new paradigm of mission", Conference on World Mission and Evangelism, Athens (Greece), 9-16 May 2005, Document n. 1.
19. John Paul II, "Message for the World Day of Peace 2001", Rome, December 8, 2000, in Interreligious Dialogue, The Official Teaching of the Catholic Church from the Second Vatican Council to John Paul II (1963-2005), 805.
20. John Paul II, "To the Diplomatic Corps", Rome, January 10, 1987", in Interreligious Dialogue, The Official Teaching of the Catholic Church from the Second Vatican Council to John Paul II (1963-2005), 410.
21. Declaration towards a Global Ethic (September 1993) as quoted by Konrad Raiser, "Global Order and Global Ethic", in Concilium 5 (2001) 22.
22. Declaration towards a Global Ethic (September 1993) as quoted by Konrad Raiser, "Global Order and Global Ethic", in Concilium 5 (2001) 22.
23. Lucas Thumma, "Seminar on Globalisation", Petri News, Bangalore; St. Peter's Seminary, December 2004, 23.
24. Pontifical Academy of Social Sciences, Acta 7, Globalisation Ethical and Industrial Concerns, the Proceedings of the Seventh Plenary Session of the Pontifical Academy of Social Sciences 25-28 April 2001, Vatican City, 29.
25. Cardinal Alfonso López Trujillo, "The Family and Globalisation", in pontifical Council for the Family, Proceedings of the International Conference of Globalisation, Economics and Family, Vatican City, November 27-29, 2000, Libreria Vaticana, Città del Vaticano 2001, 9.
26. James E. Hug SJ "Economic Justice and Globalisation", in John A. Coleman–William F. Rayan (eds.), Globalisation and Catholic Social Thought, Present Crisis, Future Hope, Orbis Books, Maryknoll, NY 2005, 62.

10

The Church in Post-Colonial Goa: The Portuguese Legacy and the Development Process

Sharon D'Cruz

The 'discovery' of an ocean route to the East Indies by the Iberian seafarers was an important enigma as it marked the dawn of the 'Vasco da Gama Epoch' in the history of Asia[1]: an 'Epoch' that drastically changed the subghat image of Goa into a thalossocratic one–at least in the colonial literature. 'Discoveries' are generally perceived to be "mere accidents in history". But, this was not the case with the Portuguese because they did not come merely as traders, "...if there were no merchants who go and seek for earthly fortunes in the East and West Indies, who would transport the preachers who take the heavenly treasures there"[2]. While the former were well known as *Conqistadores,* the latter can be termed as *Conquistadores das almas.*

Having consolidated their shoestring Empire in the East, the Portuguese established the Metropolitan Sé of the *Estado da India* at *Velha Goa.* The territorial jurisdiction of the Portuguese in Goa in the first half of the 16th century was limited to the *Velhas Conquistas*[3]. The geographical conditions of the land together with the appropriate socio-economic and political milieu enabled the Portuguese to set up an entrepôt port in 'Goa' and use it as a springboard for a delve into the Indian Ocean World Economic System. Further, the *Padroado* obligations and the close alliance between the Cross and the Sword 'morally bound' the Portuguese Monarchs to evangelize, christianize and lusitanize the "newly discovered lands", Goa being no exception to this. From here, they undertook a 'Spiritual Conquest of the East'[4] wherein they tried to christianize and lusitanize the people and give a realistic form to the *Respublica Christiana*. This was a conscious effort that was legalized by the Crown and sanctified by Papal Bulls like the *Romanus Pontifex, Inter Caetera, Regimini Militantis* etc. The missionaries assumed the role of the 'standard bearers of the faith'. The State supported them in this 'divine enterprise' of "swiftly possessing the souls and riches of the East". Both, *a priori* and *a posteiori*, assimilative and discriminative and 'carrot' and 'stick ' policies were used to lure the converts and punish the non-converts[5].

This 'conscious' effort resulted in the 'formation' of *Goa Dourada* that is aptly described as "a tiny piece of Portugal that was implanted onto the tropical soil"[6] and it was not uncommon for a casual visitor to remark, "*Aqui é Portugal.*" The *Gomantak Punyabhumi* of the yesteryears was temporarily forgotten and gradually replaced by much the touted Golden Goa paradigm, that considered Goa to be "a limpet clinging onto the West coast of India"[7]. However, it was not long before the Goans realized that they were denaturalized and denationalized to the extent of being "rendered as aliens to their own soil"[8]. The *Konkan Kashi* or the cool and refreshing land that was the "abode of the Gods" was superseded by the 'Rome of the Orient'.

But, what was ignored was that even by the 20th century, the Portuguese had been successful in alienating a small section of the Goans from their *Mai Patria*. The majority of the Goans, particularly those who lived along the peripheries of and in the *Novas Conquistas*[9] or in British India, continued to follow the Indian lifestyle and had an emotional attachment to India; they represented the *Goa Indica* paradigm[10]. It must be noted that the *Velhas Conquistas* included only 1/5th of the present day Goa. The *Novas Conquistas,* that included seven *talukas,* were acquired only in the eighteenth century and even here, only 14% were converted till 1961[11]. Before the arrival of the Portuguese, Goa was not a *tabula rasa* and hence we speak of *Goa Indica* and even *Goa Rustica.* The chroniclers and the chronicle-based historiography denied the Goan people and the hinterland a separate existence. They were relegated to the status of being mere objects and a geographical expression.

Even the Lusophiles, who were temporarily overwhelmed by the 'Latin, Christian' culture, gradually assimilated it and evolved a composite or syncretic culture. The product of the 'cultural metabolism'[12] or a recreation of "what existed among and what was thrust upon the Goans" is an essential component of the Goan diaspora or the 'Goan identity'. The presence of the Portuguese influences gave Goa an unique identity-an identity that was 'essentially different from the Indian and Portuguese identity. This is evident in the popular myths, folk culture, festivals, symbols *et al* all of which provide a 'base' to a Goan. The composite or syncretic culture that grew therefrom is termed *Goa Indo Portuguesa.* This was Indian in form but Iberian in content. The converts, for instance, followed a Lusitanian lifestyle, but they did not give up the Hindu practices. Goan Christians felt at home to seek greater affinity with their colonial brethren in religion. Incidentally, the Goan Hindus have their own variants of wounded identity and this cannot be resolved too simplistically. The Christian farmers cut paddy sheaves and took them in a procession to the village temple to be blessed by Brahman priests before the harvest.[13] Many Goans felt the oppression of the caste structure or of the traditional class structure. Many had changed their religion to escape from these structures and with the hope of improving their life conditions. The caste conflicts were obvious in the Confraternities that were created on caste-basis and the colour of the *opmus* clearly distinguished a *Bammon* from a *Charddo* and the two from a *Shudra.* The caste exclusivism is illustrated by an incident that occurred in the Parish of Guirim that had a Confraternity of Jesus and that of Our Lady of the Rosary. A friar instructed an old woman to call upon the name of Jesus on her deathbed but she was indignant and replied angrily: "*Jezú? Jezú nam! Jezú tencho!* "(Jesus? There is no Jesus, Jesus belongs to them) Obviously, she was of *Charddo* caste, and the Confraternity of Jesus was composed of the brahmins!.[14] The concept of the 'colonial other' existed whether consciously or unconsciously. But we cannot blame personalities or institutions that were involved in the 'State sponsored' venture because we have to see them "in the historical context in which they functioned"[15]. The psychology of the Portuguese has to be understood as 'Conquerors', 'Traders', 'Discoverers' and 'Christianizers,' while that of the Goans has to be considered in the context of their being the 'Discovered', 'a Conquered People', 'a Captive Trading People' and a 'Christianised People'[16]. Several aspects of Christianization and the Cultural Encounters that took place thereafter are available and these can be used for a better analysis of the Colonial Church within the paradigm of Decolonisation.[17]

In history, a few theories remain static. Theories are generally based on facts and these facts constantly change as and when 'new' sources are 'unearthed'. Moreover, theories are based on the 'historiographical constructs' that are adopted by the historians. As such, the Imperialist approach is generally contradictory to the arguments that are made by the Indologists and Nationalists, while those of the Orientalists are 'essentially' different from those of the Subalterns. In recent times, the Theory of Modernity, that focused on meta narratives and empiricism, was gradually abandoned in favour of Post Modernity: a theoretical construct that consciously ignores the foundational theories and macro-level analysis. Such an approach takes into account contextual micro-level variations. It is inter-disciplinary in approach and anti-foundational in content. The source value of Church records in recording the organization and activity of the Church in Goa are outlined by the scholars in Indo-Portuguese history.[18]

In studying the role of the post-liberated Church in the Goan context, I have made use of tradition-modernity continuum to explain the formation of a post colonial identity in what can be called a *Gemeinschaft* and has grown into a

Gesellschaft. In addressing the formation of such an identity and the expression of the same through the participation of the institutionalized Church in the various social movements in Goa, one has to take into account the historical facts as well as the Little Traditions that "existed in the minds and hearts of the people" in general and the Church in particular that were never allowed to be expressed fully either because of the close alliance between the Sword and the Cross, or because of the obligations of the *Padroado Real,* or later because of the division of loyalties between the *Padroado Real* and the *Propoganda Fidei* that was fully manifested in post 1961. But it must be noted that an identity *per se* has its base in the past and the discourse between the past and the present can be best understood by those communities who have lived through the past and have been assimilated into the present.

In the post-Republican period there was a whiff of liberalism. The global struggle with the Dutch assumed severe proportions. Besides this, the Portuguese had to deal with the Marathas, Sondekars, Mughals and other local enemies. The mainland was also engulfed by a 'hydra of nativism'[19] that took the form of spontaneous insurgencies and nationalist discourses. The revolts of the 'unsung heroes' and the ideologies of the 'voiceless in Goan historiography' need to be analyzed. Ironically, the Portuguese were unable to sustain the colonial vestiges because the sea-borne Empire was undergoing a twilight. There was a strong demand in favour of the secular clergy. The Thalosocratic State and the *gaonkars* refused to contribute for the maintenance of the Christian cult. The Portuguese had to use their own methods to extract the agrarian surplus and gain the support of the locals. In fact, the Lusitanian culture was now dependent on the local realities.

During the liberation movement, Salazar stated "...what needs to be noted in Portuguese India is the mentality, the outlook on life and the spiritual atmosphere... Goa is a transplantation of the West onto the Eastern lands; the expression of Portugal in India".[20] His close alliance with the Pope (*Concordat* of 1940) had become a subject of criticism even in Portugal as were his anti-liberal policies. Even Nehru admitted that Goa was different from India. Most Goan Christians who were faithful to the Goan Church Magisterium collaborated with the 'civilizing mission' that was emphasized by Dr. Salazar in the *Acto Colonial do Estado Novo*. The Nationalists were forced to change their domicile to the neighboring Indian territory and they along with those who rose against the Fascist Regime were condemned as 'bad Catholics' or excommunicated and even denied a Church burial on grounds of being 'communists'. What was forgotten was that one cannot understand the Latin or Christian aspect of Goa *en masse* without delimiting the geographical parameters and defining its components. Microcosm studies have to be undertaken, as a Goan is a patrilocal individual. It is important to pose new questions to the old issues and in certain cases pose a counter perspective to the dominant ideologies.

After liberation, the local, national and international press eulogised the Indian intervention in the liberation of Goa. In December 1961[21], there was an announcement that Rome had appointed the Lisbon based, Dom Jose Pedro da Silva as the new Auxiliary Bishop of Goa with the right to succeed as the Patriarch instead of a qualified and experienced Goan in accordance with the *Mater et Magistra* of John XXIII. Hence, the liberation of Goa did not cause any violent upheaval in the administration of the Church of Goa[22]. Following liberation, the Portuguese Patriarch in Goa maintained a low profile and moved out after the Second Vatican Council. At that time till 1971, there was a decrease in the Christian population from 38% to 34% while the number of Hindus increased from 384378 to 496389. Over the next decade, the number of Christians was 31% and in 1991, this figure stood at 29.86%[23]. In 1963, Msgr Francisco Xavier da Piedade Rebello then emerged as the 'natural leader': the Bishop and Administrator Apostolic of Goa[24]. Thereafter, the Church in Goa found it difficult to retain the colonial legacy. Some Christians felt that it was this legacy that gave Goa a distinct identity *vis-a-vis* the others who took the *longe duree* into consideration and asserted that the Goan identity had its roots in the pre-Portuguese setup and hence, it was not very different from the larger Indian identity. This issue rang out loud and clear during the Opinion Poll.

The political developments of the post-Liberation period have been complex. In less than a year after liberation, the Panchayati Raj Institutions were established in the Goan villages. Further, the elections in October 1962 changed the 'very nature' of the political process in Goa as they were based on universal suffrage. The Maharashtrawadi Gomantak Party (MGP), with its *Bahujan Samaj* ideology and Marathi language, was used as an expression of populism that sought to whip up communal feelings[25]. While the Hindu elite vote got divided between the Congress and United Goans Party (UGP), most of the Christians rallied around the UGP, but the MGP won with an absolute majority in the first elections and continued to rule over Goa for more than a decade. The church of Goa has been accused of encouraging a vote to keep Goa out of Maharashtra in the first Assembly elections and in the Opinion Poll of 1967. Incidentally, a large number of under-aged seminarians of the Rachol Seminary voted in the Opinion Poll against the merger of Goa.

After 1967, there were major changes within the Catholic Church at the National and International levels. The Second Vatican Council stressed the responsibility of the laity and motivated the Church to introspect into its functioning. Termed as an 'Ecumenical Revolution', it propagated the concept of 'Liberation Theology' that focused on the involvement of the Church in societal issues. To implement the decisions of Vatican II, a Seminar on 'The Church in Goa Today' was held in 1968 as a preparation for the National Seminar on 'The Church in India Today' that was scheduled for 1970. The latter gave importance to the establishment of a Senate for the priests, Diocesan Centres for Social Apostolates and a Pastoral Bulletin. At this Regional Seminar, the socio economic welfare activities of the Church were reviewed and the Church acknowledged that it had made valuable contributions to promote the socio-economic welfare of the people through Parishes, religious congregations and lay organizations through its own limited means. Further, the Church in Goa stressed Recognition,

Respect, Cooperation and Multireligious Solidarity.[26] Though it took ten years to set up a Diocesan Pastoral Council and to establish Parish Level Councils, it was a sort of 'Democratic Revolution' that took place within an ecclesiastical set-up that was led by the laity along with the Diocesan and Religious priests and nuns.[27] There were appeals in favour of indigenous saints. It was accepted that Fr Agnelo deserved to be canonized and that Fr Jose Vas would serve as a model to the Diocesan secular clergy.[28]

A scan of the leadership of the Church over the last four decades indicates that it was both enlightened and pro-active. In the '60s the Church played a pivotal role in influencing the voters. In the '70s, the Church lent its open support to the *Ramponkars* or one of the 'traditional' fishing communities in Goa who were fighting against mechanized fishing and purseing that was carried out by the trawler owners. On January 30, 1978, the Archbishop issued a Circular which pleaded that an exclusive zone of 5 kms. from the shore should be reserved for the *Ramponkars*[29]. As a sign of solidarity, several nuns and priests participated in the agitation. One of the religious who was involved in the issue stated that the "official Church which was silent upto now... for the first time in recent years had come out openly and officially against the adamant attitude of the Government and opted for justice for the voiceless poor"[30]. The then Chief Minister extended the war by supporting a rebel nun and even tried to humiliate the Archbishop by threatening to withdraw his priority pass for crossing the ferry. This largely tainted her popularity before the Christian voters, who were strongly agitated over the issue of the Freedom of Religion Bill, 1978 and the hostility of the Chief Minister to the same. In 1973, the Church raised its voice against the Zuari Agro Chemicals Limited that was situated at Zuarinagar in Vasco da Gama area on the ground that it polluted the coastal waters. Given the seriousness of the situation, the Church backed the Anti-Pollution Campaign in 1974 to fight the menace of pollution.[31] The Social Action Forums have been instrumental in organizing the clergy and the laity to participate in anti-Goan and anti development projects. The Service Centre for Diocesan Action was set up in 1976. The contribution of the Church to the development of Goa and the "collaboration with other organizations to bring about the socio-economic development of Goa was the main thrust of this Centre"[32].

Since the '80's, the Church was directly involved and has indirectly patronized several NGO's that were fighting a battle against Tourism[33]. The '80s witnessed a tussle between the *Konkaniwadis* and the *Marathiwadis* with the former asserting their stand that Konkani was the official language of Goa. On February 1, 1987[34], the Church expressed its solidarity with the pro-Konkani faction. Later, the pro-Konkani movement was used to ensure the "separate status for Goa". When the Official Language Bill was passed, the Pastoral Bulletin welcomed the compromise as "a better part of realism, though it did not hide its disappointment manifested in the use of a rather strong expression "bigamy" to describe the place accorded to Marathi in the Bill"[35]. The Church played an important role in the Anti Merger Issue. It demanded a "separate political status for Goa" and was fully backed by the United Goans Party in this regard. There were several reports that the priests gave open and worse still 'political' speeches from the pulpits[36]. Both the clergy and the laity made their presence felt at public meetings and marched on the streets against the proposed merger of Goa into the neighbouring States. The Church also raised its voice against the commercialization of the Carnival that was projected as a 'Christian tradition 'at the Carnival float that was held in Delhi in 1983 on grounds that it "jeopardized the ethical values". The Pastoral Bulletin of 1 February, 1984, openly referred to the "coming *tamasha* of Carnaval" and warned the Catholics not to allow their children to fall prey and be pleasure toys for the benefit of the Tourism industry. The Church even went a step further and protested against the celebration of Carnival in the Panjim Church square and demanded a ban on the same. At the forefront was the Diocesan Centre for Social Action that carried out the propaganda campaign against this event. The citizens along with the Christians of Margao under the

Diocesan Centre for Social Action paraded on the streets along with two MLA's, priests and nuns against the Carnival parade. After three years of an 'organised effort', the Church forced the Government to withdraw its patronage of corporate-sponsored Carnival floats. In 1993, the Central Ministry for Tourism insisted that Carnival was important for the promotion of Tourism in the State, The State took precautionary measures and set up a Screening Committee that was headed by a Christian[37]. This had an appropriate effect and since then, Carnival has been a muted affair.

The Church has vociferously opposed several developmental projects that were allegedly opposed to the interests of the Goans. It was in the forefront to oppose the coastal alignment of the Konkan Railway Corporation, as it was a threat to the fragile coastal ecology and to the 'space' and identity of the Goans. It was opined that it was passing through the thickly populated villages thereby disrupting the life of the Goans. The Church backed the 'mutinous' villagers of Salcette and other villages and was instrumental in the formation of the All Goa Citizens' Committee for Social Action that spearheaded the protests and pressurized the Court to change the alignment. Priests, nuns and lay Catholics participated in various forms of protests and extended full support to the campaign for realignment.[38] The Archbishop himself wrote a letter to the Prime Minister requesting him to intervene in the matter, while "mobs of Christians" attacked the labourers and destroyed the equipment at the KRC construction sites. In spite of all these efforts that were put in by the Goans including the Church, the anti-KRC agitation failed.

The role of the Church in the anti-Metastrips agitation is too well known to be repeated. In opposing the setting up of Metastrips at Sancoale, the Church pointed out issues of spawned hutments, sanitation, public health, overcrowding etc and directly confronted the State against the implementation of the project[39]. The logic was clear: the effluents from the imported scrap would pollute the Goan ecology. The Church encouraged the local Christians to rally around the Anti-Metastrips Citizens' Action Committee that was turned into the "public voice of the Church" overnight. Priests organised rallies and made passionate speeches at public meetings as the Church assumed an activist role. The newspapers carried the photographs of two priests who were injured in this agitation. Referring to the agitation on the Zuari bridge, the Church assailed the atrocities of the police and the Government on the 'innocent citizens'. The Archbishop personally visited those who were on a fast unto death outside the Secretariat.[40] The Church also lent its support to the anti-Nylon 66 agitation, a people's agitation that was intended to counter the polluting factory that was proposed to be set up in Keri, Ponda. The spokesman of the Church appealed to the State Government to pay "heed to the just demands of the oppressed people and to bring the crisis to a satisfactory solution".[41]

In 1990, the Archdiocese of Goa hosted a Consultation on Tourism that was sponsored by the Catholic Bishops' Conference of India (CBCI). Since then the Church has been instrumental in raising the banner of protest against the bane of Tourism in the State.[42] In the elections of 1994, the Church launched an unscrupulous attack on the political situation in the State. In his message on the Justice and Peace Sunday, the Archbishop requested the Christians to vote out the "politicians who have been supporting projects that were detrimental to the good of Goa and the Goans".

The Church has raised its voice and even imposed bans to curb the proliferation of social evils among the Christian laity. The menace of alcohol is sought to be curbed by setting up units of the Alcoholics Anonymous in the Parishes. An official ban is imposed on the serving of alcoholic drinks within the Church premises. The Diocesan Pastoral Council vehemently opposed the steady growth of alcoholism and appealed to the State Government to curb the advertisements for alcoholic drinks and the issue of new licenses for bars and liquor shops. The Church also appealed in favour of the prohibition of the advertisement of alcoholic beverages at the functions that were organized by Church institutions.[43] Periodic efforts are made to avoid the consumption or association of alcohol at and with

Catholic rituals. The Archbishop of Goa spoke in terms of a Radical Church that could serve as an instrument of Social Revolution. He periodically called upon the laity to attack the "roots" of the problems that were faced by society and "to eliminate the causes rather than the effects of social injustice". The proposal to make Goa a Free Port was openly opposed as it would be a threat to 'Goa's Sovereignty'.[44]

In the nineties, the Church in Goa had developed an 'ideology of resistance' and rallied against the politicians who wanted to sell Goa to the forces that were out to destroy Goa's economy, culture, social composition, demographic profile and identity . The Church as an institution and the Archbishop as the head of the Church in Goa periodically raised concerns about the undemocratic attitudes of the Government. The Church in Goa has had the benefit of being backed by a genre of 'conscious' laity. Recently, there was a statement that was issued by eight Goan writers and artists, who requested the Ministry of Information and Broadcasting to put restrictions on Doordarshan so that it was restrained from telecasting road shows and beach parties in Goa as a part of the Millenium New Year celebrations on ground that "the telecast is a direct attack on our cultural ethos"[45].

The post-colonial Church has taken progressive steps to promote inter-religious dialogue and to strengthen Hindu Catholic solidarity. The Church has been vehement in denouncing acts of Communalism and Communal Disharmony as is evident from the strong critiques that were made against the allegedly 'communal' activities that included the minor bomb blast in St Andrews Church, Vasco da Gama, Saleli and later in Sanvordem and the minor outbursts in Kundaim, Chicalim, Assagao, St Estevam etc. When the Hindus in India wanted the Pope to publicly apologize for the atrocities' of the Catholic Church in the colonial past, the Goan clergy denounced this as they found it unjustifiable. Secularism has been the ideal of the Church of Goa as indicated in the proceedings of the Diocesan Synod. There are efforts even among the religious in favour of Indianization and Swadeshi. In 1999, the Archbishop of Goa voiced his dissent over the

Target Asia Mission on the ground that the Church would be isolated if this target was followed. In the elections of 2002, the Church called upon the laity not to vote for the candidates who represented Communalism and corruption. The Archbishop even referred to a "Crusade against corruption"[46]. Thanks to the efforts of the clergy, the voters of Cortalim opted for a third alternative and outvoted the National Parties.

The post-liberation Church was instrumental in conscientising, mobilizing and bringing thousands of laity on the street to provide mass support to several issues that were detrimental to the 'development' and 'progress' of the State. The recent agitation against the Regional Plan 2011 witnessed the direct involvement of the Church in this anti developmental issue.[47] The colonial Church tried to be where the rulers were. The post-liberation tried to be where the laity were[48]. The Church particularly after the first two decades after liberation, has been a vigilant and pro active Church as is manifested in its opposition to several anti development movements. It is important to note that Social Action Cells are set up in several Parishes in Goa and these have been instrumental in playing the important role of 'watch dogs' in the Goan villages. Many of them have been active at Gram Sabhas and have raised their voices against the anti development forces. There are sincere efforts being made by Parish Animation Teams, Community Animation Teams, Family Cells, Social Action Cells etc in the Parishes across the State particularly after the Diocesan Synod. The Church has played a predominant role in the struggle for environmental rights, child rights, human rights and the rights of women and other marginalized sections of society. The concept of 'Justice and Peace', 'Campaign against Hunger and Disease' and the 'Preferential Option for the Poor' are among the many projects that were successfully championed by the Church on behalf of the CBCI as an institution. The Church promotes an annual campaign against hunger and disease by raising money for the needy and the poor so as to provide them with the basic human needs.[49] In December, 1984, the Church made it obligatory for the Parishes to start a fund for the relief of the poor[50]. There was an organized effort to "conscientise the people about and to launch a protest against the injustice that was meted out to the marginalized, particularly the Christians of the Schedule Caste origin"[51]. The Church has distributed her land at Baida in Chinchinim to house nearly thirty families. Several Religious Congregations and Diocesan Parishes have started farms and yet others have started technical institutes. In Ambaji, the Society of St Vincent de Paul runs a night school for the poor and the illiterate. There is an Ozanam Library in Margao and a SVP Library in Verna. In Magao, Navelim and other places the members of the SVP have free Legal Aid Cells. In other villages, they have started Medical Clinics, Rehabilitation Centres for the Alcoholics, ambulances, Old Age Homes, KG and Primary Schools etc.[52]. The members of the SVP that are animated by the parish priest champion the cause of the poor, the sick and the needy. The role of the Church as an institution in promoting charity is commendable as it runs 30 homes for the aged and the destitute, 5 hostels and boarding houses, 9 orphanages, 7 rehabilitation centres, hospitals, vocational training institutes (like St Bridget, Fr. Agnel Training Institute, Don Bosco's Crafts Centre etc) homes for the fallen women, creches, centres for the physically and mentally challenged etc. The Religious Congregations have established 6 hospitals and 5 dispensaries apart from health centres, mobile clinics etc. There are 13 primary, 6 Middle, 106 High and 13 Higher Secondary Schools, 5 Colleges and 7 technical institutes that are sponsored by the Church[53]. The Church has also taken up the responsibility of rehabilitating the prisoners in the Goan jails through the Prison Ministry and undertaking Maternal and Child Health Programmes. The Domestic Workers attracted the attention of the Church that later organized the NDWM and took up the issue of Domestic Workers in Goa[54].

It is indeed very surprising that the Church had for some time acquired a very narrow, pro Goan view. The Pastoral letter of 1995, for instance, had clearly stated that "Our proverbial hospitality is being challenged today by ever-growing influx of non-Goans into our State threatening our security and comfort". Now that the number of immigrants has increased manifold, the Church has to officially accommodate and adopt the immigrants on terms of equality into its fold and the Church has undertaken preliminary steps in this regard. Nevertheless, the Church has extended its full cooperation to the efforts to help those who had been victims of natural calamities. Among the others, the Church has extended generous financial aid to the victims of the Maharashtra earthquake (Rs. 6,20,996), Andhra Pradesh Cyclone Fund (Rs. 3,66,947), Kargil Fund (Rs. 6,56,000), Orissa Cyclone fund (Rs. 3,04,223) etc.[55].

A large section of the Christian population has joined the 'Christian' sects that are mushrooming in Goa. The display of the Roman Catholic cult has become difficult as the State no longer favours the Church and funds are hard to come by on account of the post-global crises. Few people volunteer to work in 'Gods vineyard' and even those who are recruited are not up to the mark. The Diocesan Synod 2002 has attempted to empower the lay people and tried to monitor the cult and the flock through Parish Councils, Pastoral Councils, Community Animation Teams, Parish Animation Teams, Small Christian Communities etc. But, the questions are 'Hasn't the Church that had a basis in colonialism been able to assert its liberated status in the post-modern world?'; 'wasn't the Church in a position to maintain a consensus in taking decisions that allegedly alienated the contending, 'Christian' forces that dominate the opposition party in Goa?' and 'hasn't the Church pragmatically accommodated the new challenges and come up with an institutional response to the same?'.

An evaluation of the pastoral effectiveness of the Church in Goa particularly after liberation, has definitely been on the positive side *kudos* to the 'educated' and self-confident clergy and laity of Goa. A regular opposition is voiced both from socially concerned individuals and watch groups that have been keeping an effective check on the 'abuses' by powerful interest groups. Even the religious have grown with experience at all levels and are well conscientised and equipped to continue the task of "building the kingdom of God on Earth without leaving all concerns to life beyond"[56].

This study is a micro-level study that is restricted to the State of Goa. However, the socio-religious dimension of the Church in Goa can be further studied and evaluated within the broader perspectives that are related to 'confrontation', 'governance', 'institutionalization' and 'policing' particularly after the State that was hitherto a 'standard bearer of the Portuguese State' has ceased to remain so in the post-liberation period. There is much being said and written and efforts are under way for re-writing the history of the Church from the perspective of the Third World[57]. It is argued that much that we have by way of Church history is written by the missionaries and from the missionary perspective and this is never delinked from the Eurocentic, Christocentric and Lusocentric perspective. In analyzing the role of the post colonial Church in Goa, we have to undertake a dispassionate analysis so that we are able to understand the Church within a larger historical context.

The Church in Goa started the New Year on a progressive note of renewing its commitment to promote the development of the State. She is "willing to be an active partner in this collaborative effort for regeneration" and has highlighted "her sacred duty towards humanity to help in the integral development of the human person..."[58]. Such a commitment will go a long way in putting the post-liberation Church on the 'right track' *vis-à-vis* the development process that the State is undergoing.

Notes

1. Pannikar K. M., *Asia and Western Dominance: A survey of the Vasco da Gama Epoch of Asian History (1415-1945)*, George Allen and Unwin Ltd., London, 1959
2. This statement is attributed to Fernao de Castanheda.
3. After the second Conquest of Goa on 25th November 1510, Goa was limited to the Islands of Goa that included Tisvadi, Chorao, Divar, Jua and Vamsi. These areas were under the political tutelage of the Adil Shah of Bijapur. After 1543, they acquired the adjoining areas of Bardez and Salcette.
4. Paulo da Trindade's magnum Opus is called *Conquista Espiritual do Oriente.*

5. For the conversion policies of the Portuguese refer to Kamat Pratima, *Farar Far: Local Resistance to the colonial hegemony in Goa (1510-1912)*, Institute Menezes Braganza, Panaji, 1999 and Mendonca Delio, *Conversions and Citizenry in Goa*, Concept, New Delhi, 2002 and P.P Shirodkar, 'Evangelisation and its harsh realities in Portuguese India' in T.R. de Souza (ed), *Discoveries, Missionary Expansion and Asian cultures*, Concept Publishers, New Delhi, 1994, p. 33, pp. 80-82.
6. Caroline Ifeka, 'The image of Goa' in T.R de Souza (ed.), *Indo Portuguese History: Old Issues, New Questions*, Concept Publishing Co., New Delhi, 1985, pp. 182-183.
7. *Ibid.*, pp. 190-191.
8. Cunha T.B., *Denationalization of the Goans*, 1940, Monograph.
9. These included the remaining 8 talukas of Goa that were acquired by the Portuguese only in the late 18th century.
10. Arun Sinha, *Goa Indica: A critical portrait of Post colonial Goa*, Bibliophile South Asia, 2002.
11. Even more shocking are the Statistics that are provided by the Official Census of 1891. Even after the Portuguese acquired the *Novas Conquistas*, the number of Christians in Goa was 232189 or 64.5% of the population. Sinha Arun, *Op. Cit.*, p. 27.
12. Verresimo Coutinho, *Education and Development in Goa*, ICSS, Rome, 1987.
13. Arun Sinha, *Op.Cit.*, pp.28-28. The issues on Goan identity are taken up by de Souza T.R., 'Goan culture and Identity: Historically speaking' in *Boletim do Instituto de Vasco da Gama*, Vol. 162, 1991, p. 57.
14. Teotónio R de Souza., 'The Portuguese in the Goan folklore: *Some preliminary comments*', goacom_culture.
15. Teotónio R de Souza, 'The Christian Mission in the aftermath of discoveries: Tools for shaping the colonial other' in T.R. de Souza (ed), *Op.Cit.*, 1994, p.33.
16. Anthony da Silva, 'The Discoverers versus the Discovered: Psychological Perspectives on Portuguese Goan prejudices in the 16th -18th centuries' in T.R. de Souza (ed), *Op.Cit.*, 1994, pp. 45-49.
17. These issues formed the content of the *Congresso Internacional de Historia: Missionacao Portuguesa e Encontro de Culturas*, Braga, 1993.

For a base for the study of such an aspect in Goa T.R de Souza, 'Christianisation of Goa and cultural conflicts' in T.R de Souza (ed), *Goa to me*, Concept Publishers, 2000, pp. 86-97.

18. The records in the Historical Archives of Goa like the *Rois de Christandade* and those in the Patriarchical Archives like the *Visita Pastoral* etc as well as the State and Parish records will give us a better understanding of the Colonial Church. For details one may refer to de Sousa T.R., 'Voiceless in Goan History..'
19. Roberto Bruto da Costa, *A Hidra do Nativismo*, Tipografia Braganca e cia, 1920.
20. This statement is attributed to Salazar in T.B Cunha, *Goa's Freedom Struggle*, T.B. Cunha Memorial Committee, Bombay, 1961, p.455.
21. Bulletin of the Goa Archdiocese, December 1961.
22. Teotónio R de Souza. 'The Church in Goa:*Giving to Caesar What is Caesar's?*' in goacom_history.
23. Arun Sinha, *Op.Cit.*
24. Teotónio R de Souza, *Op.Cit.* in goacom-history.
25. Teotónio R de Souz., *Op.Cit.*, in goacom-history.
26. Archdiocese of Goa, Goa Regional Seminar, Pilar, 1968.
27. Teotónio R de Souza. *Op.Cit.*, in goacom-history.
28. Teotónio R de Souza, 'Struggle for Sainthood' in *Goa Today*.
29. CP- Cr No. 2/78, 30th January 1978 and CR. No. 94/80 dated 27th May 1980.
30. Braz Faleiro, 'Ramponkars sttruggle for justice and its relationship to faith' *Religion and Society*, Vol. 27, No. 4, 1980, pp. 51-80. Anita haladi and Reggie Gomes also raise such issues in a paper presented at the Xavier Center for Historical Research.
31. Carlos da Gama, *Hacia una Evangelizacion Liberadora en Goa*, unpublished thesis, University of Salamanca, Madrid.
32. CP-Cr No. 123/76, 28th December 1976.
33. Arun Sinha, *Goa Indica: A critical potrait of Post colonial Goa*, Bibliophile South Asia, 2002, p. 115.
34. *Renovação.*
35. *Renovação*, March 1, 1987. 'Fight for *Mai Bhas' Herald*, 13 March.
36. There were several reports in the local dailies like the *Navhind Times, Herald, Gomantak Times* and in the other vernacular

newspapers regarding this. Alfred Braganza, 'The counting as I saw it: An account of the historic Opinion Poll', *Goa Today,* August 1996 ; L Cotta Carvalho, *Goa: The anatomy of Merger Politics,* New Delhi, 1966.

37. Arun Sinha, *op. cit.,* p. 116.

38. CP- Cr No. No. 55/93, 1st April 1993. Alexandre Barbosa 'Konkan Railway on a Trying Track' in *Goa Today,* November 2000 and in 'Off the track' in *Op.Cit,* August 1996.

39. Saturnino Dias, ' Issues behind the contraversial Meta strips plant in Goa', *Renovação,* 29 (15), 2000, pp. 342-44 and Diocesan Centre for Social Action, 'A statement on Metastrips' 1-15 August 1999; Claude Alvares (ed), *Fish, Curry and Rice,* Goa Foundation, Mapusa, pp.65-68.

40. The *Renovação* was virtually turned into a journal of the 'People's Movement' against Metastrips. Sinha Arun, *Op.Cit.,,* pp. 132-33.

41. Refer to the press statement dated 25th January 1995.

42. Wilson David, 'Paradoxes of Tourism in the State' in Norman Dantas (ed.) *Transforming of Goa,* Other India PressMapusa 1999.

43. Press statement issued by the Diocesan Pastoral Council, 27th July 1997.

44. *Diocesan Center for Social Action,* ' A Free Port for Goa' in *Renovação,* 1-15 August 1996.

45. *Renovação,* January 1-15 2000.

46. *Renovação,* August 1-15 2000.

47. A press report in that regard was even issued by the Diocesan Center for Media and Social Communication in the local newspapers. The Director of the Diocesan Center for Social Apostolate was in the forefront of the anti Regional Plan agitation.

48. Arun Sinha, *Op.Cit.,,* p. 116.

49. CP-Cr No. 3/75 dated 12th February 1975. The Church collected Rs. 46,874 in 2000.

50. *Renovação,*August 15 1984, p. 306.

51. CP- Cr No. 129/87 dated 4th August 1987.

52. *Vincentian Bulletin,* 1996 .

53. *Directory of the Archdiocese of Goa and Daman,* Patriarchical Curia, Panjim, 2000, pp. 243-260.

54. *Domestic Workers Link*, Vol. 5, No. 3, Dec. 1996.
55. Walter de Sa, 'The Church in Goa and Social Ministry', *Gyana*, Vol. I, No. 1, 2005-2006, p. 3.
56. Teotonio R de Souza. *Op.Cit.*, in goacom-history.
57. Lukas Vischer (ed.), *Towards a History of the Church in the Third World*, Bem, 1985.
58. *Navhind Times*, 29 December 2006.

11

Development as Quasi-Religious: A Critical Appraisal

Gnana Patrick

Introduction

We are living in an era of market-led development. The Market has become all encompassing, and has even gone to the extent of exercising a 'tyranny'[1] over the thought and activity of humanity. Development thinking, perhaps, is the most affected. The turn the Doha rounds of talks at WTO in July 2006 took by abandoning the agenda of overall development in favour of creating access for the market is a case in point.[2]

We find developmental projects undertaken disproportionately. Andhra's tryst with hi-tech industries is a good example. On the claim of development, Andhra's ruling elite took the state to the 'dizzy heights' of hi-tech development. But the project remained lopsided, and the victims of neglect are the farmers who continue to experience acute frustration (as evident in the cases of suicide). The welfare of those involved in the agricultural sector was sacrificed on the altar of hi-tech development. The huge dams built by throwing the ecosystem out of gear and displacing recklessly the inhabitants of the area of the dam are other examples.

While such experiences of development in a third world country like ours produce moral compunction in our hearts, the so-called 'developed' countries are following unethical and questionable means to support their developed status. Production of arms and dumping them on underdeveloped countries, exporting unstable nuclear plants to poorer countries, producing narcotics and smuggling them out to developing countries–are only some examples of the questionable means some countries follow to maintain their developed economy. The news that America produces marijuana as the top cash-crop, more than traditional harvests of wheat, corn, etc is symptomatic![3] That is a window to the kind of dubious practices a recklessly hi-tech developmentally oriented country can involve itself in.

Over against these cases on the ground, a section of developmental theoreticians–postmodern ones–have come to speak about the 'end of development'.[4] This manner of speaking goes along with similar discourses as 'end of history', 'end of the human', 'end of metaphysics', etc that have come to occupy the postmodern discourses. These discourses place a basic mistrust on development, calling it one among the 'metanarratives'. According to them, there is no universal knowledge or pattern of development.

While this apparently is the 'state of affairs' as regards development, it must be stated that it is again only a lopsided representation of the reality of development. Because a vast majority of humanity still remains involved and committed to development. The attempts to eradicate poverty, provide basic amenities, spread education, etc undertaken by sincerely motivated agencies that work among the masses are good examples of the other side of the story of development. Looked at from the 'developing' Indian context, the idea of development and its associated projects still grip the creative dimension of human living. As observed by Rudiger & Heiko, development-theoreticians, "... speaking with people in developing countries, development is still very much alive."[5]

It is against this backdrop of the diverse perceptions of development that this essay intends to look at the interface between religion and development. It makes an appraisal of the question, 'whether development can be treated as a form of religion. If so, in what sense? And, especially from the perspective of the marginalised people, what does it mean to say 'development is analogous to religion or quasi-religious'? This essay does not deal primarily with the question of whether religion impedes or promotes development. This has been discussed for a very long time. Richard Tawney's (*Religion and the Rise of Capitalism,* 1926) or Weber's (*The Protestant Ethic and the Spirit of Capitalism,* 1930) theses are a few of the pioneering answers to such a question. This essay does not primarily concern itself with such a question.

Development as an Enlightenment Project

Humanity has experienced several great civilizations. They all have been, in a fundamental sense, the expressions or manifestations of the basic human urge for 'bettering' of human living. By 'bettering' I mean, taking inspiration from Adorno, a 'dialectic' of comparing and confronting 'what *is* with what *could be* or what fits better.'[6] Bettering of modes of productive activities, patterns of sheltering, dietary systems, systems of social interaction, aesthetic creations, artistic expressions, and so on have been part and parcel of these civilizations. Embedded in them are also concerns for the betterment of 'self' and 'society'. These are but different aspects of the sense of 'bettering'. Such a sense and its associated activities have been, thus, part of human living all along its history.

However, this urge for betterment and the civilizational activities have not been taken to constitute the meaning of what is known presently as 'development'. Development is a modern concept, born during the post-Second World War decades, when the European concern to overcome the impact of devastations and distress ran very high. It was also the period when most of the erstwhile-colonised countries were disentangling themselves from colonial yokes and searching for ways and means of building up their countries. Welfare nation states were the phenomena of this post-colonial era. Several countries became welfare nation-states, and embarked upon a project of state-led development. India, for example, set off on the course of development with the programme of five-year plans. The Green revolution and similar transformations in India owe their origin to the idea of development as conceived by the modern state makers of India.

Though development as a project unfolded during the post-war constructive phase, the roots of the idea lie within the European Enlightenment revolution of the eighteenth and nineteenth centuries. The idea got constituted through the combination or configuration of several elements of modernity like social modernisation, industrialisation, urbanisation, enhanced communication technologies and transport facilities, Enlightenment philosophies, etc. Of them, the Enlightenment philosophies of the self and society played an indispensable role in the construction of the idea and practice of development. Enlightenment rationality, for example, was the core element of this development.

Development as Embodiment of Enlightenment Rationality

The modern concept and practice of development is an embodiment of Enlightenment rationality. Basing itself on such strong foundations as Descartes' *cogito*, which assumed the superiority of the thinking self and Kant's vision of the autonomous agent and instrumental reason, the idea of development has flourished as a modern concept, cultivating the modern self and society. It has incorporated within itself such features of rationality as cause-effect logical reasoning, subject-object scheme, faith in value-neutral objectivity, the unity of the human thinking self, fundamental faith in futuristic progress, etc. Rationality was the defining feature of what came to be known as 'scientific thinking'. The scientific reasoning deployed the instrumental reason to experiment and overpower the forces of nature and matter. Logical positivism, the high product of scientific rationality, came to exert much influence not only in the world of science, but also in social 'development'. Basing on this rationality, theoreticians began to claim with absolute certainty and confidence the course of social evolution, and began to advocate social engineering too.

Development became the most favoured child of this positivistic enlightenment rationality.

Enlightenment rationality worked on the basis of a binary of the subject and the object. The subject was a secularly triumphant self that expressed itself in systematic planning and execution of scientific projects. It was a self which had 'freed' itself from, in the words of Kant, 'self-incurred immaturity', i.e. the ability to act on its own, without being guided by an external agent. This self was the autonomous agent, which undertook several scientific rational projects, and 'accomplished' them. Development became, eventually, the site wherein this rational subject actualised itself. The object of the binary was anything external to the self. Nature, the social reality, the emotions, art and culture,–everything became objects of experimentation and utilisation. Human labour too, in and through the process of industrialisaiton, became objectified and eventually got commoditized.

The autonomy and liberty of the individual are some of the important products of enlightenment thinking. It stressed the importance of the independence of the individual as against any collective that may hold up the individual. The feudal economic system and its attendant consciousness, which stifled the individual, gave way, in the heat of Enlightenment thinking, to capitalist liberal ideas, which 'freed' the individual. These liberal ideas impacted upon the economic, political, and social systems. They, in a unique manner, influenced and transformed the religious and ethical systems and behaviours too. The idea and practice of development that arose within this Enlightenment paradigm, with its own specific care of the self and society, began to acquire religious characteristics. In other words, they became quasi-religious.

Development as Quasi-Religious

The Enlightenment-tinted interface between development and religion can be analytically explored at different levels. At a very surface level, one can think of religion as providing platforms for developmental activities. It is a fact of history that several religious organisations, structures, and institutions have been involved heart and soul in undertaking developmental projects. These activities aimed at ameliorating or mitigating social evils like poverty, social backwardness, etc. As noted by Rudiger and Heiko, at one phase during the history of development, "development intervention was largely the provision of capital to build up industries, while other aspects of underdevelopment like poverty etc. were left to charitable organisations of the churches, NGOs, etc."[7] Thus, by providing a platform for developmental activities, religion interfaced itself with the project of development, but at a very surface level.

A deeper level of interfacing would be the way both exhibited similar characteristics and, in a sense, cross-fertilised each other by playing complementary roles. Exploring this level would mean taking a more philosophical look at the way both these ideas have fecundated each other in relation to historical actualisations. The present essay would like to make some heuristic explorations on this level and see how development could be understood as a quasi-religious phenomenon.

The Teleological Element

Teleological thinking, i.e. thinking geared to an end (*telos*) and orienting human potentialities towards achieving that end is one of the anthropological capabilities that distinguishes human beings from others. In the classical metaphysical age, both of the West and East, religions offered the *telos*. Embedding them in mythological language, they presented different eschatological visions as the 'ends' of life, towards which the followers of the respective religions had to orient their lives. These eschatological *telos* were, perhaps, the sources for the emergence of the historical thinking on a unilinear pattern of progress towards a future. In the classical religions, the soul was believed to progress towards the eschatological end. Since religions always linked the attainment of the eschatological future with certain conditional 'preparedness' ('forgiveness of sins' in Christianity) in the present, they also perhaps induced a synchronic moralistic thinking among the religious followers. Thus, in a scheme of faith, the future and the present were linked. This linkage was perhaps the remote origin of the historical thinking that implied a progress towards a future. It can thus be said that unilinear historical progress towards the future, thus emerged out of religious beliefs and behaviours.

During the modern era, the language changed, but the schema remained. Teleological thinking got expressed in secular idioms. Instead of the soul, the self was considered to be progressing along a history. When the human and social sciences were born, they imagined this progression in terms of what is known as *evolution*. Anthropologists thought of progression in terms of human evolution, and social thinkers thought in terms of social ideologies. Socialism, for example, spoke of the *telos* of history as evolving towards the state of socialism.

After the era of ideologies, what fills the vacuum of *telos* thinking is that of development. As noted by Rudiger Korff & Heiko Schrader, "Development ... translates 'reason and revolution' into 'development'."[8] Development, in its unique manner, integrates this teleological thinking. It replaces the old metaphysical comprehension and eschatology with more concrete achievements of the present. And yet, it orients the modern self towards a 'developed' future. As noted by Anton van Harskamp, "it (development) has replaced the idea of a comprehensive, coherent 'grand' narrative of social 'evolution', while at the same time retaining the idea of a linear, progressive advancement apparently necessarily involving all social and living entities."[9] As noted by Harskamp again, it may be said that "Development has become a concept – and a moral appeal– functioning as the substitute for the 'old', even old-fashioned, concept of history."[10] This progressive linear advancement, inherent in development, may be deemed as one of the important elements that make development a quasi-religious phenomenon.

Unity of the Self

Progress in history implies an agent that is progressing. "Development refers to the idea of a progress that can be applied to nearly *every* social system and *every* social agent, the human self included."[11] The human self, in turn, implies a unity which can progress spatio-temporally. Any development thinking or project, in order to occur, must have an agent who is the source not merely of creativity, but also of continuity. Continuity across time and space, through the endless changes, provides the foundation also for moral responsibility of the act and the actor. All these postulate what is known as 'the unity of the self'.

In this aspect too, it can well be surmised that development functions as a quasi-religious phenomenon. Any religion has at its core a vision of the unified human self. The Upanishadic religion of India speaks of *atman*, Buddhists speak of *jiva*, and Christians speak of the soul. All these are but religious representations of the unified human self. And, this human self progresses towards what is known as the ultimate reality, be it salvation, mukti, nirvana, etc. What is implied is that the human self provides continuity and responsibility for the actions undertaken by the human beings.

Unity of the self is nurtured by religions also by cultivating a comprehensive vision of life. It combines the past, the present and the future in a religious scheme and presents a religio-moral universe, which serves, in the words of Peter Berger, as the 'sacred canopy'. A 'comprehension' is a must at all levels and in all spheres. By comprehending the external universe, the internal self is also believed to have been comprehended. The Vedic and Upanishadic philosophers saw an external *rta* (regularity) in the cosmos, and transferred it to the internal *atman*. A comprehensive vision of the external world and the unity of the self reinforced each other mutually. And these two elements are shared both by development and religions.

'Expansion of the Present'

Govert J. Buijs finds a convergence between religion and development in the manner in which both of them 'expand the present.' According to him, "... religion expands the visible present in order to endow it with the force of non-visible realities... (it) gives 'inspiration': orientation (when choices have to be made), legitimation (when choices are made) and empowerment (to carry on with the choices made). This 'expanded reality' can not be counted mathematically or tested empirically."[12] However, the impact of this is evident in the lives of the practitioners of religions. It serves therapeutically during such negative experiences of life as conflicts and frustrations.

While this is so, Buijs alerts us, religion can also run the risk of alienating human beings from the present:

Religion always runs the risk that the expanded reality not only permeates the present but that it somehow even lets the present almost vanish. The present can be suppressed by the expanded reality. People for example can withdraw themselves into what to the outsider must look like a fantasy-world. Or they act as if the expanded reality is the only thing that counts and become fanatics or even commit violence. So religion does have the inherent risk of making people less attentive to the specific situation they are in.[13]

That being the case with religion, development, in a comparative perspective, functions more moderately and realistically. With its horizontal focus, development thinking and practice expand the present more context-sensitively. The expanded present becomes a site for concrete activities, which in turn, keeps expanding the possibilities of the present in a more gripping manner. Being engaged with the present, thus, is one of the core elements of both religion and development.

As Applied Ethics

Economics and ethics, in spite of the recent academic interest shown in their inter-relationship,[14] have disparate areas of interest in the conventional understanding of a modern perceiver. While economics is taken to concern itself solely with pure economic growth in terms of production, distribution, consumption, etc, ethics is considered to be a far-away discipline concerned with morality, conscience, will, etc. While this is the apparent understanding, we are able to identify, on the other hand, a strong interest shown in the relationship between ethics and economics right from a very remote past in history. In the Indian context, we have Kautilya's *Arthasastra* speaking about economics and ethics even during the fourth century B.C. Aristotle and other philosophers of the same era have reflected on the linkage. During the modern era, the father of modern economics, Adam Smith, titled his first book (written in 1759) as *The Theory of Moral Sentiments*. The scholarly connection goes on. But perhaps the linkage has remained primarily at the scholarly level, leaving the masses to guide their economic decisions with their own intuitions.

But it was the discourse and practice of development which combined in a singular manner the scholarly and the practical interests. Both the intelligentsia and the commoner got convinced of the rationale of development and involved themselves in applying the principles of development in their practical living. Development became one of the taken-for-granted assumptions of the common sense of the modern era. This modern concept served as 'applied ethics' in the realm of human conduct. By providing a vision for the 'development' of the self, it required the individual to discipline his/her activities so that the vision could be achieved. The care of the self along the path of modern education and industry took place under the dictates of development. Development made a moral appeal to involve and commit oneself for the betterment of others too. As observed by Anton van Harskamp, "development is a moral appeal–obviously urging us to help people living in miserable economic and political conditions– as well as a kind of ideology."[15]

Development, having become a principle of applied ethics, came closer to the realm of religion. Religions promoted development in their practical guidelines and legitimised it in their theologies. As far as Christianity is concerned, developmental activities became its soul force. In the Indian context, during the post-independence era when the countries involved in building up the nation, Christianity was a trusted partner in the project. Developmental activities were undertaken in the name of social services. Theological anthropological visions, which dwelt upon the progress of the self and society flourished. The whole missionary enterprise, especially of the Protestant missionary movements of the eighteenth-nineteenth centuries, justified their work on the principle of 'civilising mission', a concept quasi-religious in nature. The missionaries of the colonial era thought that God had entrusted them with this task of 'civilising' the people of the colonised countries. A section of the colonial officials too legitimised their colonial presence on the basis of this civilising mission. This mission combined the vision of human development (through education and industry) with the religious calling. We can identify other historical projects of a similar nature. Such endeavours go to underline the relationship religion and development as 'applied ethics' had in history.

Development as Secular 'Conversion'

A call to conversion demands a transformation 'here and now'. The present moment gets radically detached from the past at the experience of conversion. Religions, especially the missionary ones, have always stressed this element of conversion. So too development... It challenges the human person to take a decision here and now in favour of a 'bright' future. As perceptively observed by Ufford, "in development, the future is declared to begin *now*. It is opposed to the past and must in fact be 'rescued' from it... The idea of a future severed from the past allows us to see the constitution of development more clearly as a work of hope."[16] It is in these ways development functions as a secular conversion.

It converts the people, almost in a religious mode. Oscar Salemink speaks of the kind of conversion taking place in capitalist development as one of 'religious conversion'. Speaking from his Vietnam situation, he observes that, "this massive *religious conversion* to a creed which sets them apart from the ethnic 'viet' lowlanders sacralises a new lifestyle imposed by the exigencies of capitalist development–austerity, moderation, frugality, thrift, calculus, and individual responsibility–under the auspices of transnational modernity."[17] Development, according to him, is "part and parcel of the multi-dimensional conversion ... along different tracks and ultimately involving a quasi-religious moral conversion to a capitalist ethos as well."[18]

Thus, we have seen some of the aspects in which development functions as religion. The religious elements in these aspects play more of a conformist role, supporting rather uncritically the projects undertaken by the development machine–an instrument smeared with the capitalist grease.

The 'Achilles Heel'

The Self-Negation of Enlightenment Development

The Enlightenment development discourse has changed its course. It has taken new attributes of market economy due, as Horkheimer and Adorno would claim, to its own inner self-negating features. The mathematical thinking inherent in development discourse makes it suffer from its self-negation. Mathematical thinking, devoid of all passions, works to reduce the world to mere mathematical formalism, "whose medium is number, the most abstract form of the immediate," and it "holds thinking firmly to mere immediacy." (246) It means Enlightenment development has been 'imprisoned' within the logic and dynamics of self-preservation.

By doing so, it enters into a dialectics of 'self-negation' in the sense that even when it builds itself up to preserve it, it empties itself of its own supports. It for example, as noted by Horkheimer and Adorno, "empties itself of all religious and metaphysical sources of value, leaving only power and self-interest as its goals."[19] Under its grip, human existence sheds its value on its own rights, and acquires value only in terms of what it produces. This self-preserving and self-negating dialectics has led, as a natural result, to the emergence of the market economy. The process started with the beginning of modernity. Descartes' *cogito* was an important moment of its genesis. Apffel's observation is pointed:

Decartes's *cogito* articulates a new style of thought, one disengaged not only from particular social contexts–from the world–but disengaged also from passions. The world is now disenchanted matter, no longer the source of humans' moral guidance... The emergence of a form of rationality where instrumental control of passions was a constitutive feature was a necessary requirement in the commoditization of labour. The latter development, alongside the commoditization of the other two factors of production, namely land and capital (Polanyi, 1944), was essential to the full-fledged development of a market economy. With the establishment of a market economy, a Cartesian *cogito* harnessed to the pursuit of self-interest deployed itself throughout the public sphere.[20]

Globalisation and Development

Led by the Bretton Woods Institutions–WB and IMF–and the WTO, the countries of the world have opened up their markets through structural adjustment programmes during the last quarter of the twentieth century under the project of globalisation. The so-called developed countries were presented as the models of development, and other countries were expected to follow them. As pointed out by Rudiger, "all nations were to follow in the footsteps of the advanced or developed nations, especially the USA."[21] India followed suit during the early nineties, and adopted the structural adjustment programmes. Liberalisation and privatisation have been the sublime policies of these programmes. Through these policies and programmes, markets of different countries have been opened up to MNCs. Correspondingly every economic institution has promoted a culture that places a high premium on consumerism.

Globalisation, the embodiment of market economy, has made development acutely market oriented. It has obtained the shrill voice of extreme commoditization of labour and marketisation of goods. It has left behind the comprehensive vision of human development, in favour of expanding the capitalist market. In accordance with these changes, development has also become a 'religion of consumerism' by preaching the 'gospel of the market'.

Gospel of the Market: Religion of Consumerism

The market has generated a religion of consumerism today. An exuberant society that delights in consumerist goods celebrates the features of consumerism. It generates an effervescence from out of the consumerist sentiments. And the effervescence and euphoria created by consumerist culture makes it a religion. As observed by Oscar Salemink, the high noon of capitalism that we experience today "thrives on the promise of absolute wealth and the hedonistic fulfilment of desire–the promise of finding paradise in consumption."[22] Oscar's observation is poignant and pertinent. He continues to say that, "like transcendental religions such as Buddhism or Christianity and like secular religions such as Communism, capitalism requires a project of *quasi-religious, personal conversion* of reverse Weberian type."[23] Oscar is of the firm opinion that the present capitalist regime, through the 'gospel of the market' converts everyone into an ardent consumer. "Development preaches the gospel of the market and holds out the promise of wealth," and "because we cannot avoid capitalist development, we are all 'converts'- as consumers and hence producers."[24]

The institutions and organisations that speak of development today have come to promote market interests. Political institutions like the erstwhile Welfare States have vouchsafed to safeguard the interests of the markets. They are no more interested in the welfare of the people. Socio-cultural organisations have come to celebrate it. Bureaucracy is geared to clear the impediments. Educational institutions churn out professionals who will fly high the consumerist values. This kind of the shift is well portrayed by Ufford when he says:

The very notion of development as a project of political engagement and responsibility is increasingly seen as anachronistic. Confidence came to be placed in the *market* as a harbinger of development and in the role of free enterprise and free trade in the quest for development. This shift to the market is much more encompassing than it seems. It aims at transforming society as a whole into a 'market society'. The metaphor of the market deeply penetrates the conventions of steering, understanding and justifying modes of operation within the non-market sector also, public and private.[25]

This shift in the focus of development is mediated through the religiosity of consumerism. Everyone is converted to this religion.

Broad-Basing Development

Development as an Enlightenment project and development as expansion of market forces have serious limitations. The former, as we have seen, is the source of the latter. Both of them are on a continuum as regards the logic of self-preservation, which is at the root of Enlightenment rationality. Concurrent upon these stages of development, there are also corresponding functions of religion. While religion played a status-quoist conformist role during the first phase of development, it tends to play a promotion role favouring market forces during the contemporary phase.

These stages of development and functions of religions, which are dominantly visible, are being critiqued from more broad-based holistic understandings. In the Indian context, the voice of Amartya Sen intones a more holistic understanding. Amartya Sen speaks of development not merely as economic growth in terms of production output and consumption, but as substantive freedom, which he defines as 'capability'. By capability he means the multiple capabilities of human beings to have long life, healthy life, ability to interact in the society, ability to be free of social inequalities and domination, ability for participation in political process, etc. Vocalising in favour of a people-centred development that focuses on human agency and social opportunities, Amartya Sen and Jean Dreze state that, "... we cannot interpret economic development merely as expansion in the production of inanimate objects of convenience–the goods and services that are (as Aristotle put it) 'merely useful and for the sake of something else'. We have to see what these goods and services do to the actual opportunities and freedoms of people, categorized according to class, gender, location, social status, and other relevant distinctions."[26]

Critical Intervention

This manner of broad-based and critical understanding of development is a matter of necessity today. It is certain that only a broad based participatory development will increase the well-being of individuals and societies, and free them from convulsions. It is also certain that only a critical understanding of development will free the whole project of development from hegemonic agenda of domination. In the words of Ufford, "Development as critical understanding is vital to reconstituting development as a global responsibility, especially as it makes us aware of hegemonic intentions and relationships parading in the name of global solidarity, but itself it is not enough."[27]

This new approach of development needs be supported with new forms of religious interventions too. Liberation theology that emerged within Catholic Christianity is one such example of critical intervention of religion in societal transformation. Basing itself on a critical analysis of the structural dimensions of injustice, this theology as a religious intervention rallied the people against oppressors and dominators. This manner of critical religious intervention is a matter of necessity today. Liberation theology must be reinvented. The major religions of the world must give birth to such liberation theologies in order to take on the hegemonic agenda of domination and exploitation couched in the present-day market-led development.

Notes

1. Cf. Pierre Bourdieu, *Acts of Resistance Against the Tyranny of the Market*, New York: The New Press, 1998.
2. Cf. Martin Khor, "Impasse at the WTO: A Development Perspective", *EPW*, Vol. XLI, No. 45, November, 11-17, 2006, pp. 4659-4666.
3. "Marijuana is U.S.' top cash crop"; *The Hindu*, Chennai edition, December 21, 2006, p. 20.
4. Cf. Trevor Parfitt, *The End of Development? Modernity, Post-modernity and Development*, London: Pluto Press, 2002.
5. Rudger Korff & Heiko Schrader, "Does the End of Development Revitalise History?", in Ananta Kumar Giri et al., *The Development of Religion, The Religion of Development*, Eburon Delft, 2004, p. 11.
6. *Ibid.*, p. 9.

7. *Ibid.*, p. 12.
8. *Ibid.*
9. Anton Van Harskamp, "Introduction" in Giri, Ananta Kumar, *et al.* 2004. *The Development of Religion, The Religion of Development.* Eburon Delft, p. 1.
10. *Ibid.*
11. *Ibid.*
12. Govert J. Buijs, "Religion and Development", in Ananta Kumar Giri et al., *The Development of Religion, The Religion of Development,* Eburon Delft, 2004, p. 103.
13. *Ibid.*
14. There is an increasing academic interest shown on the interface on or relationship between economics and ethics today. Scholars are researching on aspects of ethics that contribute to the advanrement of economic growth. Cf.
15. Anton Van Harskamp, "Introduction," p. 1.
16. Philip Quarles van Ufford, et al. "Interventions in Development", *in A Moral Critique of Development–In Search of Global Responsibilities,* Routledge, 2003, p. 13.
17. Oscar Salemink, "Development Cooperation as Quasi-Religious Conversion", Ananta Kumar Giri et al., *The Development of Religion, The Religion of Development,* Eburon Delft, 2004, p. 125.
18. *Ibid.*, p. 128.
19. Max Horkheimer and Theodor Adorno, "Dialectic of Enlightenment," in Lawrence E. Cahoone (ed), *From Modernism to Postmodernism: An Anthology,* Blackwell Publishers, p. 243.
20. Frederique Apffel-Marglin, "Rationality, the Body, and the World: From Production to Regeneration", in Frederique Apffel-Marglin and Stephen A. Marglin (eds), *Decolonising Knowledge,* Oxford: Clarendon Press, 1996, p. 146.
21. Rudger Korff & Heiko Schrader, "Does the End of Development Revitalise History?", p. 10.
22. Oscar Salemink, p. 126
23. *Ibid.*
24. *Ibid.* p. 129.
25. Philip Quarles van Ufford, et al. "Interventions in Development", p. 5.

26. Jean Dreze and Amartya Sen, *India Development and Participation*, OUP, 2002, p. 3.
27. Philip Quarles van Ufford, p. 17.

References

Apffel-Marglin, Frederique and Stephen A. Marglin (eds). (1996), *Decolonising Knowledge–From Development to Dialogue*, Oxford: Clarendon Press.

Bourdieu, Pierre (1998), *Acts of Resistance Against the Tyranny of the Market*, New York: The New Press.

Chandavarkar, Anand (2007), "Economics and Philosophy: Interface and Agenda," *EPW*, Vol. XLII, No. 3, January 20-26, pp. 221-230.

Cosgel, Metin M. and Lanse Minkler (2004), "Religious Identity and Consumption," *Review of Social Economy*, Vol. LXII, No. 3, Sep.

Dreze, Jean and Amartya Sen (2002), *India Development and Participation*, OUP.

Giri, Ananta Kumar, *et al.* (2004), *The Development of Religion, the Religion of Development*. Eburon Delft.

Giri, Ananta Kumar (2006), *Reflections and Mobilizations*, SAGE.

Heelas, Paul (ed). (1998), *Religion, Modernity and Postmodernity*. Blackwell Publishers.

Horkheimer, Max and Theodor Adorno (1972), "Dialectic of Enlightenment." Lawrence E. Cahoone (ed), *From Modernism to Postmodernism–An Anthology*, Blackwell publishers, pp. 243-258.

Mosse, David (2003), "The making and marketing of participatory development," in Philip Quarles van Ufford, *et al.*, *A Moral Critique of Development–In Search of Global Responsibilities*, Routledge, 2003.

Parfitt, Trevor (2002), *The End of Development? Modernity, Post-modernity and Development*, London: Pluto Press.

Ufford, Philip Quarles van and Ananta Kumar Giri (2003), *Moral Critique of Development: In Search of Global Responsibilities*. London: Routledge & Eidos.

12

Globalisation, Development and Religion: A Critique

Cyril Desbruslais SJ

The Birth of Globalisation

In 1999, Merill Lynch ran a series of full-page ads in several newspapers and journals worldwide, heralding the birth of Globalisation and trying, thereby, to win popular support for 'the Market Economy'. Dating the inauguration of that Brave New Age from the collapse of the Berlin Wall, ten years earlier, it hailed the death of the Old Order of Cold War confrontation between two super-powers that had put the whole world on its collective toes. We were assured that a New World Order was a-dawning, an era of peace and prosperity for all, a 'free global system'. "The world is Ten Years old", it was proclaimed in banner headlines. Then it went on:

It was born when the Wall fell in 1989. It's no surprise that the world's youngest economy-the global economy-is still finding its bearings. The spread of free markets and democracy around the world is permitting more people to erase, not just geographical borders, but also human ones. It seems to us that, for a ten-year old, the world continues to hold great promise. In the meantime, no one ever said that growing up was easy.

Excellent copy. But note how, among other things, 'democracy' is casually (and causally?) linked with 'free markets', as if to say you can't really have the former without the other. Indeed, 'globalisation' sounds like a nice, friendly word, holding out the promise of a Paradise on Earth. However in practice, as we shall see, the kind of globalisation we have makes all this true for the rich among the Americans and the Europeans (especially the big business tycoons and their families) and for their allies and hangers-on, elsewhere.

Globalisation's Roots

Globalisation is championed by the WTO (World Trade Organisation), based in Geneva, Switzerland. It had originally been called GATT (General Agreement on Tariffs and Trade), the name given to it way back in 1949, when it was founded. The new name was bestowed on it at Uruguay, in 1995. World Trade Organisation sounds more 'open', inviting and non-partisan.

And, right away, the WTO began to argue that its nascent offspring, 'globalisation', would be the surest and swiftest way to combat world poverty, promote sustainable growth and establish peace, prosperity and justice for all. Third World diplomats were, at first, impressed. They were assured that their countries would be the biggest gainers, for free trade would allow them to corner the world market with their cheaper priced goods (due to lower production costs). Some were not convinced, however. Since when, they asked, have the wealthier, stronger nations really sought the good of the Third World?

And it was not long before Asian economists began to suggest that there were 'vested interests' hiding behind the 'globalisation gambit'. An article of Joginder Singh, former Director of the Central Bureau Investigation of India, is a case in point. Backing his charges with well-researched facts and figures, he argued, "the rich nations, with [their] high standards of living [had] reached the saturation point in developing their countries and their economies," He went on,

> The goods and services they produce, in the region of $ 900 billion, are so huge that they have to find either markets, failing which their industries and financial institutions would either be in serious trouble or have to be closed down.

Good business sense suggested to them a simple expedient, whereby they could extricate themselves from the mess they had landed themselves into; do it at the expense of the weaker nations![2] And, to add insult to injury, they would do so, all the while projecting themselves as unselfishly committed to helping the poor of the world to improve their lot.

The WTO: For and Against

The TEN BENEFITS the WTO claims to offer the world at large:

- it promotes peace
- it handles disputes constructively
- it makes life easier for all
- it cuts the cost of living through free trade
- it allows for greater choice of products
- it stimulates economic growth thru increased
- its basic principles make business more efficient
- it protects governments from lobbying
- it encourages good government

The TEN DRAWBACKS of the WTO, as per the charges of its critics:

- it promotes exploitation of the Third World
- it allows environmental degradation to go unpunished
- it permits dumping of harmful goods.
- props up corrupt governments through increased trade flows.
- it blocks countries trying to ban imports of chemically modified food.
- it jeopardizes US jobs by letting in trade cheap III World labour.
- it operates in secret and is unaccountable.
- it furthers the 'americanisation' of culture.
- it's a cover-up for ruthless business.

The Seattle Protest

The first rumblings of popular discontent with the way globalisation was unfolding were heard when thousands of people protested outside the venue of the WTO ministerial talks at Seattle, USA, on November 10, 1999. Riot police had to be called in and curfew imposed while minister-delegates from 134 countries (including ours) tried to get to the closed-door discussions.

The WTO believes in, and calls for, FREE TRADE and a FREE MARKET. The protestors, on the other hand, were calling for FAIR TRADE and a FAIR MARKET. Granted, the protests were somewhat blunted for a whole congeries of widely disparate complaints jostled together to voice their grievances under a huge umbrella. We concentrate on the anti-globalisation charges.

For one thing, all kinds of problems arise when one country doesn't want to import, from another member state, beef which has been treated with suspiciously unhealthy hormones, or when a wealthy nation wants to sell its steel to another poorer country at such a cheap rate (temporarily, of course), so that no one would want to buy the more expensive local variety. In such a case, of course, the smaller, less powerful steel-producers of the poor country would be driven out of business. For every signatory to the 2000-odd page GATT agreement–still upheld by the WTO–is also bound by Article XVI (paragraph iv) which stipulates that, "Every member shall ensure conformity of its laws, regulations and administrative procedures with its obligations, as provided in the annexed agreements." Tucked among these is a rule that declares, in effect, that any local or national requirement that calls for the protection of cottage and small-scale industries, or demands a ban on certain foods on the grounds of health or environmental standards of the important-nation, could be over-ruled as in contravention of the provisions of the agreement.

US 'Bully-Beef' Tactics

An instance to illustrate what we have just talked about. Europeans, as a whole, hate US beef. This is because about 90% of US farmers, as a whole, rear their cows in cramped, confined spaces that allow them little movement. In addition, they feed them a diet of hormones. All this makes them grow fatter and faster (besides being rather cruel for the poor animal). This also raises fears among Europeans that eaters of such meat would become more susceptible to certain diseases, such as cancer. There is yet no conclusive evidence in that direction but experiments are going on to check that out. Europeans, to be on the safe side, insisted that–until conclusive evidence, one way or other, is in - the US export to them only hormone free beef and the Americans gave them a written undertaking to that effect. Imagine the horror and anger of the Europeans when they found that they had been deceived: sample tests revealed that imported US beef contained hormones! When they charged America with fraud and perjury, the US, without batting an eye-lid, retaliated by claiming that the European beef-ban was against WTO rules. In order to further pressurise the continentals, it drew up a list of some $ 900 million of European imports that would henceforth be banned in the US (including scooters and strawberry jam). On top of that, US farmers began to lobby for some $ 500 million compensation from Europe for their lost beef trade. If that is the way how the US can - and does - throw its weight about with wealthy industrialised nations, one shudders to imagine how it would treat poorer, powerless people, who cannot afford the expenses of international disputes at World Courts. The reality is actually a good deal worse than we'd imagine.

Case Study No 1: The Plight of the Igorot People

The Igorot (literally, 'Mountain People') are an indigenous folk of Bengu Province in the Philippines. For centuries, they have practised 'pocket mining' of the rich gold reserves found on their ancestral lands. The men, traditionally, dig-by hand-small, round caves into the mountains and the women and children, from time immemorial, hammer the lumps of gold-bearing rocks into less bulky, more portable sizes. Now, globalisation has stepped in and set up the Benguet Corporation, with shares equally divided between rich Filipionos, the Philippine government and US investors. New hi-tech machines now cut deep gashes into the mountains, strip away trees and topsoil, dumping piles of polluting waste into riverbeds. The Igorot people, despoiled of their mining grounds, find their water resources destroyed and can no longer grow their rice and bananas. Now they have to trudge long distances to obtain water for washing, bathing and cooking. Furthermore, instead of using water to separate the gold from the rock, as the Igorot once did, the mining company uses more 'efficient' toxic chemicals (including cyanide compounds) to do the job and flushes by-products (at little or no cost) down the river, poisoning the water and killing not only the fish that the people had once used for food but also any of their cattle that come there to drink. Investing in proper waste disposal would hardly make a dent in the billion pesos that the Company makes every year. Instead, poor rice farmers and Igorots have to lose 250 million pesos a year as their yields decline and they add their numbers to the rural exodus. Once more the poor are called to foot the bills of the rich, with a massive energy transfer from the former to the latter.[3]

Case Study N. 2: The NIKE Story

Finer NIKE products sell for about $ 100 in the US and Europe. Most of its outsourced production takes place in Indonesia, where it is manufactured at a cost price as low as $ 5.60 a pair, by hundreds of young women and girls, who are paid about 15 cents an hour. They are housed in milita like barracks, unions are banned and overtime is mandatory. In the event of protests, the army is regularly called in to enforce obedience. Cynthia Elone[4] reports that the $ 20 million paid to basketball star, Michael Jordan, for promoting NIKE shoes, exceeded the entire payroll of all the Indonesian factories that make them. When questioned about conditions in NIKE's Indonesian factories, the General Manager of NIKE, Indonesia, gave a typically evasive answer. Yes, he had heard reports of 1abour problems there but, No, he had no details. He added, "I don't need to know. It is not within our scope to investigate." What apparently was within his scope was to ensure the bucks came in, no matter what.

Case Study No. 3: The Avon Success Story

Avon is a brand name in cosmetics, popular among society ladies in the US and Europe. On August 2, 1994, TV Nation documented a very successful Avon campaign to market a product among some of the most miserable and impoverished women of the world - the thin, exhausted, prematurely aged and wrinkled women in the remote Amazon village of Santarem, Brazil. First hundreds of models were roped in to make a series of TV commercials, along side dashingly handsome young men. The campasinas, bent and wearied long before their time, due to demanding years of child-bear and back-breaking toil in the sun, were told that, by using a single jar of a miraculous product called 'Renew' (cost: $ 40), they would be able to slough of their cracked skin to release the light-skinned, sensuous woman trapped within. Indeed, special effects depicted-in a TV ad–a typical campesina peeling away years from her face and becoming magically younger and sexier and the poor women fall for it. Rosa Alegria, Communication Director of Avon, Brazil, exults, "Women do everything to buy it. They stop buying things like clothes, like shoes. If they feel good with their skin, they prefer to... buy something that is on TV, It's a real miracle!" It's certainly the kind of miracle that globalisation allows Avon and those of its ilk to perform, though it might also rank as one of the most aggressive and unethical efforts of all time to universalise consumer culture. So what if it dispenses false hopes and deprives indigent families of their basic needs? And when the campesinos realize they have been had, Ms. Alegeria would probably quip that all's fair in love, war... and business!

And Elsewhere...

In India, large-scale development projects displaced over 20 million people in 40 years. In Brazil, the switch-over from agriculture carried out by small holders, who provided enough for domestic consumption, to capital-intensive goods for export, drove some 28 million peasants onto the road between 1960 add 1980. These schemes were launched by the World Bank with the alleged aim of helping the rural poor to become self-sufficient. However, when questioned by social workers, not a single WB staff member was able to cite a WB-inspired project in which the lot of the displaced people had, in anyway, improved. A recent NGO Conference gave the following bleak report on various World Bank funded projects

In Thailand, 10 million rural people face eviction from the land where they live, so as to make way for commercial farms. Ground water is depleted and mangroves continually destroyed by export-oriented shrimp farms. Tribal people struggle for the recognition of ancestral rights in the forests of Eastern Malaya and Indonesia. In the Philippines, the government's land reform programme is systematically eroded by the conversion of prime agricultural lands into industrial estates and other non-agricultural uses.[5]

The list can go on. No doubt, these projects will bring development and again-not for the poor peasants they are supposed to benefit, but for big business and the wealthy. The *costs* of all these programmes would be borne by the lower income-groups and the impoverished. One can scarcely maintain that the World Bank and its crony, the International Monetary Fund, know nothing of all this!

Market Ideology: Fiction and Fact

Globalisation exhorts us to give up out-dated nationalities. We must see ourselves as 'peoples of the earth', true cosmopolitans, whose commitments transcend native place and homeland. In itself, this is quite an attractive proposition. But could it be one more cover-up for global-and the 'growth model' of development on which it is based?

The 'free trade' and 'free market' touted by Meriil Lynch are presented as authentic precursors of true democracy. The half truth behind this sophistry is that people best express their will by voting with their bucks than their ballots. People manifest their sovereignty not so much by voting conniving politicians into power, as when they do it through their purchases. This is appealing logic, given today's distrust of politicians and political parties and their scams and schemes to stay in power at any cost. But one key factor is being overlooked. In the market, every dollar, every euro gets a vote-not just each person, as in a traditional democratic set-up-and the more money you have, the more votes you get! Markets are inherently in favour of the rich and the big corporations, who often command more clout than governments. As markets become more global, our futures rest more in the hands of huge multi- and trans-national companies than our governments. No wonder David C. Korten entitled his distressing and devastating study, *When Corporations Rule the World*.[6]

Foreign Aid-Who Helps Whom?

"$ 146 billion: the combined income of the 528 million people living in the 43 least-developed countries of the world in 1999. $ 1 trillion, the combined income of the 200 richest people in the world in 1999."[7] These astronomical figures illustrate the yawning-and increasing-gulf between the haves and the have-nots in today's world. It boils down to saying that 200 people have almost 1000 times more money than over 500 million others altogether!

The disparity is devastatingly consequential in what William Dugger calls 'corporate libertarianism'.[8] He shows us why market-players are so drawn to corporations. Their legal nature is able to shield decision-making executives from the effects of their irresponsible actions and policies. A corporation is, thus, able to "create its own culture... [and] focus on corporate size and power."[9] Unlike real people, who are all ultimately rendered equal by death and whose accumulation of wealth can be restricted by taxes and other controls, corporations can apparently grow and exist forever as well as amass power and wealth infinitely. Thus, as the *New Internationalist* of March 1980, tells us,

> An assessment of the largest 100 economies in the world show 53 to be countries and 47 multinational corporations. More significant for the next decade, the growth rate of these companies will be three or four times that of the industrialised countries.[10]

In 1985, General Motors already had a growth sales larger than the GNP of every African country or of every Latin

American country (except Brazil and Mexico), or every Asian country (except Japan, China and India) or even of some European countries (like Sweden, Switzerland, Belgium and Austria.[11] Recently, Kohlberg Kravis Roberts (KKR), a giant conglomerate in the food industry, made the colossal bid of $ 24.88 trillion to swallow up RJR Nabisco-an amount equal to the combined fortunes of the six richest men in the US. That would have been enough to fund all Central American governments for a year, or sponsor 80 million destitute children over the planet for the same period.[12] These mega-giants, with their tentacles in every nation, unlike governments, cannot be voted out of power to give an opposition party a chance to reverse trends. They, more than any political party, run our lives, nowadays, as Barnet and Muller notes:

In developing a new world, managers of firms like General Motors, IBM, General Electric, Volkswagen, Exxon and a few hundred others, make daily business decisions which have more impact than most sovereign governments, on where people live what work-if any-they will do, what they will eat, drink and wear... and what kind of society our children will inherit.[13]

It is dangerous to allow so much wealth and power to accumulate in the hands of such profit-seeking, unaccountable megalomaniacs. The World Bank and the International Monetary Fund are UN-backed organisations, established precisely to ameliorate the conditions of poorer nations and streamline fiscal services at the international level. However, as knowledgeable social activists testify.

> If measured by contributions to improving the lives of people or strengthening the institutions of democratic governance, the World Bank and the IMP have been disastrous failures - imposing an enormous burden on the world's poor and seriously impeding their development.[14]

This is no more blatantly obvious, perhaps, than in the system of foreign aid to developing countries that they have established. Whatever be its pretensions, the whole scheme boils down to the poor nations paying back to their rich donors much more than they receive from them. In effect, it is the developing countries who are giving foreign aid to the opulent industrialised first world! Thus, Third World nations might have fared better off had the so-called First World nations *not* come to their aid at all. "Far from playing the Good Samaritan," notes Paul Vallely, "the rich world has developed a new role. Today we are Bad Samaritans."[15] And he goes on to point out that "latest figures show that the debt and interests due from the Third world are three times more than all the aid they currently receive."[16] In other words,

> To repay it [i.e. their International Debt] Third World governments are being forced by the international authorities to cut food subsidies to the poor and their health and education bud gets. After decades of improvement in levels of child nutrition and literacy, the situation of the Third World has begun to decline. The United Nations' Children's Organisation, UNICEF, has worked out that, as a result of these budget cuts a total of one million African children have died in the last decade. Throughout the developing world an additional. 500,000 children died, from this direct cause, in 1988 alone.[17]

The foreign debts of many developing countries are immense. For instance the debt of Sub-Saharan Africa is over $ 220 billion. At $ 365 per capita it is higher than the average GNP per capita which is just over $ 308. Taking India's population to be one billion from January 2000, at the cur rent rate of exchange, every Indian - including the very young, the aged and the infirm - carries an external debt of Rs. 10,000 on his/her shoulders. And let us not forget that 40% of our people still subsist below the poverty line.[18]

Can the WTO, WB and IMF Be Fair?

The WTO makes the rules by which the 'free' market works. It is controlled by the US, designed in the West and custom-built to serve the interests of the World's seven richest nations (Canada, France, Germany, Italy, Japan, the UK and US). These nations control half of the world's revenue and two-thirds of its trade. The least developed lands represent some 20% of the world's population, but generate only 0.03% of its trade. No wonder they are at a disadvantage when the former lay down their conditions.

To begin with, the Almighty Seven (and their Corporations) want a 'free market' that is, a set-up which best enhances their profits. This means no protection of local markets as this would limit the freedom of action that they would like to have, while functioning in the local economy. As globalisation is upheld, local rules, customs and regulations are pushed aside as prejudicial to the same understanding of globalisation (read big business). Such vast multi-, or trans-,nationals can thereby take advantage of their poorer, less-equipped local competitors, driving them out of business with the few efficient moves, over-ruling anti-pollution laws, offering better perks and higher wages than any local firm, while still paying out much less than would be required on home soil.

This means arranging its global, operations to produce products where costs are lowest, selling them where markets are more lucrative and shifting the resulting profits to where tax rates are the least burdensome. The ability to shift production from one country to another weakens the bargaining power of the locals.[19]

These organisations, as they stand now, merely establish better and quicker means for the rich and powerful nations to become ever more so-at the expense of the very nations they are supposed to be helping. Hence, they must be scrapped altogether, to make way for new ones, better equipped to realise their pristine goals of helping the poorer nations, or they must submit their functioning to drastic revision. Very specially must they stop demanding that all nations be bound by the same rules and that disputes be settled by world courts that involve an extremely costly and tedious process that only wealthy nations can afford.

Then there is the questionable practice of converting private debts into public liabilities that they have sanctioned. This began with Latin America in the 1980s and, after the Asian currency crisis of 1996-8, entered Thailand and then spread to Malaysia and South Korea, India is not unaffected. Putting it bluntly, the IMF forced the governments of all these countries to accept liability for private debts incurred by individual bankers, financiers and business groups in those countries who, for various reasons, were unable to pay back loans they had borrowed. Now the normal procedure in such cases, upheld by all banking institutions world-wide, is to require such defaulters to plead bankruptcy and the greedy lenders–who had thrown caution to the winds by advancing such loans (lured perhaps by the high rate of interest) would have to pay the price of their reckless loans. But thanks to the machinations of the IMF, traditional banking theory was bypassed and wealthy loaners were able to make good their losses at the expense of the already over-burdened citizens of the poorer countries!

The Either/Or Fallacy

A common sophistry of the 'growth model' advocates is that globalisation espouses the best of only two possible choices. Either we must cast in our lot with the 'free market', unencumbered by governmental restraint and opening our borders to all the world, or we must settle for the grim totalitarian model of the old Soviet States behind the Iron Curtain, where the State would decide everything, leaving us with no personal, let alone, economic, freedom, with perhaps another Wall to seal us off from the world around. If this were really the case, perhaps we would do better to opt for the present model of globalisation and 'free markets, after all.

But are we really caught up in such a Catch-22 situation? Why can't we opt for the system of Corporate Free Markets, but require them to function within a framework of responsibility? What we have now is a set-up that grants impersonal, profiteering corporations rights and freedoms above those of human persons ... and let them get away with it! This permits them to seize all the advantages of success and make the poorer countries pay the cost!

Sheer Growth Is NOT Enough!

Those who champion the growth model of development, on which today's globalisation schemes are based, assure us that if we merely produced more goods and services, all our problems with population, poverty and the environment would be solved. The fact is that, since 1950, global output has increased five-fold. The major effect of this was, as we saw, a glut of unsold goods in the hands of the rich nations - a problem they were only able to solve by the present day globalisation formula. In other words, unrestrained growth created more problems than it was supposed to solve. Of course, while world production increased, so did the population, but the former went up five-fold, while the latter merely doubled (So there was no Malthusan population growth outstripping production). At the same time, the percentage of those living in absolute poverty also doubled. Meanwhile, the assets of the world's richest 20% doubled, too, while these of the 20% poorest plummeted. In all honesty, we can't lay the blame for all this at the door of economic growth, but it just goes to show that mere growth cannot save us from our economic woes.

Unless we make some very radical changes in our production and distribution methods, the future of our ailing world will remain bleak. In the short run the rich will go on getting richer and the poor will become more impoverished. In the long run, even the rich will begin to feel the pinch, for they will either pollute the world and themselves out of existence or they will have to set drastic limits to their extravagant lifestyles. Let us also not forget that the world's resources of fuels and natural wealth are not infinite; we cannot go on wrenching wealth from Mother Nature's amble bosom forever.

Even on the "home scene" the growth model hasn't helped improve things for the common man and woman. New York, centre of the world's most successful proponent of the growth model of development, is already beginning to manifest many of the external signs of a typical Third world city; wandering bands of homeless and hungry rubbing shoulders with the bold and beautiful lifestyles of the rich and famous, sparks of random violence, an overburdened police force caught between the mafia on the one hand and corrupt politicians on the other. The same can be seen in seedy localities of Paris,

London and elsewhere in the First world. At times one wonders whether he or she has not suddenly been miraculously transported back to the slums of Kolkatta or the backwaters of Bogotá.

To sum up: the 'growth model' and its agents, the WB, IMF and WTO, coupled the kind of globalisation they are championing are no help to the poor. In fact, they are a form of violence let loose upon the defenseless, however cynically and hypocritically its perpetrators try to portray themselves as social workers, healers and saviours of the down-trodden. It's time to call the bluff.

Proposing Alternatives

The remedy is not to close the door to globalisation; a FAIR market and FAIR trade do net require that. It's not globalisation in itself that is to be blamed but the kind of irresponsible version of the same that the WTO and its cronies are defending. In place of 'the same rules for all', for the giants and the mites, the latter should be concretely assisted, rather than restricted by WTO rules.

Nor should we forget that growth is not necessarily a good thing. As the British economist, Paul Elkins,[20] has shown, there are certain conditions which decide whether it is or not.

(a) the goods or services that are being increased should be inherently valuable and beneficial to society at large;

(b) their benefits should be widely distributed throughout all sections of society;

(c) any good accruing from them must outweigh all possible detrimental effects that might be unavoidable in the process of their production.

Mention could be made, here, of Gandhiji's advice to Nehru soon after Independence. One should ensure that resources be devoted to providing the poorest of the poor with their basic necessities (clean water, a non-harmful working environment, proper housing, hygiene, etc.) before they are diverted to making more sophisticated playthings available for the rich (colour, rather than black and white TV and more opulent shopping malls and gilded arcades).

As Viktor Papanek, international planner and designer, who has worked closely with the UNESCO and other such bodies, put it, "The fact of the matter is that today there is more than enough to go around, if only it is properly planned."[21] In other words, instead of launching ourselves onto another round of frenzied production, let's concentrate on the HOW of production and distribution. This reminds us of the words of the Mahatma, "The world has enough for everyone's need, but not enough for everyone's greed."

Actually, studies carried out by the UNDP (United Nations Development Programme), have shown that quality of life is not necessarily related to a high GNP. Saudi Arabia's average GNP is fifteen times that of Sri Lanka, but its literacy rate is far lower, Brazil's per capita income is twice as high as that of Jamaica, but its child mortality rate is also four times as much! It is not HOW MUCH, but HOW that matters, not GNP but quality of life.

Small is Beautiful

Dr. E. F. Schumacher, former chief economist of the British National Coal Board, urges us to rid ourselves of the obsession with size and bigness, In his controversial *Small is Beautiful*, he suggests that we replace the system of 'mass production' with 'production by the masses'. The former, "based on sophisticated, highly capital intensive, high energy in-put dependent and human labour-saving technology, presupposes that you are already rich" before you can use it. On the other hand, production by the masses "mobilises the priceless resources which are possessed by all human beings, their clever brains and their skilful hands, and supports them with first class tools". Furthermore, it is compatible with the laws of ecology, gentle in its use of scarce resources and designed to serve the human person rather than making him or her slave of the machine. There may be some point in the objections of idealism and 'back to nature' that have been levelled against Schumacher, but this shouldn't lead us to reject wholesale all that he is pointing at. Of course, agreeing with his thesis would oblige us to try and break free from the increasing pressure of the big industrial nations who are determined to foist on us their model of development. And our own educated elite, from whom our ruling cliques are drawn, studied, for the most part, in such lands and have imbibed their principles, so they add to the pressure. It'd be even more difficult to make them alter their patterns of thinking. Are we prepared to exert alternative pressure which is not necessarily in favour of Gandhiji's back to nature rural economy and the spinning wheel?

Towards an Alternative, Rural-based Model

We are familiar with the urban-based, high-tech model of development, but it is not the only one. Ivan Illich, an educator who has worked along with Paolo Freire in Latin American villages and favellas, calls for a rural-based model of development, ideally suited for countries like ours, where the majority of people still live in far-flung villages.

Instead of investing the usual $ 100 million to construct yet another speed way between two big Indian cities, he would recommend we use that princely sum to construct a latticed work of small trails between villages, which could be traversed by 'mechanical donkeys', traveling at 5 mph and carrying loads of about a ton. If 50,000 miles of such 'kaccha' roads were laid between thousands of Indian villages, a whole network of trade and exchange would be established between previously isolated centres. This would encourage exchange, increase the quality, quantity and income of villages, promote indigenous handicrafts and cottage industries, reduce the movement to cities and move the entire rural population a step closer to self-fulfilment.

Illich denounces the kind of development that Latin America is being subjected to by big American cartels, to the detriment of other models:

Traffic jams in Sao Paolo, whilst a million Brazilians flee a drought by walking 500 miles. Each car which Brazil puts on the road denies 500 people good transportation by bus.

Every dollar spent by Latin America on doctors and hospitals costs a hundred lives. ... Had each dollar been spent on providing-safe drinking water, a hundred lives could have been saved.[22]

He could have been writing of India, we're back again to the industrialised nations, basked by our urban elites, championing a form of development that is good for the city conglomerates of our land ("India") versus the needs of our rural-based majority ("Bharat"). Little consideration is given to the 'refugees from Bharat! who crowd into India', looking for a job and a meal and having to eke out a miserable existence in slums and shanty-towns.

Two Gospels

Globalisation, as based on the Corporate Free Market Economy in today's world, is preaching the Gospel of Having More. It affirms that all that we seek, deep down, happiness, meaning, fulfilment - call it what you will is to be found in accumulating things and by limitless material gratification, even if it involves depriving certain people (deemed insignificant)of the little they have. This approach is on solid ground for it appeals to the undeniable and demonstrable capacities for greed that lurks within us and against which all of us, like St Paul, have to contend. It engenders competition, violence, hatred and racism. But there is, admittedly, something "deep down" in us that responds to the Gospel of Having More.

But there is also in us humans another-equally undeniable and demonstrable-capacity, equally "deep within" us and it provides the basis for the Gospel of Being More. It focuses on enhancing the quality of living of everyone (not just a few privileged and insensitive bloated plutocrats),is sensitive to the environment and to the millions yet unborn, our children and grand-children of tomorrow.

It is up to us to decide to which of these capacities to respond. Which is the Gospel we want to build on? Healthy societies are built on love and compassion and sharing and they thereby create an abundance of those things that are important for the quality of life for all people. Unhealthy and dysfunctional societies nurture greed and competition. They cause scarcity, deprivation and ecological imbalance and sow the seeds of their own destruction. We must choose.

And this means that religions must choose, too. For it is especially the role and responsibility of religions to make us more human, to foster authentic human and social values. However, if our religions prefer to waste their time, energy and vast reserves of money on sterile doctrinal disputes or ritualistic arguments, if they continue to nurture intolerance and divisions on earth, if they promote conflicts and terror-tactics or let themselves become the stool-pigeons of conniving politicians and their vote-banks, then they will be rejected by the people. For those who want mere opium for the masses, well, there are cheaper and more attractive versions of the same than the religious one.

And what of the Christian Church? She commands a vast network of social service institutions, schools, colleges and establishments of higher learning and research across the globe. Can any other organisation boast of such an army of allegedly committed and dedicated women and men, scattered all over the world, many in positions of power and decision-making (priests and religious)? An international Synod of Bishops, not too long ago, declared that the ministry of faith must go hand in hand with action for justice. The Catholic Church is convinced of being one of the recipients (if not *the* recipient) of the inspiration of the Holy Spirit. Millions of qualified and professional persons make up her faithful followers, all sharing in the priestly, prophetic and pastoral office of Christ. And Pentecost may be seen as God's approval of authentic globalisation. In spite of all this, if she is not prepared to take any greater involvement in the great discernment process for freedom and unity and diversity the world over–then, to paraphrase Nietzsche–she would not be worth the price of a shoe-lace.

Notes

1. In a personal conversation with the author (on record), during an interview at the Vienna International Centre on May 4, 1998.

2. In an article in the Maharashtra Herald, Pune, July 20, 2000, p. 4.
3. See David C. Korten, *When Corporations Rule the World*, Mapuca Goa: The Other India Press, 1998, p. 43.
4. Cynthia Enloe, "The Globetrotting Sneaker", in *Mainstream*, March-April 1995, pp. 10–15; see also Richard J Barnet and Johann Cavanagh, *Global Dreams: Imperial Corporations and New World Order*, New York : Simon & Schuster, 1994, pp. 325–329.
5. Korten, *When Corporations Rule the World*, p. 62.
6. Cf No. 03.
7. *Time Magazine*, quoted by Ambrose Pinto. Editorial to *Social Action*, Volume 50, No. 2, April-June 2000, pp. iii-iv.
8. In his book *Corporate Hegemony*, New York: Greenwood press, 1989.
9. *Ibid.*
10. Quoted by I John Mohan Razu, *Transnational Corporations as Agents of Dehumanisation in India*, Delhi, Cambridge Press, 1999, pp. 7-8.
11. Cf. The Marxist Review, January-February, 1987; quoted by Razu, *Transnational Corporations as Agents of Dehumanisation in India*, p.8.
12. Cf. *The Multinational Monitor*, March 1969, p. 4: quoted by Razu.
13. George W Ball, partner of Lehman Brothers and former US Under Secretary of State (1961-66) went on record admitting that multinationals and transnationals "have the power to affect the lives of people and nations." Cf. Razu, Ibid.
14. Korten, *When Corporations Rule the World*, p. 171. According to World Bank Debt Tables, corroborated by the Reserve Bank of India Report on Currency and Finance, 1998–99, India's external debt has escalated alarmingly, from US $ 20 billion in 1970, to US $ 77 billion in 1980 and further to US $ 97 billion in 1999-that's a debt burden something like Rs. 300 on every Indian, young or old, healthy or infirm. And let us not forget that India's per capita income is about US $ 310.
15. Paul Vallely, *Bad Samaritans: First World Ethics and Third World Debts*, Maryknoll: Orbis Books, 1990, p. 4.
16. *Ibid.*
17. *Ibid.*

18. Arun Ghosh, "External Indebtedness, Capital Flows and the Problems of Financial Integration", *Social Action*, Volume 50, No. 2, April-June, 2000, p. 111.
19. Korten, p. 126.
20. Cf. Korten, p. 39-40.
21. Quoted by Adam Daniel Pinnerty, *No More Plastic Jesus: Global Justice and Christian Lifestyle*, New York: Maryknoll 1979, p. 2.
22. Quoted by Finnerty, pp. 48-49.

13

Environment: Whose Development?

Walter Fernandes SJ

During the last two years India and the rest of the world have experienced several disasters that some call natural though their link with the degradation of the environment is difficult to deny. Among them are the unprecedented floods in Europe and the inundation of Mumbai, Chennai and New Orleans during 2005 and the worst floods of half a decade in Assam for two successive years. One may not stretch this thesis too far by linking tsunami with climate change because one does not know its exact causes but it is difficult to deny its link with snow in Abu Dhabi the same day. These and other events should make one sit back and reflect on the type of development that has led to environmental degradation and to the marginalisation of the poor.

It is also an invitation to a search for alternatives to the system that results in such events. As a help to such a reflection, we shall begin with a note on different schools of thought involved in the debate in the environment before looking at some recent events. We shall not limit ourselves to the urban events that make headlines but go beyond them to the ongoing impact on the rural poor because while the environment has today become a major issue but the way one understands it depends on the class one belongs to. Events affecting the middle class receive greater attention than those affecting the voiceless rural poor. That is why our starting point is the environment primarily as the livelihood of the poor. Its deterioration affects them as much it destroys nature.

Types of Environmentalists

How one looks at the implications of development-induced environmental degradation depends on where one stands on the issue of resource use. There are at least four stakeholders in the debate on the environment, the most important being the communities whose sustenance the natural, particularly common property, resources (CPRs) are. The tribals and other rural poor who sustain themselves on land, water and forests, the fish workers who live on the marine resources, the Dalits a majority of whom work on land owned by others, as such depend on its sustainable use and a favourable climate, and other communities like the quarry workers have nature as their sustenance. To them the environment is an ecosystem with human communities at its centre. These resources have traditionally met their food, fodder, medicinal and other needs. Around them they have built their cultural, social and religious systems and their very identity. A symbiotic relationship has developed between them and nature. As a result, they have used the resources judiciously, treated them as renewable, preserved them as sustainable and have recognised their own right and that of nature to a life with dignity.[1]

On the opposite side are many urban environmentalists to whom the environment is "beautiful trees and tigers"[2] and its deterioration is air and water pollution and deforestation. The communities that sustain themselves on them do not enter their thinking. Some would even like to preserve nature from them. For example, those opposing the Forest Rights Bill that is before the Parliament assume that the tribals are the real destroyers of wildlife and that one has to protect it from them. The urban environmentalists also oppose the third stake holder, the industrialist who treats land, forests and water as raw materials for his own profit and to produce consumer goods for the middle class whose lifestyle depends on them. In between is the fourth stakeholder, the official bodies like the Forest Department and the Pollution Control Board dealing with the resources. By and large these three stake holders are more concerned about water, air and forests than the communities that depend on them.[3]

Environment and Development

The debate around the environment and development has to be situated in the context of the contest between the stakeholders. Most planners view development only as building the infrastructure and maximising profit. Forests, land and water would then be only raw materials. But the communities that sustain themselves on them belong to the 70% of the population that lives in the informal economy while the legal, administrative and economic systems are based on the formal system. The two emanate from opposite, even contradictory, foundations. The formal is based on the concept of property, the individual and the written word. Profit is its moving force. The informal system, especially tribal, is based on the resource, word of mouth and legitimacy by the community. Sharing and equity are its foundations.[4] To the formal sector their livelihood is a commodity and a raw material to produce goods for over-consumption by the middle class. Profit depends on rendering them productive and for this purpose they alienate the resources from the communities that sustain themselves on them. For example, they view land only as a place of cultivation and building and ignore the agricultural labourer, the trader, the barber and others who live on it by rendering service to the village as a community.[5]

In the past religion legitimised such monopolisation. For example, much of the thinking on development was justified through the Judaeo-Christian misinterpretation of Genesis 1.26 which was viewed mainly as God's command to dominate nature. Ignored was the fact that this command included also equitable distribution and the access of all to the fruits of creation. Development is thus based on the assumption that the natural resources are raw materials meant to be exploited to ensure the investor's profit. "It is western Christianity that has taught us to see ourselves as the centre of things with the right, even the duty, to conquer, subdue and have dominion over nature. Early scientific thought reinforced this view of ourselves, by seeing the earth as the centre of the universe, with the planets, the stars and the sun all circling round it."[6]

Its result has been destruction of nature that is the livelihood of the poor and the consequent impoverishment of the communities whom the God of history created in His own image (Gen. 1.27) and on whose side He has shown Himself (Lk. 4.18). For example, the outdated drainage system was certainly a major cause of the Mumbai floods of 2005. The unprecedented 97 cm of rain in three days caused by climate change was the second. However, the damage could have been kept within reasonable limits if the greed of the real estate speculators had not led to the reclamation of the Mahim and Bandra creeks that were rivers through which excess water from the city flowed out to the Arabian Sea. Once the builders filled them to put up high rise buildings, the excess water could not flow out of the city. That greed is seen also in the price that land fetches in Mumbai. 20 acres on which the textile mills stood once were sold in late 2005 for around Rs. 700 crores, or Rs. 35 crores per acre. Another 16.2 acres are expected to fetch Rs. 40 to 50 crores each in January 2006. Using the pretext of the 1983 textile workers' strike the owners had closed them down in order to sell the land as real estate.

Land, Water and Displacement

Another consequence of treating land and water as commodities alone, is the displacement of people's for dams, industries and other projects, in the name of national development. The post-independence Governments used the enabling laws enacted by the colonial regime to make it easy for the entrepreneurs to take control of land. These laws have their foundation in the *Permanent Settlement 1793* and continued in various legislative measures from a Calcutta law of 1824 to the *Assam Land Rules 1838* and culminated in the *Land Acquisition Act 1894* (LAQ).[7] These laws are based on the eminent domain of the State which is called *terra nullius* (nobody's land) in Australia. The White colonisation of the Americas, Australia, New Zealand and southern Africa was based on the principle that anyone can occupy land belonging to none. The Australian judiciary has struck it down as unconstitutional since what the coloniser occupied was the livelihood of the communities inhabiting it[8] but it continues to be the basis of Indian land laws under its American interpretation of eminent domain. Its first facet is that all natural resources like forests, as well as land with no individual title belong to the State. Its second facet is that the State alone has the right to define a public purpose and deprive even individuals of their assets in its name.[9] Their land can thus be acquired without their permission for the profit of the entrepreneur.

Post-independence Governments have kept these colonial laws intact and have even made them more stringent. For example, the Government of India amended the LAQ in 1984 to make it possible for the State to acquire land for private companies. Using this change the State has acquired land for Enron whose corruption is well known, the Tata Steel Plant in Gopalpur and 15,200 acres at Kalinga Nagar in Orissa and for numerous other private projects instead of getting them to buy the land they required. They thus get land at a low price while they would have to pay more if they bought it directly.

The National Water Policy 2002 is another example. It focus is on water as a resource for irrigation and power and on building large dams. Its objectives are exploitation of the hydro-potential at a faster pace, maintaining a minimal share of hydro-power in the national system, enabling inter-state and inter-regional transfer of power and encouraging private investment in this sector. So it suggests basin-wise investigation and planning of the hydro-potential and privatisation of water but has very little to say on drinking water. The policy ignores this aspect and treats water only as a commodity for irrigation and power to the profit of the private sector.[10]

This private profit-driven enterprise is given concrete shape in the projects being planned. For example, on 14th March 2002, the then Union Minister for Power outlined in the

Rajya Sabha plans to build 11 hydro-electrical projects (HEP) in the Northeast because it has 58,971 MW of hydel potential or 38% of India's total (*The Assam Tribune,* 15th March 2002). On 24th May 2003, launching the 50,000 MW Hydro-Electrical Initiative for the Northeast former Prime Minister Mr. A. B Vajpayee said that the region should become India's powerhouse (*The Telegraph,* May 24, 2003). According to Mr M. Debnath, former Member-Secretary, Narmada Board, at least 48 HEP were under study in the Northeast in 2001.[11] There is another list of 138 possible dams in the Seven Sisters of the Northeast and 23 in Sikkim[12] to produce power for export to the rest of India and to Southeast Asia (*The North East Times,* February 11, 2002). That they are taken seriously is seen from the fact that the Chief Minister of Arunachal Pradesh praised the decision to go ahead with work on one of them even before getting central clearance though it is against the law, because it will bring revenue to the State (*The Telegraph,* February 2, 2002). Many of these massive dams will be privately owned.

Thus, revenue, much of it to be spent on the administration, is what impels the States to permit this plunder. They ignore the fact that the Northeast is one of the 25 mega-biodiversity zones of the world and one among 18 biodiversity hot spots. Also ignored is the fact that the region which is home to various ethnic groups has witnessed armed ethnic conflicts for decades mainly because of land loss to immigrants and to development projects. Its fallout is militarisation because of which development itself is located within a defence perspective.[13]

Many dams will be in Arunachal Pradesh whose tribes live on community owned land according to their customary law but the State does not recognise these CPRs as their livelihood. Because of this disjunction between the legal and social reality they have lost much land to the immigrants as well as to development projects and will lose more to the dams but most of them will not even be compensated because their CPRs are considered State property according to the eminent domain. This is true also of other States. For example, by the early 1970s the tribals of Tripura had lost 60% of their land to the Bangladeshi Hindu immigrants. More of it was acquired for the Dumbur dam but out of about 9,000 families displaced by it, only around 2,500 were compensated. The rest were not even counted among the displaced because they lived on the CPRs. The unrest in Tripura is attributed mainly to their impoverishment that followed from it.[14]

Such massive land acquisition in the name of national development is not limited to the Northeast but is true of the whole of India, especially its tribal areas. The eminent domain ensures that what the State calls public purpose gets priority over the people but it does not oblige the State to rehabilitate those whom it deprives of their livelihood. It has resulted in massive land loss since independence. In Orissa more than a million ha were acquired 1951-1995, in Andhra Pradesh around 1.2 million ha and more during the last decade. In West Bengal 2 million ha, in Gujarat 3 million ha and in Assam 700,000 ha have been acquired 1947-2000. In most States around half of it is CPRs that are the livelihood of the rural poor. Since they are considered State property, its losers not only do not get compensation but are often not even counted among the displaced (DP) or those deprived of their livelihood without being physically relocated (PAP).

The exact number of the DPs/PAPs from 1947 till today is not known. They are more than 4 millions in West Bengal, 2 million in Orissa, 3.5 millions in AP and many more in other States. The All India total is around 60 million. Only around a third of the DPs have been resettled. In Orissa 35.27% of the DPs in 1951-1995 were resettled[15] against 28.82% in Andhra Pradesh[16], 33.63% in Goa[17], 9.8% in Kerala[18] and fewer in West Bengal, Jharkhand, Gujarat and Assam.

Forests and Development

Equally important are forests that have met more than half of the food, fodder, medicinal and other needs of the rural poor in general and of the tribals in particular. Because of this dependence, a symbiotic relationship had grown between them and the forests and they had built an economy, culture, social and political systems around them that ensured that they were treated as renewable resources. However, to the State they are a commodity and a raw material that was given to the industrialist at highly subsidised rates. Because of the industrialist found it cheaper to destroy them than to replant them. That began the vicious circle of sequential exhaustion. The industrial agent began by cutting forests near the village and from there went to the next village, the next block and the next district. Then he began the sequential exhaustion of species. For example, after exhausting bamboos for paper, he took to soft wood species like mangoes.

Impoverished and deprived of their land, those whose livelihood it was, fell in to the hands of the moneylender who accompanied the industrial agent, lost their land to him and often became bonded labourers. For sheer survival they began to destroy the forests and cut trees for sale as firewood or for timber often as bonded labourers of the contractors. That symbolises not only loss of forests but also their alienation from their culture of treating them as renewable. They go beyond losing their vested interest in its preservation to develop a culture of their destruction for survival.[19] This transition from constructive to destructive dependence is basic to the loss of forests. As a result of these processes India's tree cover declined from 40% in the mid-19th century to 22% a century later and to around 13% today.[20]

Climate change is another result of deforestation and of environmental degradation. It is not an issue of clean air but of people's lifestyle. The rich countries that account for most ozone layer destroying emissions refuse to reduce them for fear of affecting their lifestyle. The USA that causes a fifth of all greenhouse gas emissions has rejected the Kyoto Protocol that demands the reduction of such emissions by 15% before 2010. The other countries accepted it initially but later changed the discussion to clean mechanisms thus diverting attention from the livelihood issue. Clean mechanism is a euphemism for transferring their outdated technologies to the poor nations. They may be cleaner than that of the poor nations but will soon be outdated but the "donors" get credit points that exempt them from reducing the emissions within their own borders. They have been asking the poor countries to sacrifice some of their development in order to reduce emissions but through credit points for clean mechanisms, they exempt themselves from this obligation. They refuse to recognise that over-consumption in the Global North and by the middle and upper classes in the poor countries causes poverty in the South.[21] Instead of developing its own clean technologies, India has yielded to the temptation to import "clean mechanisms" from the rich countries and has joined the biggest offender, the USA in rejecting the Kyoto Protocol.

Globalisation of Intensification

These processes are being intensified by globalisation that depends on a consumerist society. It is called a "free market" economy but in reality it is the freedom of a few countries to impose their lifestyle on others in order to get control of their markets and natural resources. A sign of it is the growing disparities in the global income and resource use. According to estimates, in the late 1960s, 32.5% of the world's population accounted for 87.5% of its income. In 1978 the global income was US $8.5 trillion and the world population 4.4 billion, thus giving a per capita average of a little over US$ 2,000. But roughly $7 trillion of it, or 82%, was generated in the North which contained around 25% of the population. The 75% living in the South shared the remaining $1.5 trillion. A decade later, 784 million of the world population of 5,101 millions or 15.4%, had an income of $13,394 bil-lions or 78.2% of the total of $17,135 billions. According to estimates, in the 1990s 80% of the world's income was enjoyed by 15% of its population.[22] Income is one of many signs of differential access to the re-sources. In the mid-1990s 17% of the world's population living in the rich countries used 70% of the global energy, 75% of its metals, 85% of its wood and 60% of its food. That is basic to environmental degradation.[23]

The recent Agreements that are intrinsic to globalisation legitimise such inequalities in the name of a "free" market. Among them are the Convention on Bio-diversity signed at the Earth Summit of Rio de Janeiro, 1992 and the World Trade Organisation that emerged from the GATT negotiations completed at Geneva in December 1993 and signed at Marakash, Morocco, on April 15, 1994. Through such Agreements those who over-consume the resources, ensure that the poor preserve the environ-ment on their behalf. These Agreements are also a part of the process of extending the culture of a consumerist society to countries like India. It has resulted in a more intense attack on the environment. Integral to it are projects that India has initiated, including those related to forests, that will further destroy the people's livelihood. For example, studies on the World Bank Forestry Programme in Madhya Pradesh show that in reality it is meant to turn forests into plantations for industrial raw material. The tribals and other forest dwellers are denied access to these "plantation forests". Even when access is granted, they are unable meet their food, fodder and medicinal needs because almost exclusively commercial species are planted in them.[24]

The Poor and Women as Victims

While all feel the impact of environmental degradation most of its victims are the poor in general and women among them in particular. For example, out of the estimated 60 million persons displaced or deprived of their livelihood by development projects since independence, 40% are tribals who are a little over 8% of the country's population, at least 20% are Dalits and another 20% are other landless rural poor like the fishing communities and quarry workers.[25] That situation continues because there is greater attack on their livelihood after globalisation. For the focus today is on mining for private companies in Middle India and for major dams in the Northeast[26]. Around 90% of coal and more than 50% of most other minerals are in the tribal regions and the effort is to exploit them. Which will result in massive tribal displacement.[27]

The same is the case of other forms of environmental degradation. For example, the Mumbai floods affected all but almost all those who died because of the landslides were slum dwellers who had to occupy the worst land. The neglect of the African Americans during the New Orleans floods is well known. Urban pollution has increased because of the encouragement given to individual vehicles. In Delhi alone they deposit more than 2,000 tonnes of pollutants everyday that result in health hazards especially of children. Every class suffers but the middle class can have some recourse to health care while the poor can rarely afford the costly medicines.

Even among the poor, the impact is felt more by women, children and aged persons than by men. For example, a study of the DPs/PAPs of development projects in Orissa and AP showed a steep rise of more than 100% in five years, in air pollution and stress related ailments and water borne diseases. The impact was on women and children than on men, because of higher malnutrition among them after the loss of their land and forests. Even after their loss the woman is expected to continue to play her role of ensuring regular supply of food, water and medicinal herbs to the family, organic manure to the fields and fodder to the cattle. She is unable to fulfil this task after the loss of forests, the source of food and herbal medicines.

In case of the displacement of the people, their livelihood is not replaced. If some economic resources are replaced, they invariably go to man. For example, the project rarely gives a job to the DPs/PAPs. If it does, it is limited to one job per family, almost invariably to men, considered its head. Tribal and Dalit women had enjoyed a higher social status and greater economic autonomy than their counterparts in caste societies did, though they were not equal to men. This relatively high status depended on the partial control they exercised over the CPRs. After their alienation the woman is unable to work outside her home since the projects do not give her a job. If resettlement is land based, land is allotted to individuals, invariably to men except in women headed households since men are considered heads of families. Thus she loses her economic autonomy and is reduced to being a housewife alone, unable to make an economic contribution to the family economy. Slowly she loses her decision-making role since with individual *patta* becoming the norm of land ownership after resettlement, power is transferred to the man and from him to his son.[28]

Together with land and forests, women also lose access to their traditional work without any alternative. With the alienation of this source of their sustenance they cannot grow or collect the food that the family needs and have to buy this and other basic needs. However, influenced by the outsiders who come to the project, men spend a substantial amount of their earnings on clothes, entertainment and other trivia, thus leaving a relatively small amount for the woman to run the household. Malnutrition is its consequence, particularly of girls and women because over time, women internalise the ideology of their subordination and follow the dominant caste custom of feeding elders, men and boys and girls in that order and themselves eating last. In case of food shortage which is common when they are deprived of their livelihood, women have to starve and girls get less food than the others do.[29]

Besides, deprivation of their livelihood often results in additional workload for women but less food for the family. For example, with deforestation for industrial needs and development projects the distance of forests increases, and so does women's workload. In Orissa and Chattisgarh the distance of forests had increased from around one km from the village to more than five km in a span of two decades. So women had to walk the extra distance to collect less food because children and older women were unable to accompany them. The combination of higher workload and malnutrition affects their health too but because of the extra workload, they are unable to visit the health centre since it is open only during the day when they have to work in the fields or forests. As a result, many pregnant forest dweller women are forced to work till a week before child delivery and begin to work again within a week after it.[30]

Conclusion

The above discussion on the environment and development shows that deprivation of their livelihood and deterioration of the environment understood as natural resources has had an adverse impact on the poor in general and on women in particular. More often than not they lose their livelihood to the benefit of the better off sections of society. Deterioration of their status and environmental degradation do not have to be automatic consequences of modernisation if the communities, whose livelihood it is, continue to have some control over its process. That requires a search for alternatives to the present type of modernisation and to the natural resource and capital intensive pattern of development. In making this statement we assert that, what causes environmental degradation and deterioration of the status of the poor in general and of women in particular, is not modernisation in itself but its present model controlled by one class. One cannot fight against modernisation and development because the poor and women have as much of a right to change and modernise themselves as men have. What is required are environment friendly alternatives that are supportive of the subalterns in general and of women in particular.

The first challenge in this search is a new understanding of and approach to development itself. Today it is identified with economic growth and results in processes that marginalise the subaltern classes in general and women in particular. Some of its assumptions can be questioned, for example the need for individual vehicles at the cost of public transport. The consumerist society too needs to be questioned. One can also ask whether the present projects are the best means of meeting even genuine needs. For example, does one have to displace the poor in the hill areas in order to supply drinking water and irrigation in the coastal areas? Would developing low priced desalination technologies for its 7,000 km coastline not be alternatives to it? Is hydro-electrical power the only option in a country that has 300 days of sunshine? Why does the country import solar technology of the 1970s instead of developing low-prices alternatives? What a city needs is street lights, not necessarily electric lights. But the human and industrial waste is sent into the rivers and oceans and then money is borrowed from abroad to clean them. Instead recycling plants can ensure that costly processed water is not used for cleaning houses and toilets and for watering the garden. Recycling can provide the fertilisers for the gardens that are imported today and gas based street lights for the city.

One can give many more concrete technical alternatives. What is required is a new thinking on development. One has to go beyond economic growth and share markets to demand that the benefits reach every class. Christians need to reinforce their belief in the creation and its use as a resource to be developed for the benefit of all. That will be a method of fulfilling the mission of Him who came to make all things new.

Notes

1. Ramachandra Guha. "Forestry Debate and Draft Forest Act: Who Wins? Who Loses?" *Economic and Political Weekly,* 29 (N. 34, August 20, 1994), p. 1192.
2. Anil Agarwal. "Ecological Destruction and the Emerging Patterns of People's Protests in Rural India," *Social Action* 35 (N. 1, Jan-March 1985), p. 54.
3. Ramachandra Guha and Madhav Gadgil. "What are Forests for?" in Walter Fernandes (ed). *Drafting a People's Forest Bill: The Forest Dweller-Social Activist Alternative.* New Delhi: Indian Social Institute, 1996, pp. 36-39.
4. B. D. Sharma. *Tribal Development: The Concept and the Frame.* New Delhi: Prachi Prakashan, 1986, pp. 8-12.
5. NCHSE. *Rehabilitation of Displaced Persons Due to Construction of Major Dams: Volume I.* New Delhi: National Center for Human Settlements and Environment, 1986, p. ii.
6. Freda Rajotte and Elizabeth Breuilly. "What is the Crisis?" in Elizabeth Breuilly and Martinmer (eds). *Christianity and Ecology.* London: Cassell Publishers Ltd, 1986, p. 6.
7. Sanjay Upadhyay and Bhavani Raman. *Land Acquisition and Public Purpose.* New Delhi: The Other Media, 1998.
8. Frank Brennal. "Parliamentary Responses to the Mabo Decision," in M. A. Stephenson (ed). Mabo: *The Native Title Legislation: A Legislative Response to the High Court Decision.* St Lucia: Queensland Univ Press, 1995 p. 16.
9. Ramanathan, Usha. 1999. "Public Purpose: Points for Discussion," in Walter Fernandes (ed). *The Land Acquisition (Amendment) Bill*

1998: For Liberalisation or for the Poor? New Delhi: Indian Social Institute, pp. 19-20.

10. Manju Menon. *Large Dams for hydro-Power in Northeast India: A Dossier.* Pune and Delhi: Kalpavriksh and South Asia Network on Dams, Rivers and people, 2003 (mimeo), pp. 3-10.
11. M. Debnath. "Need for Development of Hydro-Power Potential in India with Special Importance to North Eastern Region," *Seminar Papers, 10th Annual General Conference of Engineers,* Agartala: August 10-12, 2002.
12. Manju Menon, Neeraaj Vagholikar, Kanchi Kohli and AshishFernandes. "Large Dams in the Northeast: A Bright Future?" *The Ecologist Asia* 11 (N. 1, Jan-March 2003), pp. 3-4.
13. Sanjib Baruah. "Take the Jungle to the Law," *The Indian Express,* March 9, 2005.
14. Subir Bhaumick. "Tripura's Gumti Dam Must Go," *The Ecologist Asia* 11 (N. 1, Jan.-Mar, 2003), pp. 84-85.
15. Walter Fernandes and Mohammed Asif. *Development-Induced Displacement and Rehabilitation in Orissa 1951-1995: A Database On Its Extent and Nature.* New Delhi: Indian Social Institute, 1997, (mimeo) p. 135.
16. Walter Fernandes, Nafisa Goga D'Souza, Arundhuti Roy Choudhury and Mohammed Asif. *Development-Induced Displacement, Deprival and Rehabilitation in Andhra Pradesh 1951-1995: A Quantitative and Quantitative Study of Its Extent and Nature.* New Delhi: Indian Social Institute and Guwahati: North Eastern Social Research Centre, 2001. p. 87 (mimeo).
17. Walter Fernandes and Niraj Naik. *Development-Induced Displacement in Goa 1965-1995: A Study of Its Extent and Nature.* New Delhi: Indian Social Institute and Panjim: INSAF, 2001, p. 62 (mimeo).
18. Jose Murickan, M. K. George, K. A. Emmanuel, Jose Boban and Prakash Pillai R. *Development-Induced Displacement: Case of Kerala.* New Delhi: Rawat Publications, p. 133.
19. Mdhav Gadgil. "Forest Management, Deforestation and People's Impoverishment," *Social Action* 39, (n.4, Oct-Dec. 19879), p. 358.
20. FRI. *The State of Forest Report.* Dehradun: Forest Survey of India, 2004.
21. Walter Fernandes and Nafisa Goga D'Souza. "Climate Change and Tribal Sustainable Living: Citizens' Concerns, An

Introduction," In Walter Fernandes and Nafisa Goga D'Souza (eds). *Climate Change and Tribal Sustainable Living: Responses from the Northeast.* Guwahati: North Eastern Social Research Centre and Vishakapatnam: Indian Network of Ethics and Climate Change, 2001, pp. 3-5.

22. Walter Fernandes. "India's Socio-Economic Situation and the Poor," *Paper presented at the National Assembly,* Yesu Krist Jayanti 2000, Bangalore, September 20-24, 2000.
23. John Desrochers. "Complementary Insights on Colonialism," *Integral Liberation* 1 (N. 3, Sept. 1997), p. 141.
24. Bittu Sahgal. "Colonisation Continuum: The Never Ending Story," *Paper presented at the International Conference, Colonialism to Globalization: Five Centuries After Vasco da Gama.* New Delhi: Indian Social Institute, February 2 6, 1998.
25. Walter Fernandes. "Rehabilitation as A Right: Where is the Policy? *Social Action* 55 (N. 2, Apr-June2005), p. 125.
26. IWGIA. *The Indigenous World 2004. Copenhagen: International Work Group for Indigenous Affairs,* 2004, p. 316.27 IBM. *Indian Mineral Year Book.* Nagpur: Indian Bureau of Mines, 2000.
28. Stan Thekkekara. "Historic Adivasi Sangamam at Mananthavady," *Social Action* 43 (N. 1, Jan. March 1993), p. 89.
29. Nafisa Goga D'Souza. "Development, Displacement and Marginalised Women," in Walter Fernandes and Sanjay Barbora (eds). *Changing Women's Status in India: Focus on the Northeast.* Guwahati: North Eastern Social Research Centre, 2002. pp. 85-86.
30. Anil Agarwal and Sunita Narain. "Women and Natural Resources," *Social Action* 35 (n. 4, Oct. Dec. 1985), p. 305.

References

Agarwal, Anil (1985), "Ecological Destruction and the Emerging Pattern of Poverty and People's Protest in Rural India," *Social Action* 35 (N. l, Jan.-March), pp. 54-80.

Baruah, Sanjib (2005), "Take the Jungle to the Law," *The Indian Express,* March 9.

Bhaumick, Subir (2003), "Tripura's Gumti Dam Must Go," *The Ecologist Asia* 11 (N. 1, Jan.-Mar), pp. 84-89.

Baviskar, B. S. and D. Attwood (1998), Who Shares? Co-operatives and Rural Development. New Delhi, Oxford University Press.

Brennan, Frank (1995), "Parliamentary Responses to the Mabo Decision," in M. A. Stephenson (ed). *Mabo: The Native Title Legislation: A Legislative Response to the High Court Decision*. St Lucia: Queensland University Press, pp. 1-25.

Debnath, M. (2001), "Need for Development of Hydro-Power Potential in India with Special Importance to North Eastern Region," Seminar Papers, 10th Annual General Conference of Engineers, Agartala: August 10-12.

Desrochers, John (1997), "Complementary Insights on Colonialism," *Integral Liberation* 1 (N. 3, September), pp. 141-145.

Fernandes, Walter (2000), "India's Socio-Economic Situation and the Poor," *Paper presented at the National Assembly, Yesu Krist Jayanti 2000, Bangalore, September 20-24*.

Fernandes, Walter (2005), "Rehabilitation as A Right: Where is the Policy? *Social Action* 55 (N. 2, April-June), pp. 123-137.

Fernandes, Walter and Mohammed Asif (1997), *Development-Induced Displacement in Orissa 1951-1995*. New Delhi, Indian Social Institute (mimeo).

Fernandes, Walter, Nafisa Goga D'Souza, Arundhuti Roy Choudhury and Mohammed Asif (2001), *Development-Induced Displacement, Deprivation and Rehabilitation in Andhra Pradesh 1951-1995: Its Extent, Nature and Impact*. New Delhi: Indian Social Institute and Guwahati: North Eastern Social Research Centre (mimeo).

Fernandes, Walter and Niraj Naik (2001), *Development-Induced Displacement in Goa 1965-1995: A Study of Its Extent and Nature*. New Delhi: Indian Social Institute and Panjim: INSAF.

Fernandes, Walter and Nafisa Goga D'Souza (2001), "Climate Change and Tribal Sustainable Living: Citizens' Concerns: An Introduction," in Walter Fernandes and Nafisa Goga D'Souza (eds). *Climate Change and Tribal Sustainable Living: Responses from the Northeast*. Guwahati: North Eastern Social Research Centre and Vishakapatnam: Indian Network of Ethics and Climate Change, pp. 1-15.

FRI. 2004. *The State of Forest Report*. Dehradun: Forest Survey of India.

Gadgil Madhav (1989), "Forest Management, Deforestation and People's Impoverishment," *Social Action* 39, (N. 4, Oct-Dec.), pp. 357-383.

Goga D'Souza, Nafisa (2002), "Development, Displacement and Marginalised Women," in Walter Fernandes and Sanjay Barbora (eds). *Changing Women's Status in India: Focus on the Northeast.* Guwahati: North Eastern Social Research Centre, pp. 81-91.

Guha, Ramchandra (1994), "Forestry Debate and Draft Forest Act: Who Wins? Who Loses?" *Economic and Political Weekly* 29 (N. 34, August 20), pp. 1192-1196.

Guha, Ramchandra and Madhav Gadgil (1996), "What are Forests For?" in Walter Fernandes (ed). *Drafting A People's Forest Bill: The Forest Dweller-Social Activist Alternative.* New Delhi: Indian Social Institute, pp. 33-67.

IBM (2000), *Indian Mineral Yearbook 2000.* Nagpur: Indian Bureau of Mines.

IWGIA (2004), *The Indigenous World 2004.* Copenhagen: International Work Group for Indigenous Affairs.

Menon, Manju (2003), *Large Dams for hydro-Power in Northeast India: A Dossier.* Puneand Delhi: Kalpavriksh and South Asia Network on Dams, Rivers and people (mimeo).

Menon, Manju, Neeraaj Vagholikar, Kanchi Kohli and Ashish Fernandes (2002), "Large Dams in the Northeast: A Bright Future?" *The Ecologist Asia* 11 (N. 1, Jan-March), pp. 3-8.

Murickan, Jose, M. K. George, K. A. Emmanuel, Jose Boban and Prakash Pillai R. (2003), *Development-Induced Displacement: Case of Kerala.* New Delhi: Rawat Publications.

NCHSE (1986), *Rehabilitation of Displaced Persons Due to Construction of Major Dams: Volume I.* New Delhi: National Center for Human Settlements and Environment.

Rajotte, Freda and Elizabeth Breuilly (1986), "What is the Crisis?" in Elizabeth Breuilly and Martin Palmer (eds). *Christianity and Ecology.* London: Cassell Publishers Ltd, pp. 1-18.

Sahgal, Bittu (1998), "Colonisation Continuum: The Never Ending Story," Paper presented at the *International Conference, Colonialism to Globalization: Five Centuries After Vasco da Gama.* New Delhi, Indian Social Institute, February 26.

Sharma, B.D. (1978), *Tribal Development: The Concept and the Frame.* New Delhi: Prachi Prakashan.

Thekkekara, Stan (1993), "Historic *Adivasi Sangamam* at Mananthavady," *Social Action* 43 (n. 1, Jan. March), pp. 88 92.

Upadhyay, Sanjay and Bhavani Raman. 1998. *Land Acquisition and Public Purpose.* New Delhi: The Other Media.

14

The Railway Bridge of Shrirampur: From Listening to Speakingas Embodied Hermeneutics

CHRISTIAN BAUER

Allow me to begin with a true story of the conversion of a theologian that almost looks like a fairy tale. [1] Once upon a time a young European theologian went to India. This young theologian was very familiar with the contemporary theological discourses on so-called 'postmodern' thinkers like Lyotard, Foucault, Derrida, etc. Because of these highly intellectual discourses on difference, pluralism and alterity, he was very sceptical about the possibility of cross-cultural understanding. He was convinced that the gap between Europe and India would be too deep and wide very to be bridged.

But this young European intellectual was in fact converted by experience, experience of cross-cultural friendship. The empirical place of this 'conversion' was the railway bridge of Shrirampur and it happened not in one single moment, but step by step. At this particular place, he often met a young Indian teacher of the same age and they sat on that bridge doing nothing but telling stories of every day life in their two different worlds. Slowly the sharing of these stories made them become good friends and the young theologian slowly and steadily realized that a cross-cultural understanding could actually take place.

This young conceited European intellectual is the one writing this article and I must admit that this railway bridge was a true eye-opener for me. I want to share this experience of disclosure since it answers some fundamental questions of cross-cultural encounter and development: How can we mediate conflicts in a pluralistic world full of tension, gaps and fractions? What are the conditions for the possibility of cross-cultural understanding and development, especially in India marked by its diversity and extreme contrasts? How do we deal with plurality of cultural, economic and– not the least- religious differences?

Compassionate Listening

As a second step, I would like to switch to a practical procedure which tries to answer these questions by solving concrete problems in a pragmatic way: the so called mediation method. Mediation is a up-coming, well structured and psychology-based procedure of conflict resolution. But for me it is more than only a technique with a certain set of tools, it is a social attitude–and as a theologian, I would add: it is a pastoral attitude, even a way of spirituality.

Mediation does not want to solve people's conflicts, but enables them to solve their problems themselves by opening up a space for them to take life into their own hands. Mediation is not yet the solution, but its procedure offers conditions for the possibility of an encounter, for new contact and real change. Mediation is characterized by one key word: listening. It is a listening that goes beyond the normal hearing. Marshal Rosenberg, the father of non-violent communication, who is mediating post-war conflicts at Kosovo at present, speaks even of a hearing that is "compassionate listening."

Hearing to Speech

In her famous book *The Journey is Home* the American theologian Nelle Morton gives an impressive example of the power of compassionate listening:[2]

> It was in a small group of women, who had come together to tell our own stories, that first I received a totally new

> understanding of hearing and speaking. I remember well how one woman started ... trying to put the pieces of her life together. She talked on and on .... After a silence she looked from one woman to another. "You heard me, you heard me all the way." She looked directly at each woman ... and then said slowly: "I have a strange feeling you heard me before I started. You heard me to my own story." ... I had been experiencing something I never experienced before. This woman was saying, and I had experienced, a ... hearing that takes place before the speaking, a hearing that is far more than acute listening. A hearing engaged in by the whole body that evokes speech–a new creation. The woman had been heard to her own speech. (p. 127).

For Nelle Morton, this kind of listening as a "hearing to speech" is truly "political" (p. 210), because it is "equivalent to empowerment" (p. 128): "We empower one another by hearing the other" (p. 128). This one-another relation is very important, because hearing-to-speech is never one-sided. "Once a person is heard to speech, she becomes a hearing person" (p. 210). In this context Nelle Morton sketches the outlines of a "Hearing-to-Speech theology of liberation":

> Every liberation movement rises out of its bondage with a new speech on its lips. This has been so with women coming together seeking to get in touch with our own stories ... which we have discovered welling up from within, from underneath, from out of our past ... But to evoke our story to speech, women experience ... a ... great listening ear .. that hears without interruption ... until we experience at the lowest point of our lives that we are sustained (p. 55).

Nelle Morton identifies this "great listening ear" (p. 55) with God, and in this way she creates a new metaphor for God on the background of her own experiences: God as the "great ear at the heart of the universe and of our common life – hearing humans to speech" (p. 128). "Though hearing and speaking", Nelle Morton says, "women sense the possibility of doing theology out of own experience" (p. 83). This experience-based theology creates a new speech about creation: "We began hearing one another to speech. We experienced God, as Spirit, hearing human beings to speech, to new creation.... The creative act of the spirit was not word speaking, but hearing, hearing the created to speech" (p. 82). In this way, Nelle Morton is able to turn our traditional idea of creation: "In the beginning was not word. In the beginning was the hearing." (p. 82).

Embodied Hermeneutics

Concluding this brief article, I would like to return to the Railway bridge of Shrirampur and to my cross-cultural disclosure-experience, which took place there. We did not tell *any* stories, but we were telling *our own* stores–and this hearing and speaking opened up the space for a new speech of encounter for me. I still have got my ideas on a 'postmodern' theology, but now these discourses on difference, pluralism and alterity root deeper: deeper in a non-discursive field of cross-cultural face-to-face experiences.[3]

Therefore we need an embodied discourse of hermeneutics, which does not take place beyond our different worlds, but *within* the tension, gaps and frictions of our own worlds. We do not need a hermeneutical "fusion of horizons" (Hans-Georg Gadamer) on an abstract level, but we need embodied encounters of citizens of different worlds of meaning. Not ideas, theories and concepts encounter each other, but authentic human beings, who hear one another to speech. And we cannot 'make' these experiences by a master-plan of understanding, but they may happen here and there, now and then–granted by grace. Such an encounter leads to the authentic liberation and development of the whole person.

Conclusion

Situating myself concretely on the railway bridge at Shrirampur, I, as an young European intellectual explore and experience the power of compassionate listening which has enabled him to empower the both the listening and the speaking.[4] Basing my self on Nelle Morton, these random reflections plead for a liberation that is hermeneutical and embodied and a development that is based on authentic encounter between human beings.

Notes

1. This article is fondly inspired by and dedicated to Prof Kurien Kunnumpuram, with best memories of our cross-cultural encounters. See Kuruvilla Pandikattu and Rosario Rocha, *Bend Without Fear: Hopes and Possibilities for an Indian Church: Essays in Honour of Professor Kurien Kunnumpuram SJ*, ISPCK, 2003.
2. Nelle Morton, *The Journey is Home* (Boston 1985).
3. Kuruvilla Pandikattu, *Dialogue as the Way of Life: Bede Griffiths' Attempt at Integrating Religions, Cultures and Sciences*, Kuruvilla Pandikattu, Mumbai: Zen Publications, 2001, pp. 34-35.
4. Rosario Rocha and Kuruvilla Pandikattu, *Dreams and Visions: New Horizons for an Indian Church: Essays in Honour of Professor Kurien Kunnumpuram SJ*, Pune, JDV, 2002.

Index

C

T